SPIRITUALISM

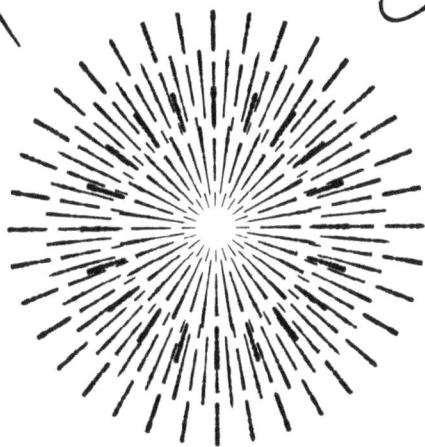

THE OPEN DOOR

to the

UNSEEN UNIVERSE

Spiritualism:

The Open Door to the Unseen Universe

Being Thirty Years of Personal
Observation and Experience concerning
Intercourse between the Material and
Spiritual Worlds

By

JAMES ROBERTSON

— 1908 —

San Francisco

THIS unabridged edition has been newly typeset and edited; some punctuation has been adapted to more closely conform to modern American usage. Original British spelling has been retained. The text was compiled from various print versions in the public domain of the original 1908 book.

PREFACE

No other movement which has originated during the past sixty years has exerted so powerful an influence upon contemporary thought as modern Spiritualism has done.

No man within the ranks of British Spiritualists can better tell the story of its growth in these islands during the past thirty years than the writer of the following pages; few could tell it as well.

Having been intimately associated with him during the period covered by his pen, there is no question in my mind as to the accuracy of his statements, while their illuminating lucidity leaves nothing to be desired. Personal experience in the matters detailed in the ensuing chapters is necessary for correct judgment. My friend possesses such experience, and speaks, consequently, as "one having authority." Himself a business man of repute in his great city, Glasgow, his words are weighty and full worthy of respect.

To those of us who have fought in the ranks of modern Spiritualism for many years, often blinded by the dust and deafened with the din of conflict, this book will be a treasured record of the history we have been making, though not always comprehending. To all students of the movements of the times—ethical and religious—and particularly the advance of psychical knowledge due to the services of Spiritualists, the work will be a welcome and instructive addition to their libraries.

The material of this volume originally appeared in the columns of *The Two Worlds*, under my editorial supervision, and it is with the utmost confidence and pleasure I commend the record of my dear friend's valuable experiences to all and sundry the wide world over. The positive testimony of one candid mind is of far more worth than the non-committal opinions of the prejudiced or timorous. Herein speaks a man who knows, one who is not afraid of the truth he has found.

J.J. MORSE.
MANCHESTER, June 1908.

INTRODUCTORY NOTE

The future life is a subject which certainly concerns everyone, and if there is to be found evidence which transfers our knowledge of it from the domain of speculation to that of certainty, it is surely a duty to submit such evidence to the inspection of all. Spiritualism, to the minds of many, may seem a very obscure and nebulous thing, but already it has commanded attention and brought the conviction to millions of thoughtful truth-seekers that its phenomena solve the great problem of continued personal existence after bodily death. The conditions of trance and clairvoyance are facts in nature, not theological inferences, and they show that the people of the other world can open its gates, enlighten mankind by revelations, and prove their presence visibly and audibly. We may not, as yet, see clearly the full significance, the sequence of this knowledge, but it is our duty to investigate continually, as it is only by searching in obscure realms that the great scientific facts with which we are now familiar have been brought to shed their blessings on human life. Spiritualism does not seek to found a new sect, it simply seeks to widen our knowledge of the great realm of nature. In sending out this volume of observations I do not attempt to solve all the difficulties which I raise. I am quite willing to admit that my thoughts may seem to lack connection, nay, may even appear inconsistent one with another; but I shall be satisfied if what I have set down will cause others to think and investigate in a realm which has brought to me much joy and tranquil peace.

JAS. ROBERTSON.

GLASGOW, July 1908.

Contents

Spiritualism:

The Open Door to the Unseen Universe

CHAPTER I

THE STARTING POINT

The year 1876 was to me the most eventful year in my life's history. The clouds which had obscured my vision melted away, and I was brought into a realm which has ever since yielded me intense delight. Men often grapple with a subject, wrestle with it, and exhaust it, and themselves, but the realm into which I was introduced was so limitless and inexhaustible, that after thirty years' dwelling there I find it ever opening up new continents to view, and fresh people to mingle with—I feel that I shall never tire of its boundless treasures. I am no visionary, and have no predisposition to superstition, no wonder-mongering in any department, so that when this land of splendours opened to my sight, I did not lose my senses, but looked it fully and squarely in the face, and recognised that here was an unfoldment of Nature's processes which hitherto had been hid from me. I never could live on unreality. Poetry might for a season ring the changes on my emotions, but calm reflection deadened the power of the most glowing strains when these could not be linked on to facts that could be verified.

I did not start with any thought or desire to enter on a road which would reveal to me a world beyond the gates of death, nor did I believe that there was in this universe of ours, or ever had been, such evidence as would establish such a fact so that it might be grasped by human senses. I had long ceased to regard the books called sacred as being in any way historical or authentic, and felt that the present day was as much entitled to witness the occurrences narrated in them as any past age. I had made brave struggles for long to believe what the Church called truth; had sought to catch the faith that was preached, but reason ever cast these teachings aside as being in no sense a revelation of truth. I had reached the position of many others on these questions; I was neither a believer nor altogether a disbeliever. They did not appeal to my reasoning faculties, and so I wandered for years, without finding a permanent home where faith and reason might lie down together in unity.

The Secular school, with its presentation of one side of man's nature, did not satisfy me. I might be charmed at moments with the intellectual presentation of facts, but felt that even here there was no abiding place for me. I welcomed such truths as sincere and lofty souls like George Jacob Holyoake would so gracefully present, but ever a something would be lacking. I had reached a position, mentally, where I felt that all schools of thought were groping in the dark, and that there was no authentic light anywhere which could dispel the gloom.

I had heard of Spiritualism at a distance, but all the talk about spirits coming to tables was, to my mind, only lunacy abroad, and it never crossed me that here could be found any possible solution of the great question of human immortality. I had even tried to read D.D. Home's *Incidents of My Life*, but cast it aside as wretched drivel, unworthy of the serious attention of rational minds. Swedenborg seemed a strange character, but as the writings of the ancient prophets, and their claims, were unbelievable, the modern seer had no message for me, just then. The philosophers have said that the impressions made upon us by any circumstance, or combination of circumstances, depend upon our previous state. I had been educated in the school of the senses, rather than in the school of imagination. I had but one desire, to know the truth; but one fear, to believe in a lie; and, therefore, neither Home's remarkable incidents, nor Swedenborg's life, appealed to my mode of thought. I had to wait a season before I recognised how valuable to the world were the experiences of both men.

You will naturally ask what special circumstances brought about such a resetting of my mental furniture as to cause me to accept the evidence offered by Modern Spiritualism. What occurred in that eventful year, 1876, will show you the pathway on which I walked, and found the Gate Beautiful. In the early part of September 1876, the British Association met in the city of Glasgow. Spiritualism had claimed the attention of eminent scientific workers like Professor Crookes, as he then was, and Dr. Alfred Russel Wallace, both of whom had for long experimented and given the fruit of their research in the volumes now so well known as *Crookes's Researches into the Phenomena of Spiritualism*, and Wallace's *Miracles and Modern Spiritualism*. Dr. Wallace's whole cast of thought had been remodelled by the new marvels with which he had come into touch. His courage and enthusiasm were so great that he laboured to bring the subject privately before his scientific *confrères*. Tyndall, with his luminous mind capable of peering into most intricate and far-off domains, had no eye to see what was at his doorstep, of paramount importance, and with all his friendship and esteem for the great work of Wallace in the domain of evolution, he went out of his way, in the famous Belfast address (one of the most masterly ever offered to the members of the British Association) to have a hit at Spiritualism, by saying that the science of the Middle Ages "was almost as degrading as the Spiritualism of the present day." Huxley had said to Wallace that while not disposed to get up a Commission of Lunacy against him, he could not get up interest in the subject. I have so much admiration for the splendid services of Tyndall and Huxley that I cannot afford to sneer at their lack of vision.

John Morley, still to the fore, and once again a Cabinet Minister, when editor of the *Fortnightly Review*, in 1874, invited Dr. Wallace to write an article on Spiritualism. The article was a long one, and appeared in May and June 1874, under the title, "A Defence of Modern Spiritualism"; it is now incorporated in the volume to which I have referred. The publication of such strong statements, attested by a man of the first rank in experimental science, no doubt caused a considerable amount of opposition on the part of those who had already settled the question of a future life, before looking at the evidence Wallace presented.

The British Association is divided into sections, and it was perhaps difficult to find one which could permit of a tabooed subject like Spiritualism being introduced. The difficulty was solved, however, by the Anthropological Department opening its doors. Here Professor Barrett read a paper on "Some Phenomena Associated with Abnormal Conditions of Mind," and under this title he managed to introduce many of the spiritual evidences which had been so much talked about. Dr. Slade, the medium for slate-writing, had only recently arrived in this country, and the striking phenomena manifested in his presence, which had caused considerable commotion, were referred to at great length in Professor Barrett's paper. Dr. A.R. Wallace, who was President, for the year, of the Anthropological Section, and chairman of the meeting, was loud in his praise of the paper, and spoke of the author as a thoroughly trained man of science, who had been reared under the eye of Tyndall. The paper, to his mind, was a record of facts, and he objected to anyone speaking unless be had facts to offer. Crookes, W.B. Carpenter, Groom Napier (for whom Lord Brougham had written his famous preface to his book on *Nature*, in which he said that, "amid the cloudless skies of scepticism, he saw a rain-cloud no bigger than a man's hand—it was Modern Spiritualism") were amongst the speakers. There was much heat displayed by the opponents of the subject, and some distinguished people, amongst these Professor Lankester, said it was a degradation to science to admit such a topic within the walls of a learned society. A storm was raised which took some years to calm down. Magazine articles representing both schools of thought abounded. Prejudice fought against knowledge. Materialism combated the evidence of man's spiritual powers. The men who preached the largest liberty and who spurned such words as "impossible," as being unscientific, were loudest in the exhibition of narrow prejudice. Tyndall, at Belfast, had said that science had built one wing of the many-mansioned house which man in his totality demanded. But he failed to recognise that Spiritualism was seeking to build another wing of the mansion not made with hands, eternal in the heavens. Culture is a very fine word, but it loses its claim to be reverenced when it is one-sided and not all-sided. The old spirit which ruled the enemies of Galileo and Bruno seems to show itself again in modern scientific men, who would be the first to combat the ancient intolerance. A matter like Spiritualism, which combines verification with intuition, should be at least looked at in a temperate spirit. The apostolic injunction as to entertaining strangers who might reveal the angelic nature is not unscientific. Knowledge once gained casts a light beyond its immediate surroundings. There is no discovery so limited as not to illuminate something beyond itself.

I have said Professor Barrett's paper raised a storm. Professor Lankester, who was a member of the Selecting Committee, had, it seems, been outvoted when Professor Barrett's paper was admitted. He felt that the reputation of the Association had been besmirched, and with his strong prejudice he determined to take some steps to crush out this new superstition. We have ever to give credit to opponents for being honest. Doubtless the crimes which have been committed in the name of religion were the work of honest men, but prejudice blinds the senses, so that matters are not seen in their true light. As Stainton Moses has wisely said, "When knowledge has progressed in even a slight degree, the ignorance of a Lankester will be impossible."

The opportunity for striking a blow at Spiritualism soon presented itself. Returning to London after the close of the British Association proceedings, he met his friend Serjeant Cox, who told him of the marvellous writing he had got on closed slates in the presence of Slade, and advised him to go and see the reality for himself. With his strong bias against the possibility of anything abnormal occurring, Lankester, accompanied by Dr. Donkin, went to visit Slade—as a detective simply, and not as a truth-seeker. When the writing was taking place he seized the slate, without waiting, and said the whole thing was a piece of jugglery. He did not want to be convinced, did not seek for explanations, lost his temper, and rushed to Bow Street Police Court for a summons against the man who, he claimed, had obtained his money by false pretences. A letter was sent to the Times, detailing how he had exposed to the full the spiritual imposture, and the world at large, who take the newspapers as the repositories of all true knowledge, felt that the subject had at last received its quietus. The letter was telegraphed to all the press, and one Monday morning, in the latter part of September 1876, I read it in the *Glasgow Herald*, while crossing in the steamer from Granton to Burntisland. I remember that the feeling which came over me was one of satisfaction that this palpable attempt to trifle with the sacred feelings of humanity had been crushed; for above all things I detested trading on the hopes, the affections, and the fears of mortals. I was satisfied that Spiritualism was a delusion, which had nothing behind it but trickery and fraud. A few minutes later, before the steamer had completed its short passage, there came across my mind what now I can only call an inspiration; for quite suddenly I asked myself: "What can be behind all this? Why do some people believe in it? Can there be some obscure force manifesting itself which weak minds are by some stretch of imagination associating with the work of dead people?"

I then and there resolved, as Robert Dale Owen had done before me when he first came into contact with the phenomena, that I would probe the matter, and settle for myself whether this was a probability, or a certainty, or a delusion.

I did not know in the least how I would go about it, where I would find the field for my exploration, but I was determined to look for it. The idea dominated me for several days until I returned to Glasgow. So strong and determined was I that on returning to business I said to my colleague, "I am going to investigate this Spiritualism." He looked up at me with a smile. "Leave it alone," he said; "it will, in six months, put you in a lunatic asylum." I was not the type of man to be cowed by such fears. I had faced other problems until they yielded me some satisfaction. The old faiths which had darkened my early life had been discarded; I felt pretty much like John Sterling when he said, "I would plunge into the bottom of hell, if I were sure of finding the devil there and getting him strangled."

7

The way opened for me in a most unexpected manner. I had had for years a close friend with whom I had wandered in the realm of doubt and denial. We thought together, discussed many of the problems of life and being, warming ourselves at times with the great thoughts we found in literature. Some time before this we had been attracted by the preaching of John Page Hopps, and although we admired his spiritual rationalism, neither of us had ever heard his name associated with Spiritualism, and it never crossed our minds that this was the source of his bright message. My friend and I had become members of the East End Church, which Mr. Hopps had been the means of founding; but he had himself left Glasgow a few months before. To this friend's house I went on the Sunday after the thought of getting at the bottom of Spiritualism had come to me, and as he was out I looked at his bookcase and saw a volume, *Miracles and Modern Spiritualism*, by Alfred Russel Wallace, which I at once took down from the shelf and began to peruse. My friend soon returned, and I asked him, "Where did you get this book?" The name of Wallace had struck me as an important one to be associated with such a subject. I had a kind of cloudy recollection that he was associated with Charles Darwin in the theory of evolution, and was one of the leading scientific minds of the day. My friend told me that a customer had called upon him during the week, "A person of sense," he said, who had loaned him the book to read and invited him to some meetings which were held regularly in the city. I asked him if he had read it, and he said no, that he had been too busy. I at once said, "Will you let me read it first, and I will tell you what is in it?" to which he readily acquiesced. I took the volume home, and night after night I dipped into its pages. I had been for so long dwelling in an atmosphere which had no place for the miraculous that I confess the first part, "The Scientific Aspects of the Supernatural," did not appeal to me. Hume was

8

not to be readily displaced, nor Thomas Paine. The title was, after all, a misnomer, as the author argued for all the phenomena being really "natural, and involving no alteration whatever in the ordinary laws of Nature." What, however, stirred me was the "Notes of Personal Evidence." To find a man of his calibre vouching for the extraordinary incidents there recorded as having taken place was indeed most startling. Could these things be possible, after all? I was not carried away, however. I did not yield myself to the charmer. I had refused to accept the ancient stories of spirits; why should I accept the new on the authority of any person, however good and great? It was personal experience I wanted, not the statements of others; and if these were not forthcoming for me, then I must still dwell in a world of doubt as to continued personal existence after the death change.

CHAPTER II

FIRST EXPERIENCES

On the next Sunday my friend and I found our way to the Trongate, and after ascending some four or five flights of stairs, we found ourselves in a square, low-ceilinged room, with a few seats, without backs, which were in front of a desk. I looked around at the people, to see if I could see any marks of intelligence, expecting to see some long-haired cranks or other oddities; but no, there were some twenty-five or thirty average-looking men and women, whom I might have met anywhere. It did not strike me, however, that here was a new and brilliant truth which was capable of putting a new soul into religion and transforming the world. It was all commonplace and humdrum, without much sign of burning zeal or enthusiasm. The speaker for the evening read his paper, which could only be called commonplace; it was not marked by oratory, or even warmth of delivery. At the conclusion, questions were invited. I had not the temerity to rise, as at that time I was rather diffident in expressing myself, but one gentleman went dead against the whole subject, saying: "We have a religion already. What could be better than the Bible to lean on—a revelation for all time had been given us—Jesus was the all in all for man to know?" My opportunity had now come; I rose and stated my position, that I had ceased to believe in the Bible as being infallible, or even authentic history; that if there was to be gained in this world of ours any evidence, palpable to the senses, which would establish the fact that the departed lived on, and could manifest to mortals, I, for one, would appreciate such evidence as a priceless boon. I cannot say that I had got anything from my visit—I perhaps expected to see something, and not to listen to words only. Nothing was offered me by the chairman which would place me on the way to getting the needful evidence, but the relief was at hand. A number of the audience were in the habit, I found, of attending the East End Unitarian Church, and one of these, a lady, who knew me by sight, came up and said: "You have seen nothing, Mr. Robertson, it seems. Well, I am willing to come up and give you a sitting, being somewhat of a medium."

I eagerly fell in with the suggestion, and the next night had drawn a company together to witness the marvels that were to be forthcoming. I cannot say that I altogether expected that I would have brought home to me conclusively that our conscious life does not perish with the death of our physical body; I was neither excited nor expectant. I scarcely expected that what would be forthcoming would have much, if anything, in it. The trend of my mind was that great discoveries were more likely to come from universities or apt scholars, than from a body of unlearned, humble people. I had forgotten the old story of the fishermen of Galilee, and the wonderful movement that sprang from that unlettered body of men. Had I dreamed that I was going to meet with some facts which were likely to revolutionise my whole life, I would have been excited, and have lost, perhaps, the even mind with which all things should be viewed.

We sat round a table in one of our bedrooms, the subject being too undignified for us to bring it forward in our best room. At moments there was a feeling of being ashamed at having any connection at all with a subject held in such contempt by the world. We formed a circle of eight persons, six being our own group, not one of whom had ever come near the matter. The lady medium had brought a young friend with her. She told us wonderful stories of what the spirits had done, and we sat for fully an hour, joking and laughing, but there was not the slightest appearance of anything abnormal occurring. Not a rap was heard, not a table tilted. I was getting pretty nearly convinced that there was not much chance of anything extraordinary happening when cool, critical minds were observant. But in this I was soon undeceived. That table did at last behave in a strange manner. It tilted from side to side independently of any pressure brought to bear.

It became light and heavy by turns, and the tilts responded to questions that were asked. There was certainly the clear manifestation of intelligence, and that not of the sitters. The names of old friends were spelled out, and incidents which some of the sitters had forgotten were referred to. Some years before, death had taken from me a boy of promise, whose departure had caused me to think, for a season, that life could have for me no further joy; he was said to be present, and nothing could convey to an outsider how that table seemed to leap for joy; at one moment going, as it were, into my wife's lap, and anon into my own. I certainly, as well as the rest of the company, was a bit upset, and we had got more than we bargained for. It seemed a somewhat crude way to introduce us to the denizens of the spiritual world, but there were the facts, and where were the theories which would cover the ground, without letting in the spirits?

No unseen force known to science could lift a table when desired. What made that table so heavy that at times we could not press it down, and what lightened it so that it seemed like a feather? The great forces of nature, though under law, never manifest personality, while the force that moved that table claimed to be someone we had known, who had passed through the crisis called death. I confess sleep did not come to me readily when it was all over. I bad been suddenly thrown against facts, regarding which I had practically possessed no information. I awoke to the possibility of experimental proof of a future life, and an indescribable emotion filled my being.

Was I standing on the threshold of a great discovery, likely to colour all my future thought and life? Had I been dwelling in darkness, while the light of spiritual facts might be obtained for the asking? The past still held me, however; there arose the old questionings as to the probability of such an important truth forcing itself on my attention by such apparently absurd manifestations. I walked for days in a peculiar, unsettled frame of mind: all my old beliefs were in a state of flux.

That table had upset me more than I would admit to anyone. I wished at some moments that I had not seen it move, but soon there came better thoughts. It is wise to know all of truth. When my perturbation was greatest, I got from a library Serjeant Cox's two volumes, entitled *The Mechanism of Man*. When I had perused these I seemed to realise that we rush ofttimes against the very thing we need, and that our life is made for us, and not by us. This book dealt with what the author calls psychic force, and in it the phenomena of Spiritualism are occasionally accepted to the full, but the intelligence manifested is not regarded as that of spirits, but of the sitters. The only effect the book had upon me was to cause me to feel that the author had failed to justify his theory, and I finished with the impression that had I met such evidence as he had set down, I could be no other than a Spiritualist.

When I left the Trongate after my first visit, I had no idea that I should ever go back again, but my anxiety was great to learn more of the message. I had worked my way from darkness into twilight, and now twilight was giving place to day. The full import of great discoveries grows, and I was approaching tranquility. I did not benefit much from the hall lectures, but I met with those who had had a varied experience of spirit return, some of whom told me I had avoided much mental friction through having previously cast off the old creedal beliefs.

The great prop and stay of the spiritual cause in Glasgow when I became an adherent was James Bowman, a well-known photographer of the city. Reared in Secularism, and with the most intense devotion for Robert Owen, whom he had known, and still loved as one of the most glorious products of the human race, his own mind, as if it had been a photographic plate, had been gradually cleaned, and had been prepared to catch impressions from the light of truth. He literally revelled in the facts of Spiritualism. His intensely joyous nature had found a further source of joy, and this world to him with spirit communion was the brightest of all possible worlds. His purse was ever open to defray the wants of the Society, and he it was who furnished the room, and let the Society use it rent-free. Though there was a president (an old man of some scientific ability), and a secretary and treasurer, James Bowman was practically the Society. He would spend hours with anyone who called upon him, in seeking to explain matters to them. Yet the man himself was ever anxious to take a back seat, contented if he thought the Cause was progressing. He was not profound by any means, but he more than made up for this by the richness of his heart. He had a genius for benevolence, and many obtained his help who scarcely deserved it. When mediums such as Mr. Morse had been brought to the city, he it was who provided the cost in the most hearty spirit. With what reverence he would talk of "Tien," and with what familiarity he would converse with "The Strolling Player," the two spirits who most frequently speak through Mr. Morse when he is entranced. Spiritualism had given him a new world, and out of the fullness of his heart he could not do too much for it. He had brought to Glasgow at one time Kate Fox, the medium through whom the rappings had originated at

Hydesville, and brought as many prominent persons as he could to witness the phenomena that took place in her presence. At all the meetings his rich bass voice could be clearly heard. He was no speaker, and did not ask many questions. He was happy when a hymn was called for him to lead off, and then he would listen contentedly. He eagerly welcomed me, and did his utmost to help to establish me in the faith.

I saw nothing for a few weeks, although circles were held at the rooms. The doors were not opened at once, wisely I believe now, for all who wished to witness the marvellous phenomena. Preparation of some kind is necessary before introduction to a spirit circle. Each new visitor brings with him or her certain conditions, which affect the power that is at work, and to this fact is attributable the crop of alleged "exposures" which have thrown odium on the name of Spiritualism. "Take thy shoes from off thy feet, for the place whereon thou standest is holy ground," might well be taken as a true maxim.

There are some words in a letter of Professor de Morgan's, one of the greatest mathematicians of his time, which are well worth pondering over by Spiritualists. Alfred Russel Wallace in his own home had the most remarkable kind of evidence, and he naturally thought that if any of his scientific friends would witness the facts they would be satisfied; and so he brought in Professor W.B. Carpenter, but the phenomena were weak, and again with Professor Tyndall nothing remarkable took place. De Morgan, in writing to Dr. Wallace, said to him: "I doubt whether inquiry by *men of science* would lead to any result. There is much reason to think that the state of mind of the inquirer has something—be it internal or external—to do with the power of the phenomena to manifest themselves, It may be a consequence of the action of incredulous feeling on the nervous system of the recipient; or it may be that the volition—say the spirit, if you like—finds difficulty in communicating with a repellant organisation, or, maybe, is offended. Be it what it may, there is the fact." These words from such an authority are valuable, and not the least unscientific. De Morgan himself had met the evidences, for in the preface to his wife's book, *From Matter to Spirit*, he said: "I am perfectly convinced that I have seen and heard, in a manner which would make unbelief impossible, things called spiritual, which cannot be taken by a rational being to be capable of explanation by imposture, coincidence, or mistake. The Spiritualists, beyond a doubt, are in the track that has led to all advancement in physical science; their opponents are the representatives of those who have striven against progress." I had not advanced to this plane of thought at the beginning of my investigations, of course, yet I felt that there was something to unravel, and if a mind largely free from credulity and superstition could probe the matter I should succeed.

Our group, consisting of my brother-in-law and his wife, the old friend of whom I have spoken, my wife and self, sat in circle for several times without the least token of anything abnormal being given. I thought it strange that we ourselves should not have a repetition of our first night's experience. We called again for the services of the lady who had first helped us, when at once we had a repetition of the messages, if anything with stronger force. I kept saying, "Why should not this evidence come to myself?" We then began to sit with our own family only, and gradually we got phenomena of a kind we did not want. The bells in the house began ringing without any probable cause. We were annoyed, and wished they would cease. Night after night we were disturbed, and I felt that if this was all the spirits could do, we would be as well without their presence.

Mr Bowman at last invited us to one of a series of séances which had been going on in the hall for some time, at which Mr.

Robert Duguid was the medium; and at this gathering, I, for the first time, was conscious of the great reality. There I came into contact with spirit people, with some of whom I have kept up communication to this day, each one with a distinct personal manner, ever maintained, and revealing human characteristics about which there could be no doubt. "Sabo," who had been a negro slave, was the most marked personality. We got his story of how he had been stolen from his native Africa, shipped on board a slave trader, and how he had to undergo the lash till the cruelties he experienced brought release in death. A gentle, loving soul was "Sabo," full of quaint wisdom, and free from the vengeful spirit which marked some of the other controls. When speaking he always had the medium sitting on the top rail of the chair, and when he relinquished his speech the medium sat on the chair in regular fashion. "Blackhawk," a North American Indian, was of quite another stamp; a man of strong feeling, almost fierce at times in his denunciation of the cruelties which had been perpetrated on his people. He had not reached the spirit world in a contented mind, and though he told us he had got over his ferocious feelings, the coming back to earth recalled the old fierce spirit. Character, most strongly marked, was revealed in all he said; the style of utterance was bold and graphic. You could not help believing that you were in the presence of a powerful personality. "White Star" was another of the Indian band to whom we were introduced; but again we met with quite another stamp of individual. You almost felt relieved at the departure of "Blackhawk," as of one who had the power to crush you. Not that he was always thus; there were times when he was subdued, and pointed out deep spiritual truths. "White Star" was all poetry; the love of nature ran through all that he said. The Great Spirit, whom he had worshipped in the woods, was ever the theme of his discourse. The "happy hunting ground" of his earth religion had been more than realised in the beyond. When we asked questions which could be answered by a yes or no, little luminous lights would be shown in response all over the room. This would be repeated again and again. I can recall my emotions on returning home from this gathering; almost feel again the thrill which went through me. I was deeply impressed with the fact that what I had heard did not spring from some hidden source in the medium's being. I knew I had been in the presence of those whom the world had called dead. It was a momentous con-clusion, but I could not escape it.

I was now on the way, certain almost that knowledge would be added day by day. My appetite was whetted, and I began sitting with my own son, then a lad of ten years of age, and I was soon rewarded beyond measure. "Sabo" used his lips, and gave forth messages in the same manner as those coming through Robert Duguid. He also saw a board, which was held before him, and from this read out to me what was written; questions of a profound character were asked and always answered in an intelligent manner. At last I had got what I had desired—the evidence in my own home. The matter did not stop, however, with speech; what are called physical phenomena abounded. Articles were moved from place to place at times, the chair bottoms would be removed from their settings and heaped on the top of the table, while all this time I held his hand, no other person being in the room. We had been sitting on Saturday nights, and one evening I asked whether it was possible to bring anything from outside the house. Soon we had some leaves brought from the neighbouring garden. Later on I was conversing with the spirits, when a flower-pot was lifted from the top of the piano, where it was standing, and turned upside down on my lap, the earth falling on the floor. I feel that I then got sufficient evidence of a physical kind to satisfy me for all time. It literally abounded for a season in all directions, and I had little idea that it would ever cease, or I might have tabulated it fully at the time.

The following night was Sunday, and Mr. J.J. Morse had been engaged to speak in the Trades' Hall, Glassford Street. This was the first time I was privileged to hear this time-honoured trance-speaking medium, and I need hardly say that the wealth of expression, the profound setting forth of spiritual mysteries to which I then listened, opened up a new vein of thought. It was the most powerful eloquence I had as yet heard, and I felt that with such an instrument the world must soon awake. That it helped me greatly to grasp the meaning of Spiritualism is undoubted. Phenomena without a rich philosophical setting would soon pall, but when there is a perennial stream of wisdom flowing, we can be forever content.

My brother-in-law was at the meeting, and I told him about the flower-pot being lifted by unseen hands the previous evening. He was anxious to go home with me to see if it would be repeated. The three of us sat in the dark, when the usual shifting of chair bottoms and pitching about of cushions took place, and while we were in the midst of our sitting, we were summoned to go to the next room for tea. When the light shone into the room, we looked and saw that the flower-pot had disappeared from its place over the piano, and was nowhere to be seen. After tea we resumed our sitting, wondering where the flower-pot had gone, when soon after it was again placed in my lap. We knew that to tell such a story to outsiders would only cause us to be laughed at. It seemed such an incongruous thing that spirits should play such antics, but they evidently knew how necessary it was for us at this period to meet with facts which would appeal to our senses. Some of my friends thought I had been too ready in accepting the spirit hypothesis, but I do not consider it is evidence of superior talent to remain for years a doubter or inquirer, when the facts presented all point so clearly in one direction. Credulity is not a quality of mind which anyone would laud, but scepticism, in face of clear evidence, is as bad. The lame, hesitating person who is never sure about anything, who doubts the senses of hearing, seeing, and touch, is not the rational inquirer.

CHAPTER III

STORM AND PEACE

At the time of my investigations during 1876, Spiritualism occupied a prominent position in the public press, which, with one accord, seemed to delight in publishing all that could affect the subject adversely. Dr. Slade was placed at the bar, and many friends gathered round him and gave their testimony as to the reality of the phenomena taking place in his presence. Amongst them were Dr. Alfred Russel Wallace, Serjeant Cox, and Dr. Wyld, who detailed what had occurred. The magistrate who heard the evidence admitted that it was overwhelming, but held that it was inadmissible; the law did not admit that such powers as Slade claimed were possible, and had framed statutes long ago to punish the offenders. The result was that Slade was sentenced to three months' imprisonment. An appeal was made, however, bail being forthcoming, and Slade was liberated for a time. When it came on for hearing again, Serjeant Ballantyne, in his day one of the most famous pleaders at the Bar, was retained for the defence, and the charge was thrown out on some technical point. But the opponents were not inclined to let the matter drop. A new warrant for Slade's apprehension was being made out, when his friends felt that little good would come of prolonging the fight, so they had him quietly removed to Dover, whence he crossed to France and Germany, where his wonderful gifts were tested by Professor Zöllner and other savants, the results being published in Zöllner's work, entitled *Transcendental Psychics*.

Another prosecution of the same period was that of Dr. Monck, a powerful medium, who had been for long creating considerable sensation in the midland counties. Under some obsolete Vagrant Act he had been seized and imprisoned in

Huddersfield. Dr. Monck had been a Baptist minister, and all his life had been subjected to strange manifestations, which interfered with his clerical work. He got many friends to stand by him, and though pronounced guilty, an appeal was lodged, and he returned to London, where crowds gathered round when he spoke at meetings. The Ven. Archdeacon Colley has recorded the wonderful materialisation phenomena which occurred in his presence; how these materialised forms came, as it were, from his body, remained in sight for a considerable period and talked with the sitters. Money was subscribed sufficient to fight when the appeal came on, but the conviction was confirmed. The Rev. W. Stainton Moses, long known as "M.A., Oxon.," who afterwards became the editor of *Light,* was one of the staunchest supporters of Dr. Monck, and has detailed some of the wonderful evidence he got in his work entitled *Psychography.* In an appeal for funds to carry on the defence, he wrote: "An attempt, well considered and well organised, is being made to crush out all investigation into an unwelcome subject, and to revive musty statutes, with their obsolete enactments and penalties, to prevent men from exercising an inherent and sacred right, viz., the pursuit of knowledge and the search for truth. If the attempt succeeds, other unpopular subjects will share the same fate, and the dogmatism of priestcraft, rapidly dying out, will be followed by the dogmatism of materialism, which is more intolerant still."

The other persecution which characterised the year 1876 was that of a working man named Lawrence, a man of neither position nor education. He was convicted, and as, evidently, he had few friends, he suffered the imprisonment awarded. That he was one of those rare instruments capable of blessing others is undoubted; a modest, sensitive soul who, in his normal condition, had few words to say, yet when influenced by superior friends who had passed on he gave forth streams of sublime wisdom, and tests of personal identity. When he came out of prison, a retired Indian judge, A.T.T. Petterson, who met with him a short time before, arranged for a series of séances, and took careful reports of what fell from his lips while he was in the trance condition. Oriental and historical people came and spoke through him, and manifested much of the character known regarding them. These addresses, which were printed in *The Medium* and *Daybreak*, were gathered together, and form a considerable volume entitled *Essays from the Unseen* and the critical student must admit that, whatever their source, they are scholarly, reverent, logical, and comprehensive. All types and conditions of people seemed able to manifest through him. At some moments, while in the trance, he would snatch up a pen and dash off sketches and maps to illustrate his subject, some of which are artistic productions. Besides this, the most varied handwritings would be penned, facsimiles of those of departed worthies. It will scarcely be believed by future ages that in 1876 a man capable of expressing so much that was lofty would have been cast into prison as a vagrant, but although Professor Crookes and Dr. Wallace, amongst men of science, had asserted that the facts were real, the great body of scientists were materialists, and were convinced, as Tyndall had said, that "no baser delusion than Spiritualism ever obtained dominance over the weak mind of man."

While all this noise of persecution was abroad, I continued my sittings at home. My old friend, from whom I had received Wallace's book, mingled no more with us, as he was clairvoyant, and became afraid because of some of the sights presented. While sitting with him one day in the Unitarian Church, he described to me a certain spirit form which stood over the minister, and my own psychical powers beginning to develop, the name "Lessing" was spelled out through my hand. The minister, whom before this I had sought to interest in the subject, was not over friendly, as on one occasion when I had told him of some of the marvels I had witnessed, he said that he would not believe them, though he should witness them with his own eyes. On this occasion, however, I ventured to give him the description which my friend had got, and the name which had been given me, when he acknowledged that at that time he was particularly engaged with Lessing's works. As for myself, I do not believe I had ever heard the name of Lessing at this period of my mental development. My friend, however, as I have said, let the subject drop. He thought I was too deeply interested; that there were other matters more worthy of my attention, while to me it was the one subject which eclipsed everything else. We sat with a young lady who, coming from the Highlands, had been long familiar with second sight, and could tell of wonderful events which occurred amongst those who would have shuddered at the name of Spiritualist. We ourselves would hear raps on the pictures on the wall, and get some letters, if not words, on the slate, which we had placed under the table.

Amongst the spirit visitors who came to us was a person who gave the name of "Alfred Taylor," from whom we received the statement that he had been a scholar of Cambridge University, but dissipation had destroyed his chances of success. We got this story written for us through a pencil which we tied to the end of a walking stick.

Another character who invaded our sittings was an Irishman, named "James Murphy," who used my son's lips to tell his story. "James" was not at all truthful, and would force himself in when not specially wanted.

He seemed to take great delight when he managed to deceive. To avoid being troubled with strange spirits we arranged with "Alfred Taylor" that we should always feel certain of his presence if he began his writing with a Latin quotation, and many were the pointed epigrammatic sentences which were written down. We generally knew when some other spirit was seeking to find an entrance, although the writing itself had no marked characteristic. One night the assertion was made that "Alfred Taylor" was present.

When we asked for the test of his presence, the usual pointed quotation, "James Murphy" was evidently put out, and after some hesitation he wrote down "Be jabers." It was a real revelation of an individuality which had not been changed by death. That we could have invented such people as "Alfred Taylor" and "James Murphy" is simply impossible; they were spirits on the Borderland, getting some measure of satisfaction by coming into our presence.

Our lady friend after a time was entranced, and many were the beautiful addresses which were given through her lips, all exhibiting a lofty spirit of purity and piety. Some lines of the sweet poems which were poured forth still linger in my memory after all these years. An old friend of hers controlled, and recounted some incidents which had occurred in her early life, such as how he had taken a copy of Paine's *Age of Reason* out of her hands, which she had been seeking to read secretly. All of this was a surprise to her when she came out of trance. Altogether I found her a most valuable instrument for spirit people who were capable of blessing us; but, unfortunately, I happened to tell a friend, who knew her family, of the consoling messages we were receiving. He conveyed the fact to her relatives, from whom came the command that she must have "no more connection with a subject which was devilish." The lady was herself dominated with the Christian idea: the Deity of Jesus must not be touched. She has since then made some mark in literature, and no doubt remembers those pleasant gatherings, when we thought not of dogma but were contented to be bathed in the loving magnetism of the superior spirit people.

These experiences were gathered during the first three months of my spiritual awakening. I felt that no power could ever crush out of me the sense of the reality of the facts. Carlyle had harsh things to say of Spiritualism, because of lack of knowledge as to its bearing on modern thought and life; yet he did say a true thing when he uttered these words: "The weak thing, weaker than a child, becomes strong one day if it be a true thing."

Spiritualism, from its first glimpse, has never appeared to me other than a religion, a fuller revelation of man's relationship to the world of spirit, and therefore one step nearer to God. If Jesus of Nazareth, who "brought life and immortality to light," and pointed more clearly man's true relationship to the Infinite, is recognised as the founder of a new religion, surely Spiritualism, which has widened the doors of communication between the two worlds, and permitted us to hear the music of heaven, is worthy of being called a divine religion. If it has contradicted some unwarrantable, unsupportable, and baseless ideas, which have floated down the stream of time, it has replaced them by others more worthy of acceptance. Man could never have fallen from a state of perfection, never could be estranged or lost from God.

We have been tearing out each other's eyes, as Carlyle says, over "Plenary Inspiration," while the Bible, of whose inspiration doubt is impossible, is open before us. The light of knowledge comes to earnest souls in all ages, and the earnest-hearted and wise of our day are ever writing new chapters of the Book of Revelation.

Darwin and Spencer and Huxley have had poured upon them a large measure of inspiration, which they have verified by looking at God's handwriting, which shows that man has evolved from lower forms of being, and has progressed from the lowest estate to his present civilisation by inherent power of growth. Our history is not a retreat; it is a march forward. Mythology fancies a "fall," history records an ascension. Whether that nebulous haze which Tyndall talks of had within it the potentialities, the prediction of all that has since occurred, or whether, as Dr. Wallace postulates, there was a period in the evolution when a divine something was implanted from the source of Power which separated man from the world below him, we may not know. The men and women, however, who have laboured to read God's handwriting were inspired searchers obedient to the command of truth as much as the patriarchs, prophets, and apostles of olden times.

The spirit people, who use human lips, declare that sin, or evil, is due to imperfection, which can only be eradicated by normal growth; that "man makes his own future, stamps his own character, suffers for his own sins, and must work out his own salvation either here or in the hereafter." Immortality, the spirits say, is not bestowed on account of certain beliefs, or any sacrifice, but is evolved from and a direct continuance of the physical being. They hold with Paul that there is a natural body and a spiritual body, which the ego or soul personage presides over; that at the crisis or evolution of death we slough off the earthly covering, and march into a world where we shall find our fitting place. Spiritualism declares emphatically that the spirit world is peopled with just such souls as are daily going out from earth, and that the commencement of the spiritual life is just where the last hour of earthly life leaves you. If you go out with a prayer and a blessing, you enter the spirit world with a prayer and a blessing. If you go out as the miser does, with his hands clutching his gold, you will go out with the gold on your heart. If you prepare yourself for any course of life, then death will find you just as you have prepared yourself. Every spirit enters the spirit world dwarfed or beautiful according to its spiritual nature; for every deed of earthly life the spirit itself shall bear the exact resemblance of what that life has been. Clairvoyants see these conditions; spirits, through mortal lips, tell the universal tale. There is no word of miracle, no hint of being affected by beliefs; but amendment is possible through the yearning for higher things. The undeveloped must climb innumerable steps, with humbleness and diligence and pain, and in that new condition there are many whose soul growth is increased by assisting the soul growth of others. Delight comes to all who extend the helping hand to those who need such help. Much of this was revealed to me during my first few months' association with the subject.

Mr Robert Duguid became a weekly visitor at my home, and while we had many lofty and soul-stirring addresses on the spiritual life, and the need of presenting ourselves pure in the sight of God and His ministers, there were brought to our circle at times, by helpful souls, those who had not yet awakened to the change of death, who had gone out of life sodden and degraded, with scarce a thought other than for animal enjoyments. In this work of redemption were engaged some of those Indians who seem to have a mission, and whose magnetic powers enable them to reach more readily those who are close to the earthly atmosphere. We had brought to us on one occasion a soldier spirit who had had his leg shot off at Balaclava. After his discharge from the army he had lived in Ayr, where by deep carousing he had managed to separate soul from body. When he had controlled the medium, he spoke about the darkness he had been dwelling in so long, and wanted to know where he was. He had no conception that he had passed through the change of death, and when we told him he had died he was loud in his protestations against such an idea. We were "a set of fools." He was as "much alive as any of us." And then he began to speak about his great thirst, praying that we would give him just a drop of something to steady him. He would go for it himself, but that he had lost his leg. We sought to awaken him to his true position, but in vain. With all our arguments he seemed to have the best of it. With one hand in the medium's pocket, he rattled the money that was there as the best evidence that he was not a dead man. When we refused to supply him with the drink, he pleaded for some tobacco, "just a chew" would satisfy him, he said. He rose in indignation, saying he had got into the society of a lot of Methodists; but, strange to tell, the fact that he was without a leg while in the body seemed to have an effect on the spirit, for the medium's body fell on the floor, and the voice kept lamenting his helplessness through lack of limb, and again beseeching us to meet his terrible craving. The attendant spirits no doubt effected his release from controlling the medium, and, as we were told at a subsequent period, his eyes were opened to his true position, and the first steps taken to march into the light. This was but one of many such cases, which showed how the spiritual, like another atmosphere, acts upon this world of ours, swaying, governing, and directing it according as we invite good or evil spirits. That hypnotic, or mesmeric, control is possible between mortal and mortal is now pretty well admitted, and it is but a step from this to admit the hypnotism from the unseen, by which undeveloped spirits in some way gratify their appetites in measure by obsessing sensitives in the earthly life. The fact is there, whether we shut our eyes to it or not. Better to face the problem with knowledge than to ignore the subject. Knowledge is power in every realm of being, and law, not caprice, rules the world. Even as the law of science declares, like attracts like, so the spiritual law declares that if you are governed by evil spirits, it is because your thoughts are evil and inviting to them.

Statements, such as I make, are often repudiated because everyone has not met with similar occurrences. Every new idea which has blessed the world was waiting, like Spiritualism, for recognition. Most persons have been taught that spirit communion belongs to the past; that although Moses and Elias were said to have spoken to Jesus on the mountain top, that was a miraculous occurrence, and had no relation to Nature's laws. But, after all, spirit intercourse is as natural as the sunlight shining upon us, or the air we breathe, only men have not known it. When Swedenborg spoke forth the things he had seen and heard in spiritual places, the world would have none of it; he was but a dreamer of dreams. When Blake with his spiritual vision painted his pictures of those unseen ones who stood before him, or penned the spiritual melodies which were sung in his ear, he was a madman. Many persons in all ages have seen the faces and heard the voices of the departed, but, after being refused credence, they have kept their experiences in their own minds. How difficult it is to see the green fields if the window through which we look be encrusted with the dust of many years! How difficult, therefore, to see what is around us if the windows of the soul have been closed!

CHAPTER IV

THE LITERATURE OF SPIRITUALISM

Of the many surprises which came to me in my investigations, none were greater than to know the deep wells of knowledge that were embedded in the literature of Spiritualism. I had walked through life almost unconscious that any men or women of great worth had contributed to it, or had acknowledged the facts to be real.

From my earliest days Robert Owen was one of the names I held in honour; I had conversed with those who had known him closely while labouring at his philanthropic schemes, and while myself a believer in Christian dogma had regretted that such a good man had not recognised the true religion. I do not know that I was a believer in his fundamental doctrines, that man came into the world like a sheet of paper upon which anything could be written, good or bad; that he was entirely a creature of the circumstances under which he was placed; but it was the high-souled man I loved for his unselfishness, ever seeking to mitigate the woes of humanity. What a delight it was for me to read that such a lofty soul had met with facts such as mine, and was able to say that "the sum of his whole lifelong endeavour to bless and improve his fellow men paled before that mighty illumination which brought to him the assurance of immortality, and the certainty of reunion with all we have loved and lost on earth, in another and better world." There have been few men who have earned the same loving regard from their disciples as Robert Owen. I have never met a soul who came into personal touch with him (and in my earlier years I knew some of his closest companions), but who spoke of him as having a calm settled love for all that was honourable and good; that an air of wisdom and sweetness was in all he did or said. Instinctively, all felt he was a great man, and those who ranged themselves under his banner, secularists many of them, laboured for progress, though they believed that it ended with the tomb. That a man like Owen in his latter years got to know that the lever which moves the earth has its fulcrum in the unseen has given me a special joy.

Of spiritualist literature which is not likely ever to perish are the books written by Owen's gifted son, the American statesman, Robert Dale Owen. The clear evidence of spirit return in his case dissipated the materialism that had ruled his life. The truth at all costs was the maxim of his life, and when he met it in the form of Spiritualism, he worshipped it, and devoted his life to its expansion. The old miracles taught him by his pious mother, the daughter of Glasgow's famous citizen, David Dale, he had long discarded, because they were represented as being violations of natural law. But the phenomena which he met, however wonderful, now appeared as part of nature's processes. The believing heart which the exclusive claims of Christianity had destroyed, was his once more. All the facts that his earnest penetration gathered are lucidly set down in those priceless volumes *Footfalls on the Boundary of Another World*, and the less known work, *The Debatable Land*. The man or woman who faces these records will find it difficult to discover a weak spot in the chain of argument, or to brush aside the great realities there presented. Robert Dale Owen became one of the most religious of men. The deep things of God absorbed his thought, and he became satisfied that the Master Soul was indeed opening the eyes of His children to the happy destiny that is theirs when the clash and din of earthly life are over. He knew for a certainty that the soul's progress begun on earth continues through the great chain of existence, and that all souls will ultimately rise to purity and happiness in the realm beyond.

Spiritualism appeared of tremendous importance when I reflected that all the controversial books written and all the preaching from the pulpits had never brought any belief as to God and immortality to those who denied; while there was no genuine evidence on record of the unbeliever becoming a believer through Christian effort, Spiritualism, despised and rejected, had worked greater wonders than centuries of preaching. A most potent fact is this, which would startle the world were it to become earnest in its thinking on religious questions.

Perhaps a greater surprise to me than even the works of Dale Owen, were the more phenomenal books which were penned or dictated by men who were not scholars like him, but who had matriculated at the university of the spirit. *Hafed, Prince of Persia*, had but just appeared when I entered the ranks. Here was a most wonderful narrative. relating to life on earth and in heaven, which was said to be dictated by one who had been a personal follower of Jesus of Nazareth. The medium who, week after week, poured forth the wonderful story, was but a working man, a joiner by trade, without scholarship, had never travelled, and could not be called a reader of books. Surely a remarkable incident to occur in these modern days. I obtained the volume before I saw the man David Duguid, and felt it was a most enchanting book. I wondered what the great man, to whom those pictures of a past age were revealed, could be like; for it was a tremendous claim to make that the real authors of the book had been contemporaries and companions of the Man of Nazareth. I soon got to know all the people who had been associated in its production, not one of whom was either a scholar or had any pretensions to scholarship or literary gifts. These men were persons of the best moral quality, who would never dream of perpetrating a deception; but deception was out of the question, for even had whole libraries of books been at their command, such questions as are put in that volume could not have been met. Training and culture of the most extended nature would have been requisite. The volume gave a simple and rational explanation of the instrument's growth, how step by step the spirits had been able to influence him, until the work was produced. The plates which illustrate the text are as wonderful as the literary matter. I have looked at the original drawing of these and seen the signatures of the friends, whom I got to know well, on the back of the cards, which signatures were placed there before the spirits made their drawings. The hands of the medium were tied behind his back, the room shrouded in darkness, with all the members of the circle joining hands, in a ring, while the invisible artists effected their work. But, perhaps, as wonderful as this is the fact that inscriptions are correctly put down in Hebrew, Greek, and Latin, by the entranced man, when no one present had the least knowledge of either Hebrew, Greek, or Latin. The nineteenth century with all its wonders has not much that is more marvellous to record than the production of this remarkable book.

Mr. Hay Nisbet, a well known printer in Glasgow, had been associated with David Duguid since their first investigation into the matter. He it was who took down the words as they fell from the medium's lips, and who made the corrections which were dictated by the spirits when it was read over to them. Mr. Nisbet I knew well for years, a true-hearted, religious man, who might be called a broad-minded Christian, and who, to the last, did not forsake his church. On his invitation I attended some of the meetings, and several times witnessed the production of messages in Greek, Latin, and Hebrew, as well as the direct spirit paintings, many of which, in those early years, when the regular circle was not disturbed, were really artistic gems. The association of the medium with certain old Dutch artists is as well established almost as any fact could be. There were many tests as to their identity, carefully tabulated by Mr. Nisbet, and nothing has ever since overthrown this collection of facts.

At my first sitting I witnessed phenomena which I have never forgotten, and I can recollect saying to myself, when I saw a globe of light travelling from the end of the room, and assuming the form of a human hand when it reached the table, "There never can come to me in all the future years anything which will weaken or make me deny what I am now witnessing." It was, I think, almost my first experience of physical phenomena, and though I have ofttimes since seen the full form built up, nothing impressed itself so markedly on my memory as this first event, which, with many others, in those early years of inquiry, satisfied all doubts, and produced a calm spirit on this great question which has never deserted me. Darwin once said, "With regard to a future life everyone must draw his own conclusions from vague and contradictory probabilities," but though once I would have echoed his sentiments, I now had perfect assurance that the question had been settled—for me at least, for all time.

The great books of Andrew Jackson Davis presented to my view such a luminous philosophy, such a scientific view of Nature's processes, that I had to recognise that real scholars did not need to matriculate at an earthly university; that great teachers from the world of spirit could send down their illuminated thoughts through such sensitive natures as were capable of receiving the afflatus. There is scarcely in all history anything so wonderful as the presentation of such a body of truth as was given to Davis. A shoemaker's apprentice, with scarcely the rudiments of ordinary education, he was utilised to present astounding descriptions of God, man, creation, the solar and astral systems, the mystery of force, life, and being, the order of creation, in eloquent burning words, and to express thoughts almost beyond earthly comprehension. There was sublimity in every line, yet he, the normal lad, knew nothing; neither scientific terms nor the simplest facts known to schoolboys. The boy of sixteen could not even spell the words he used. No fact could be better attested than that of the manner of the production of *Nature's Divine Revelation*, and nothing more astounding was ever presented to the world. Had we not the faculty of overlooking the most transcendent things, the world would have stood in awe and wonder before such an important event as the production of this book. It is true that on its appearance, some sixty years ago, there was some little commotion over it in America, which got as far as one or two popular journals here; but all this was soon forgotten, and the man remains largely unrecognised and unknown. It is a volume "not for an age, but for all time." Each new generation will find, as other and better ideas come into circulation, that Davis had already dealt with them. The "Descent of Man," as described by Darwin, was clearly portrayed by this lad, who was reared in the school of destitution. No human teachers taught him; only God and His ministering spirits. This volume, which discoursed of suns, stars, systems, astronomy, geology, physiology, and every known science, was followed by others, the matter of which was dictated to himself and written down when his faculties had been unfolded still further by the spirit teachers. All inspirations of past ages sink into insignificance before those of Davis.

Swedenborg, a spiritual medium, who had the education of universities, did reveal some things regarding the spirit world when his spiritual faculties were opened up in mature years, but the ascended Swedenborg was able to express through Davis's faculties something more comprehensible and nearer to man's state than he did when on earth. The time must surely come when these stupendous revelations, which throw light on man's onward march, will commend themselves to every civilised nation. As yet, Davis, surely the profoundest scientist, the loftiest teacher of religion, is not at the head of any church, temple, or university. The greatest phenomenon of the ages is to be found acting as a consulting physician, for body and soul, as he describes his work, in the city of Boston, where I found him a few years since.

I have in my possession a volume of the *People's Journal*, published in this country in 1847, a magazine which had amongst its contributors John Stuart Mill, Sir John Bowring, Harriet Martineau, and other notable writers, and there I find an article penned by Parke Godwin, a well-known *littérateur*, and the son-in-law of Bryant, the American poet, wherein he writes of Davis's first great work: "It carries the doctrine of progressive development into all spheres with the most rigid and unflinching logic, and as a mere work of speculation is full of the highest interest. It could only have been written by a man of extensive acquirements and the most vivid and vigorous imagination. But if we suppose it to be what it purports to be, the spontaneous utterings of a clairvoyant, it becomes one of the most extra-ordinary works that was ever published." How much I owed to Davis in those early years of inquiry! What rapture and gratitude were called forth at the thought that such inspiration was given to mortals in these days! The whole subject appeared in a new light. I could understand Shakespeare better; could recognise how much real inspiration had been streaming from the unseen, which properly tuned sensitives had caught up and interpreted in their own language. I did not take these writings as being in any sense infallible; to me they were but human and incomplete, but they were studded with mighty truths, and, in spite of all imperfections, were the best interpretation and revelation of the inner life that the world had yet had.

I revelled in spiritual literature. It was to me so rational, comprehensive, and soul-satisfying. Davis did not stand alone, a single figure in the firmament of marvels, for Hudson Tuttle's *Arcana of Nature* and *Arcana of Spiritualism* revealed the same quickening power at work. There were other volumes that told the story of spirit action on mortals which also had their charm, and amongst these were the poems of Lizzie Doten, who gave evidence through her mediumship that in the mysterious depths of the inner life all souls can hold communion with those invisible beings who are our companions for time and eternity. She translated the messages of the spirits into human language in the most melodious tunes. "Edgar Allan Poe" came back again through this woman, with all his old poetic imagery and fire, and though other poets, "Robert Burns" amongst them, came to her side, "Poe" is there without a shadow of doubt. His "Farewell to Earth" is not a mere poem of the imagination, but a record of his life. In it he says:

> I will sunder, and forever,
> Every tie of human passion that can bind my
> soul to earth,
> Every slavish tie that binds me to the things of
> little worth.

You feel that those poems given by "Poe," "The Streets of Baltimore" and "Resurrexi," are not imitations of some master, but strains from the souls of ministering spirits.

Amidst all my reading I kept up the communion with spirits week by week. My soul was stirred, and life altogether presented a brighter and loftier aspect. A new phase of being was mine. I was never alone, for there streamed through my mind thoughts and aspirations which acted on my mode of life. The sublime philosophy sustained by the daily facts submerged all gloom and doubt. I had a key to all religions, and could call none of them false, but only imperfect expressions of those great problems with which in all ages men had sought to grapple. The "Thus saith the Lord" of the Bible days was but the outcome of the fervour which possessed the speaker when the exhilaration of spirit presence came upon him; but humanity can only tell the heavenly story in earthly language, which ofttimes fails to give the true shade of meaning.

CHAPTER V

ALEXANDER DUGUID

I was brought into touch during 1877 with another seer, in the person of Mr. Alexander Duguid, a brother of the mediums of whom I have spoken. Alexander Duguid at this time resided at Kirkcaldy. Being a person of pious mind, deeply imbued with what is called Christian truth, he felt called to come to Glasgow when he heard that his brothers had taken up with this heresy of Spiritualism. But his coming to Glasgow sent him back a changed man; the "new superstition," as Spiritualism is sometimes called, had destroyed the old one, and henceforth he also was to become a labourer in the spiritual vineyard. The spirit friends who used the voice of his brother Robert soon began to influence him also, and it would have been difficult to recognise any difference between the "Sabo" and "Blackhawk" and others who spoke through the brothers—Robert in Glasgow and Alexander in Kirkcaldy. Themes that I had discussed with the spirits in Glasgow were taken up by the spirits in Kirkcaldy, and fully entered upon. The mundane affairs of our lives seemed to be familiar to them, and great surprise was mine ofttimes when I joined in with the sitters at Kirkcaldy. Alexander was, normally, the most cultured of the three brothers, but his reading had been neither varied nor extensive. With what delight I joined in this Kirkcaldy gathering, where ofttimes I was brought near the gates of heaven!

In this modest little bedroom we held converse with some of the great ones of earth. I know how much Spiritualism has suffered through the introduction of great names, while the matter presented fell so much below the earthly standard; but even these imperfect productions are often intimations of what might have been had there been more effective instruments upon which the spirits could pour their inspiration. I am as certain as I am of anything, that I have held converse with "Joseph Priestley," the discoverer of oxygen, whom religious bigotry forced to flee from Birmingham to America on account of his Unitarian opinions. Through the medium his master mind grappled with great problems, and revealed personality most clearly. Incidents of his earthly life were recalled, and the real human soul was made patent to us. I do not think any of the other sitters had ever heard his name, though he had been visiting them a long time before I joined the circle. I had no doubt about the man, so many traits making his identity clear. I used to wonder what could be the meaning of all this stream of eloquent wisdom being poured out for the benefit of the few persons of no importance who gathered there. But the spirits saw the wisdom of it all, and knew that it was not in vain.

Once a month or so Mr. William Oxley, of Manchester, made one of the group who listened to the heavenly truths. He took down the story of an ancient Druid control, who gave some graphic pictures of our country in prehistoric times, and it was published by him in the pages of a magazine called *Human Nature*. Mr. Oxley was a man of some scholarship. He had been a Methodist, but through certain spiritual experiences he had drifted to Swedenborgianism. If Methodism is an emotional religion, Swedenborgianism is an intellectual one, and he studied Swedenborg's philosophy as well as his theology. Swedenborgians, as is well known, while admitting the fact of spirit agency, choose to class it as the work of disorderly spirits. When Mr. Oxley met with the facts of Spiritualism he recognised at once something more profound and orderly than his late friends had grasped. He made the discovery, with his scientific and philosophical bent, that Swedenborg himself did not fully comprehend his own seership; that he had not penetrated beyond the spiritual-natural spheres; that, like other seers in the domains. or physical and spiritual things, he had to leave his visions for others, who will continue to apply them to the elevation of mankind. Mr. Oxley, under inspiration, translated the *Bhagavad Gita*, an ancient Hindu poem, which he published under the title of *Philosophy of Spirit*, and later on he wrote and published a work on *Egypt and the Wonders of the Land of the Pharaoh*, which was the outcome of a visit to that classic spot. So that it can be seen he was a man of some attainments. For years, at a circle in Manchester, he had been engaged in taking down, week after week, the matter which flowed from the lips of a control, and which was published in some five or six volumes. This work, which is entitled *Angelic Revelations concerning the Ultimation and Destiny of the Human Spirit*, contains much of a symbolic and mystical nature.

One of the striking facts concerning its production is that the spirit at the circle at Manchester gave instructions to Mr. Oxley to go to Glasgow, and get the spirit artists, who worked through Mr. David Duguid, to furnish the illustrations for each volume as it was prepared. These illustrations are all of an allegorical or mystic character, which require some interpretation, and the sitters at Glasgow had no knowledge of or sympathy with this particular phase of spiritual thought. Yet each time Mr. Oxley went to Glasgow there was produced by direct spirit action, in the same manner as the direct paintings were produced, these most suggestive bits of artistic work There are few facts I have met with that made a stronger impression on me. There was no possible loophole of escape from accepting these pictures as the spirits' work. Mr. Oxley was not the type of person to be imposed upon, but the character of the illustrations alone was the best test of their spirit authenticity.

Mr Oxley, like myself, found the Kirkcaldy circle full of charm; there ever breathed amidst its members a spirit of calm receptivity. It was an opening into the higher realms of life. Great souls poured out their wealth of thought; the fountain of knowledge and exalted spirituality seemed to be inexhaustible. Among others, "John Stuart Mill" told us he was still at work on problems regarding the social amelioration of the world; that his writings contained a spiritual germ, though unknown to himself at the time of writing, and that they had done a work and might do more; that now his promptings were given to all toilers for human welfare, who might be susceptible to his influence. He often referred in tones of admiration to Gladstone, with whom he was in the closest sympathy. "Harriet Martineau" spoke to us of how she had failed to grasp the truth of continued existence when on earth, and in glowing strains dwelt on her unexpected awakening to the joys of the higher life. At every meeting she would put forth her ideas, so different in manner and idioms of speech from the other spiritual visitors. There was continual reference to her work on earth, and to those with whom she had laboured. I have been present when many who were familiar with her life's history wore with us, and these would cross-examine the intelligence, only to find the strictest accuracy in the statements made. Once the Rev. William Bennett, then Unitarian minister at Aberdeen, said to me, "I cannot doubt what is presented, but cannot realise it. Could I only feel the truth as you do, I would preach it from the house tops. Once let Bible infallibility be weakened, and much of the fabric falls to pieces. Without Spiritualism I can see nothing which can prevent the world drifting into Agnosticism."

The medium knew nothing of Harriet Martineau's life or character, while my own knowledge of her history was of the most limited kind. I knew that she had dabbled in mesmerism, which had not brought her, as it has others, into the brighter light of spirit existence, and that she had to the end of her earthly career called herself a materialist. Now, when she came amongst us. there were continual expressions of regret at her blindness while on earth.

After one of the meetings during the latter part of 1877, I sent a short report of the sitting to *The Medium*, then the leading spiritualist newspaper, in which I said: "The sublime thoughts expressed roused within us feelings akin to the heavenly; that while regretting her earthly intellectual errors, she promised now with enlarged powers and more glorious aims, still to toil for all that was best." I said I could convey but little of the wealth of language, the golden thoughts in choice phrases, which had been expressed. I was surprised to find within a week or two in *The Medium* some questions asked me through the newspaper by Henry G. Atkinson, her old friend and collaborator. He wanted to know, "After what manner was the address of 'Harriet Martineau' made?" "I presume," he said, "the intellectual errors referred to the views we published together in the *Letters on the Laws of Man's Nature* in 1851, and reproduced in the *Autobiography*, in respect of which, if 'Harriet Martineau' was alive and able, she could not have failed to send me a message." My response to Mr. Atkinson was briefly as follows: "I regret my incapacity to carry in my memory all that was said, and re-state it in consecutive form. Whatever may have been the principles conceived and jointly promulgated in the *Letters* referred to by you, I have no knowledge of, not having read either them or the *Autobiography*. Only 'Harriet Martineau' herself can tell the motive which prompted her to express her opinions to the body of sitters at Kirkcaldy. What I have set down, however, is perfectly clear, that she, 'Harriet Martineau,' had misconstrued the real meaning of spiritual existence while in earth life; that the perpetuity of the individual in a super-earthly condition, with power to act, and a sphere of individual action, congenial and fitting, had never until now opened its reality to her most aspiring dreams. I have no doubt, were the way open, the first one to whom she would think of imparting her newly acquired knowledge would be he, who, to a large extent, had shared her thoughts and sympathies in the past; but most probably the conditions have not been forthcoming for her to communicate directly with you yourself." I added, that should he "trouble himself to go to Kirkcaldy, he would there be enabled to prove for himself the existence of the real, living, conscious personality of his friend, 'Harriet Martineau.'" Mr. Atkinson was then an old man, residing in France, so that the opportunity offered was never taken advantage of.

All the experiences which I have noted came to me without money or price. Alexander Duguid was a working saddler, who gladly shared the bright knowledge that had come to him without thinking of any reward. The same remark applied to the brothers, David and Robert, in Glasgow, who spent themselves to bless others, without a thought of the money question. I shall have further opportunities of referring to the remarkable mediumistic gifts of Alexander Duguid, both in the matter of clairvoyance and materialisation.

CHAPTER VI

PERSONAL DEVELOPMENTS

During 1877 I kept up my attendance at the Spiritualists' Hall on Sundays, and was often called upon to speak on the subject which now engrossed all my thoughts. I continued to attend the East End Unitarian Church in the forenoons, of which place I was treasurer. There came, however, a period when I felt that no good purpose was served by dividing my energies; that Spiritualism contained all of truth that was in Unitarianism, with the addition of facts that appealed to all the faculties.

I had now begun to be conscious of the spirits' presence in my own person. Gradually the spirit people were able to make me feel that they could come into touch with me. My hands would be moved to make responses to questions asked, and I would be lifted from my seat and forcibly shaken by the unseen powers. Clairvoyants would see spirit hands touching me, and I would feel the fingers of my ascended boy on my forehead. Hundreds of times have I put up my hand to touch this something on my head, which, to my senses, was quite objective. Ofttimes when I would be carried away by some impetuous feeling, the finger touches would come and bring the needed reflection, followed by calm and rest. Through all the years has this phenomenon continued with me, calling forth feelings of gratitude. In the hours of gloom and sadness, when there is only the memory of the open vision, the touches come to cheer me up and make me conscious that I am not alone. At other times I find myself muttering strange words which I do not comprehend, and mediums who are influenced by Indian spirits often respond to them, and keep up a seeming conversation in a language unknown to me. When sitting with my wife and family my boy would use my lips to utter his feelings towards us, ofttimes rhyming out his story of gladness. I have never had the gift of rhyme, and to produce anything which would be at all rhythmical or harmonious would be an effort slowly accomplished; but under this influence the rhyme would rush along without volition on my part. The addition of personal spiritual contact in this way was of immense value. Travelling as I did at the time all over the country, day by day I led a charmed life, conscious of the companionship and help of the ministering ones. I would sit alone at nights in hotels, and commune with those friends with whom I had been brought into contact at the spirit circle. I would feel the strong "Blackhawk" or the gentle "Sabo," and ofttimes in my heart thanked God for Spiritualism and all it had brought me. It absorbed all the religious faculties of my nature, and blended philosophy and religion in harmony. I felt I was privileged in knowing of a religion which combined all that science had to teach and all that philosophy could expound. I knew that nothing could ever disturb its basic facts, that the dead came back and refreshed the lives of the living.

The old order of supernatural prophets, oracles, and special seers had gone, and now inspiration had to be looked at in the light of reason. Spiritualism had done with mystery and miracle, and sought to give a rational interpretation of the processes by which the souls of men had been lighted up. It pointed to men and women that other great continent, from which could be transmitted thoughts, feelings, and ideas, without the use of physical wires, thus linking together the seen and the unseen.

Spiritualism has embraced all the truths relative to man's spiritual nature, capacities, relations, duties, welfare, and destiny; all that is known, or to be known, relative to other spiritual beings, and the occult forces and laws of the universe. Insensibly, to us it has been seeking to build up the land of righteousness, in which the world might dwell in harmony. It is thus all-comprehensive. Its great practical aim has been the quickening and unfolding of the spiritual or divine nature in man, to the end that the animal or selfish tendencies may be outgrown. Man's salvation, or harmony of being, is only to be attained by growth, slow and steady, never losing hold of any good thing till a better has been found to take its place. Spiritualism encourages the loftiest aspirations, and energises the soul by presenting only exalted motives. It prompts to ever higher endeavours, and inculcates noble self-reliance. It seeks to free man from the authority of book or creed, its only authority being truth, its interpreter reason. It can have no binding creed; every individual must be a law unto himself and draft his own creed, not seeking to force it on others. Its aim is not to build up an isolated sect, but to enter into and verify by its inspiring truth all organisations of men and urge them onward. Surely such aims are worthy of the consideration of all men who desire the kingdom of heaven on earth, and wish to be in harmony with what should be recognised as real religion.

The surroundings of the Glasgow Trongate meeting-place were anything but aesthetic, yet, to me, it became a veritable Loretto shrine. It was the place where life and immortality were constantly brought to light; where the stone had been removed from the sepulchre of my mentality; and where death was revealed, not as a story of gloom, but as one of gladness. What mattered the surroundings? As an ancient poet has said:—

> And this I know, whether the One True Light
> Kindle to love, or wrath consume me quite;
> One glimpse of It within the tavern caught;,
> Better than in the temple lost outright.

When wending my way up the long flight of stairs, I ofttimes thought, what would the outside world say of me were it told that my object in visiting this place was to hold converse with the denizens of another world?

On Sunday evenings there were addresses delivered, and during the week select gatherings were held, when we looked into the faces and felt the hand-clasp of the immortals. For us there could be no more talk of the "bourne from whence no traveller returns." We had learned more on this matter than the great Shakespeare himself. With all our faculties we had tested the phenomena, and doubt was destroyed forever. We had done with faith; we no longer blindly followed the authority of others instead of using our own perceptions.

There were many instruments who were acted upon besides the brothers Duguid, and amongst them was a sterling, thoughtful man named William Birrell, whose devotion and enthusiasm was a noble example to us all. Many times would this man walk in from Hamilton and back again, so that he might be present at the meetings. He had a fine type of face and head, like that of some noble old Greek. The spirit people come to him and lifted him out of great darkness into a marvellous light, and now, by the unfolding of his spiritual faculties, he himself could see and describe the spirit people and be controlled to express their wisdom. For many years he had been an Atheist, but coming touch with James Nicholson, who will be known by some as a sweet minor poet, the subject of Spiritualism was brought under his notice. The talk had chanced to fall, on one occasion, on mediums and spirits, and the wonderful things which were said to take place through their agency. Mr. Birrell, at whose house the meeting took place, naturally said: "Why not try here, and now, to get these marvels amongst ourselves?" A small table was at hand and they gathered round it, whereupon Mr. Birrell was almost immediately entranced and began to describe the condition of the people in the spirit world.

Mr. Nicholson has given the details of this séance in a little book which he published, entitled *The Vision of Mirza*. Mr. Birrell, who was a mechanic, had many inventions presented to his spiritual vision, some of which he patented, but without financial success, for though, intellectually, what I should call a great man, he had little capacity for business. Quite a number of his useful inventions which came on the market and found a great sale were first shown to me by the spiritual inventor. He was too simple and honest, however, for the commercial world, and he would walk round and reveal his ideas openly, often getting them copied before he had obtained any protection. Governors for steam engines, railway brakes, limelights, and dozens of other inventions came to him. When I first knew him he had patented an automatic limelight apparatus, which seemed likely to be a great business success. It was a most ingenious appliance, and every part of the idea had been put before him by the spirits. Eventually, however, he never made much out of it.

Financial success never came to him, but he was ever bright and contented. He used to rhyme out long poems, many of which had the real fire in them. I could fancy Robert Burns to have been such a man as William Birrell, and Burns was said to be the spiritual author of the sweet Doric lays which came through him. I recollect Mr. Birrell once delivering an address in trance, clear and penetrating, and at the close of "G.V. Brooke," the actor, one of his controls, in order to give a fuller illustration of the subject which had been dealt with, gave, with fine dramatic effect, through the medium, the soliloquy of the King in *Hamlet*, in which he speaks of forgiveness as not being possible while he holds the fruits of his misdeeds in his possession. The soul of the great actor seemed to manifest itself with the old fire. What a rousing effect it had on us!

Mr Birrell's ordinary trance addresses were slowly spoken, but under the control of "G.V. Brooke" there came forth a veritable torrent of living power.

CHAPTER VII

SOME STRENUOUS WORKERS

At this time we had several visits from Miss Annie Fairlamb, of Newcastle-on-Tyne, a young woman who had been developed as a medium for the building up of fully formed materialised bodies. Newcastle had caught the spiritual fervour, from which had sprung up some valuable instruments. Miss Fairlamb was a modest, simple-minded, light-hearted girl, who regarded her spirit controls as dear friends. The importance of the work in which she was engaged did not seem to affect her gaiety, and she was delighted simply at the joy she gave to others by her powers as a medium. Materialisation seems the most difficult of all the spirit phenomena for ordinary mortals to believe in. That Jesus was seen by His apostles after His death does not seem to help the present age to a comprehension of it, though to the early Christians so important was this re-appearance that Paul said if it were not true, then all his preaching was in vain. It was what is known as the resurrection, or re-appearance, that was the great fact with the early Christian Church—a fact considered of even greater importance than the ethical teachings associated with the name of its founder. Renan and Strauss have, of course, dissected this story of the resurrection, and cast it aside as not having sufficient evidence to support it, which is not to be wondered at in this age which seeks to test everything with the point of the dissecting knife of science before giving it credence. If materialisation be a fact in nature, the disproving of this one special case does not affect its truth in the slightest. One swallow does not make a summer, nor does the re-appearance of a miraculously born man help the world to accept or deny materialisation as a natural fact having any bearing on men of ordinary birth. Spiritualism has no place for the miraculous. In nature no law is ever violated, and every event which occurs must be taken to be a part of nature, until proof to the contrary is supplied. As Huxley says: "The day-fly has better grounds for calling a thunderstorm supernatural than has man, with his experience of an infinitesimal fraction of duration, to say that the most astounding event that can be imagined is beyond the scope of natural causes."

> *There is no great and no small*
> *To the Soul that maketh all;*
> *And where it cometh all things are;*
> *And it cometh everywhere.*
>
> *I am the owner of the sphere,*
> *Of the seven stars and the solar year;*
> *Of Caesar's's hand and Plato's brain,*
> *Of Lord Christ's heart and Shakespeare's strain.*

If Renan and Strauss can dislodge the ancient story of Christ's rising, it is not so easy to get over the clearly-tabulated statements which Sir William Crookes has set down regarding the resurrections of the present day. The modern disciples are not Galilean fishermen, but shrewd and capable observers, argus-eyed for facts, and facts alone. Abstract reasonings cannot decide any questions bearing on concrete matters. Clairvoyants see forms; a substance of some kind is presented to the spiritual eye. There is a spiritual substance dispersed throughout the universe which assumes many forms in Nature; and in the spirit circle, where harmony and passivity reign, this ethereal substance, too fine to be seen by the naked eye, is thrown off by the medium and sitters to such an extent that the spirit, by force of will, can manipulate it to a given form. The spirit clothed in this, now visible, aura, is seen by the sitters in bodily form, seemingly with all the external organs. To acquire knowledge, to extend the chain of progressive development, is what we reach this life for, and surely to seek for knowledge of that other life and its people is as legitimate as to seek to learn to know how plants breathe.

Miss Fairlamb at the aforementioned séances would get behind the curtain, and in course of time these people from another world would appear, clothed in light, gauzy material, which we were allowed to handle at our will.

The controlling spirit was a tall Scotsman called "Geordie," who had spent most of his life in Newcastle. He would come out amongst us and talk to each quite freely, would write on the paper which was presented, and would even shake me forcibly with his hands to show how strongly he was built up. These circles were made up of sitters who were familiar with Spiritualism.

They were passive and cool of head, and to them the return of the dead was the most certain of facts. When strangers were present the phenomena were weakened, the spirit forms did not get so far from the curtain, and had often to retire inside to gather power. As a conclusive test that the form and medium were separate personalities, the curtain would be lifted at times and both medium and spirit seen together. During these manifestations we had Miss Fairlamb tied in every conceivable way, and at the end of the sittings we always found the tapes, which were tacked down to the floor, in the same condition as we had left them. The spirit "Geordie" spoke with a broad Scotch accent, while the medium had all the tones of a native of Newcastle. There was no point of character in the one which could be seen in the other.

Another control was a little black girl called "Cissie," whose portrait I have seen, taken by a spirit photographer in London. I have looked many times closely into the little black face, and in subsequent years I got to know her well. These two were the spirit managers of the circle, and they often made way for the friends of the sitters to appear, among whom we very often recognised our own departed. The importance of this was simply incalculable. It was one of the most transcendent facts of all the centuries. One night we made an attempt to get a photograph of "Geordie," by arrangement. Mr. Birrell, the spiritual inventor, had brought with him his limelight apparatus, which we thought could be safely used for the purpose. Miss Fairlamb got behind the curtain as usual, and soon "Geordie" was walking about in our midst. Mr. Birrell sat behind with plate and lamp ready to act when "Geordie" would give the word that he was ready. The strong glare of light was thrown on to the figure, when suddenly a noise was heard behind the curtain as if the medium had fallen from her chair. "Geordie" rushed in, and for some moments a commotion was heard. We were rather alarmed, and felt perhaps we had gone too far. "Geordie" was heard speaking rapidly to the medium, then he rushed out and said, "Mr. Robertson! Mr. Robertson! come quick, the lassie is ill!" I at once rose and followed the figure inside, expecting to see him behind the medium; but no, he had suddenly disappeared from view, no doubt giving back to the medium the elements he had used in making up his form. I found the medium on the floor, moaning, and evidently in some sort of faint. Some power seized my arms, and for more than ten minutes I made rapid passes in front of her, when she gradually came to herself, and spoke to me, much to my relief. She was ill for some days, and I myself was limp and weak, much of my life-force having evidently gone out to help towards her recovery.

In 1878 I was brought into touch with London Spiritualism, and met Mr. James Burns, the editor of *The Medium*, which was then the principal journal issued in the interests of the Cause. Mr. Burns was a Scotsman, the brother of a prominent Glasgow merchant. His was a striking personality. He was a man who laboured with all his faculties for the establishment of Spiritualism on a high and noble basis, and it would be difficult to estimate all he did for the Movement to which he devoted his life. He had the eye to see the tremendous importance of this revelation of the return of the dead, and he laboured unceasingly with tongue and pen to set its glories forth. In his fierce independence of spirit he would truckle to no party, but held on his way, despite a perpetual struggle with poverty, ever speaking courageously for his unpopular cause, and firm in his trust that the world must someday welcome it with grateful heart. His writings not only displayed fine literary talent, but his depth of mind and strong intuitions enabled him to present the profoundest of problems in the most clear and lucid light. Mesmerism, phrenology, and psychology he revelled in, and indeed he might have occupied a chair in one of our Universities with distinction. He kept the light of the Spiritualistic Cause burning when it seemed as though a breath would have blown it out. He never despaired, never slackened, but held on his way amid impediments that would have discouraged other men. In spite of a strong personality and a tendency to have his own way, which caused him at times to fight in strange fashion with his most loyal friends, he was utterly unselfish, and would continually forget his own needs to render help to others. From one corner of the land to the other he would travel to speak on behalf of his beloved cause without thought of the tax on his strength of body and without thought of monetary gain. He was proud of the fact that he was a Spiritual teacher with a noble message to the world.

To produce for years the bright paper to which he was editor, and at the same time to spend himself so freely in other directions was indeed marvellous. He was a man lofty in morals and spirit, and with all the fire and untiring energy which mark the pioneer of progress. He was earnest, sincere, and whole-souled in all he said and did, and if, as I have said, he was at times impetuous and extravagant in some of his ideas, it was but part of that zeal which characterised him in all that his hands found to do, and by which he "allured to brighter worlds and led the way." A real hero and martyr was this man, whose great worth was scarcely recognised till death had promoted him to that land about which he had written so forcibly.

All mediums found in him a friend. Mr. and Mrs. Wallis, Mr. J.J. Morse, and many other public advocates of our movement had the benefit of his fostering hand to guide and direct them in the early stages of their development. Mr. Morse, after the spirits had begun to entrance him, was an assistant in his printing and publishing office, and it was at Mr. Burns' rooms that those fine addresses dictated by "Tien Sien Tie," the Chinese philosopher, were first given. The old volumes of *The Medium* contain some of the most wonderful tests of spirit identity given at this time through Mr. Morse, some of which have been recently tabulated and republished by Mr. Edward T. Bennett, who was for twenty years assistant secretary for the Society for Psychical Research. Numbers of strange spirits came to these gatherings in Mr. Burns' rooms, who told their story and set forth their identity, which, upon inquiry, was invariably found to be authentic. No one, knowing the honesty and devotion of Mr. Burns and the lifelong candour of Mr. Morse, can read these cases of spirit identity without feeling with conviction how many from the other side of life have striven to make, and indeed have succeeded in making their existence known to the world here below.

About this time I was invited to the Sunday service at Doughty Hall, London, where I had the privilege of saying a few words on the question of paying mediums a fee for their services. This I advocated strongly, as by the help of mediums who had come to

Glasgow and who needed recompense, I had been strengthened in my faith, and so, no doubt, had many others. At this gathering I met a Mr. Lambelle, a man with great spiritual gifts, who had been for several Sundays delivering a course of lectures on the "Origin of Religious Rites and Ceremonies," in which he dealt with the different religions of the world in a most learned fashion. For weeks I had been reading these lectures with delight, brimful as they were with the most comprehensive knowledge of the subject. The thoughts and the facts which were presented with such fine colouring did not come from Mr. Lambelle himself, who had not had the advantage of scholarship, but from those on the other side who knew of these matters, and he merely used his organism to telephone them to earth. The medium had been a working blacksmith at South Shields, who while sitting in a circle had become entranced, and had gradually been developed to become the mouthpiece of lofty souls in the spirit world. Mr. Burns, who had visited him in the North, induced him to come to London to assist him with the conduct of *The Medium*. The wages, however, of the Spiritual worker are usually starvation, and soon Mr. Lambelle had to return to his old occupation, and use the hammer instead of the pen. The spirits did not give him up, however, and occasionally he preached in a little Unitarian Church in his native place, where he gained many admirers. Soon the Unitarian Association took him up, and he became the "Rev." W.H. Lambelle, and for many years he has been a respected minister of the above-named body. He used to tell me that he never prepared any sermon. The matter flowed to his lips, and he gave it expression as a mouthpiece merely. No doubt there are many speakers who have not gone through the development of the spirit circle who feel this controlling power, but would not care to think that spirit beings were the authors of their thoughts.

I paid several visits to Mr. Lambelle in his own house at South Shields, and many of his inspired utterances have not yet faded from my memory. Later on, he was present at my own house, when his spirit friends talked to me and showed strange glimpses of character to which I may have occasion to refer again. The outside world looks on Spiritualism as a field where money is to be made, but the true story is the reverse of this. Had one been able to gain sufficient for the bare wants of wife and children, a fine instrument like Mr. Lambelle would not be in a Unitarian pulpit today, but rather a clear exponent of the spiritual gospel. The great truths he has learned in Spiritualism, the knowledge of certain facts he has gained, and the conscious presence of individual spirit guides must be ever with him and influence all his utterances in the pulpit.

The night after my visit to Doughty Hall I was invited to take tea with some Scotch friends, a Mr. and Mrs. McKellar, who had found a solace in the spiritual gospel, and while there Mrs. M.H. Wallis dropped in on a friendly visit, carrying her first baby in her arms.

Before Mr. and Mrs. Wallis were married, they used to attend circles which were the means of bringing them together, and after their development they took up the work of Spiritualism in the East End of London, occupying the place of an old and valued worker, Mr. Robert Cogman, who had passed over. They had a hard struggle at first, and for some time Mr. Wallis had to go back to his ordinary labour, but the spirits needed his services, and he again took up the work of Spiritualism, and had set out on his first tour in the provinces when I met Mrs. Wallis.

At this period she had no thought of becoming a public worker, being content to share with friends the blessed realisation of spirit ministry. While at Mr. McKellar's house she was in-fluenced by the son of our host, who took the hands of his mother and father and poured into their ears a message of counsel and affection. The tears stole down their cheeks while they listened to the old endearing tones spoken through the lips of another.

Seeing my old friends comforted in this way, I no longer wondered at people devoting themselves so deeply to Spiritualism and sacrificing so much for their faith. Since then many friends of my own who have gone to the land beyond death have come to me in like manner through Mrs. Wallis, assuring me of their continued affection, and of the precious gift of life beyond the grave. Their return has many times healed the old wounds of parting and filled me with new life and inspiration. It is not in crowded assemblies, but in our home circles, that the joys of spiritual communion are realised at their fullest. To get near to the lost loved ones of our homes and look without fear into the gloomy chasm into which Death snatched them, and to be conscious of their continued love and life, is indeed a restoration greater than all else that could come to mortals. The infinite goodness is revealed, death is seen as but part of evolution. and with the awakened eye we become conscious that those whom we thought lost forever are ours still.

> There shall never be one lost good! What was
> shall live as before;
> On the earth the broken are; in the heaven, a
> perfect round.

A faith founded on facts like that of spirit return can never be submerged by all the ignorance and calumny that may assail it. It becomes part of our lives, a perpetual presence, a knowledge which cannot become weakened like the old faiths of our fathers. Heaven is truly brought to earth, and songs of gladness echo through the souls of those who have been blessed by this great knowledge.

CHAPTER VIII

FRIENDS IN THE CAUSE

Almost from the first hours of this new revelation I have been making friendships with the inhabitants of that other land: friendships which must be enduring, for those purified souls have shaken off all the selfishness which corrodes earthly connections. They are ever ready to extend the helping hand to mortals, and, understanding human frailties, know how prone is the ungrown soul to fall back into the slough of sordid desires. They have caught a nobler patience, and wait faithfully to recall us to the narrow path where alone is to be found true happiness. Loving themselves last, they are our true helpers in times of trouble. I do not wish this to be understood in the narrow sense that only those who are familiar with spirit return are as the elect to have this boon of angel guardianship, but that all the time the spirits work with all mortals, trying to lead them upward and onward. In impulses and dreams is their influence felt, though the source of such influence is but seldom recognised. It is part of the order of Nature, this spirit guardianship. yet many never know of the care with which they have been tended until they open their eyes on the spirit side.

It has been my lot to know many of my helpers and inspirers. I have seen some of their faces, have ofttimes heard their voices, and penned their loving sentiments, without voluntary wish of my own. They are as real to me as the friends of earth. I know their characteristics so well that I cannot be mistaken in their identities, and nothing in the universe is more real to me than the fact that these people do objectively exist. This fact for me cannot be shaken in the slightest by any theories of "subliminal" consciousness, or "secondary personalities." I know those in whom I have put my trust, and am sure they will sustain me to the end of life's journey.

That all mortals have some spiritual faculties awaiting awakening, which link them on to the unseen, seems certain, just as we are all more or less poets when the strains of some minstrel warm our blood. The poet Burns we call normal, but no great gulf separates him from many of the instruments whom the spirit people have utilised to speak forth the message of immortality.

During 1878, there came among the Glasgow friends at the Trongate meeting-place a young man named David Anderson, who was destined to do some good work in the Cause. He had met with many strange experiences during his life, the causes of which Spiritualism explained to him. In a marked degree, he had the peculiar organisation which enabled spirits readily to make him their mouthpiece. It is often a slow process for the spirits to shape the instrument they have selected according to their requirements, and at first, spirits from the borderland used to entrance Mr. Anderson—undeveloped spirits—from whom we had difficulty in freeing the medium to make room for wiser souls to assume their place in the work.

One of these former spirits was "John Connelly," an Irish shoemaker, who had been a Roman Catholic while on this earth, but who had failed to pay much attention to the moral teachings of his church. "John" was quaint and original, with little or no reverence for priesthood of any kind, and he had got little beyond the knowledge that some change had come over him, though what it was he could not understand. His spirit surroundings were of the most material kind. He felt he was still at work, making shoes, and it was most difficult to make him understand that there were higher things than this to be attained in the new life, things of the spirit. He was a bit rough in speech, and when we sought to inculcate moral principles, we were called a set of preaching Methodists. As time went on, however, there was an improvement in his surroundings. He told us that he was no longer engaged in shoemaking, but was at work gardening, pulling up weeds; symbolising, no doubt, that much of the ignorance and sin of his past life would have to be uprooted before advancement would be possible. He was a complete picture of a living man, with all his loves and hates, in whom, however, there were the dormant germs of goodness. I knew "John" for many years afterwards, and he became a wise teacher, whose peculiar mode of speech, rough but honest, ever bore some touch of epigrammatic wisdom. He told all his family history, and asked me many times to call on a daughter he had in Donegal, but I never followed up this bit of evidence. I regret it now, but at that time I had so many tests that the importance of this one did not dawn upon me. It is doubtful, however, what special piece of evidence would be considered satisfactory by those who will not believe.

The principal guides of Mr. Anderson were, however, of a loftier type. At first there was one who gave the name of "Richard Hall," an American clergyman and a prominent anti-slavery advocate, who had been placed outside the pale of the Church for some of his heresies. The teachings which flowed from this source were of an elevated stamp, breathing a tone of piety towards God and of love towards men. What graphic pictures he gave us of the men who had toiled for the abolition of slavery—William Lloyd Garrison, Wendell Phillips, Theodore Parker, and others, whose courage and philanthropy ultimately triumphed over the malignity and blindness of their fellows. We all felt as if in close touch with the real actors in the scenes which were described. There was a fine warmth of sentiment about those first controls which kindled the better nature in us; they were broad in thought and yet devout, ever pointing out the way whereby the highest human blessedness could be reached. "Richard Hall" continued with us for only a season, some other spiritual mission calling him away, but the fragrance of his presence remains even now.

A stirring control, who gave the name of "Harbinger," took up the position which "Richard Hall" had vacated. We often wondered who this fluent orator could be, but when we asked for his name we were told a man's name was of little moment, his teachings and whether they appealed to our intellect and encouraged us to lead a nobler life being the great question. One night a reference was made by him, seemingly unintentionally, to a personal incident in his own life, which gave us a clue to his identity. He spoke of banishment; of relief from his troubles being at hand, when the cup of joy was suddenly snatched from his lips; of how he had been followed for years by shipwreck and disaster. We recognised in the speaker Thomas Muir, of Huntershill, an advocate of the Scottish Bar, who, for some outspoken sentiments regarding Parliamentary reform in 1793, was tried for sedition, and sentenced to fourteen years' banishment in Botany Bay. This brave outspoken hero nobly met the fate which was not uncommon at that time, when Toryism triumphed, and men had to suppress their more liberal thoughts. The story of Muir was indeed a sad one. After he had laboured at teaching in Sydney for some time, the brave sentiments of his defence at his trial reached George Washington, and stirred his heart so that he sent a ship to bring Muir to America. Shipwreck overtook the vessel on its voyage between Sydney and America, and he was thrown on foreign shores, where he had to wander about for years without a friend to help him. "Harbinger," as we had called him, acknowledged that he was the Thomas Muir whose story had stirred so many hearts. I never had any doubts as to the personality of this loving influence, whose giant heart had forgiven the wrongs done him while on earth. He had laboured for the better day, and already he saw the dawn of something still brighter even than his dreams, when love and justice would play a fuller part in the expression of human life.

Controls such as "Harbinger" were far beyond the medium in intellect and knowledge. They were indeed profound on all questions they handled, and we who listened to their words of wisdom had sufficient reverence to acknowledge that we were sitting at the feet of our masters.

There was one friend of another stamp, however, who always came during the evening—one who was much like ourselves, and with whom we had quite a feeling of comradeship. He had no great burst of eloquence, but with slow speech he gave forth many useful lessons. His name was "Jacobs," and he told us he was a Jew. At times he was somewhat cynical in speech, and in all he said we saw a thorough detestation of shams. He made continual war against many of the dogmas called Christian, in a way that was most penetrating. Despite his cynicism, there was something friendly and personal about him. He would do anything to serve his fellows, and having had some medical education on earth, he, whenever occasion offered itself, was ever ready to give medical advice, which was always of the most valuable kind. He could see right into the human body, locate the disease, and prescribe the necessary remedies. Hundreds of people have been truly blessed by him. I have often seen articles brought to "Jacobs" from the person of sufferers, and he would only have to touch these to understand the personalities of the sufferers and the troubles with which they were afflicted. I have never known "Jacobs" to err on any point. Sometimes there was a difference between the orthodox medical diagnosis and that of "Jacobs," but even in these cases I found our spirit friend correct, and the authority wrong. Those who have never come into touch with clairvoyance and psychometry will be apt to put all this down to the wildest dreaming, but how can they know that it is not possible? How much can any of us know of man's spiritual possibilities? They who say these things cannot be, have simply not explored a realm of nature which has many secrets to yield up. They may look like magic, but they are veritable facts. After all, are they more wonderful than the fact that the sun can make an impress on a sensitive plate? This photographic influence pervades all nature. In the world around us are imprinted not only our characters, but even our deeds and thoughts, and it only needs the psychometric photographer to reproduce these pictures.

> Then let your secret thoughts be fair;
> They have a vital part and share
> In shaping worlds and moulding fate,
> God's system is so intricate.

I do not suppose Carlyle knew exactly what he meant when he said: "On the hardest adamant some footprint of us is stamped in; the last rear of the host will read traces of the earliest van." This is not merely a poetic metaphor, but a psychometric fact. You cannot walk in and out of a room without leaving a portion of your influence there. You cannot sit on a chair but the chair receives from you that which can convey to the sensitive reader the idea of your presence and your mental peculiarities. and sometimes even more than this. How few would have believed a few years ago in the possibility of the phonograph reproducing the sound of the human voice and repeating it as often as desired. Modern physical discoveries point to powers and possibilities which belong to the world of nature. Psychometry belongs to the new era of the awakening of the spiritual faculties in man.

In all the city of Glasgow there was no more valuable person than this man David Anderson, the letter-carrier. Pulpit ministrations are seldom of value to the aching heart, but through this man of genuine modesty, simplicity, and sincerity, consoling messages were sent from friends in the higher life to those in sorrow here below. He was a source of rich blessing to many, and so unselfish was he that in ministering to the wants of others he forgot to guard sufficiently his own physical frame. Conviction took the place of doubt when, with his fine spiritual vision, he was able to depict the features of some loved one, and to convey a message of hope and cheer.

To this man, perhaps, I owe more than to any other spiritual worker. In mundane affairs he was able to perceive and to lighten the clouds that oppressed me, and for years his control was the one medical person in whom I felt I could place reliance. Oftentimes I used to think what a loss it would be when he should be taken from our midst. I have never known a man who exhibited in so large a measure what I should call disinterested benevolence. The spirits were to him ever the closest of companions, and they sought to minister to him all through his irksome journey through this life. My close fellowship with him was never weakened during its five and twenty years' duration, and the manly man who gained my reverence at the first was ever held by me in the same veneration.

Disease for a long time had him in its grip, and though his spirit friends did much to prolong his life, they could not keep him in the form forever.

There are few incidents, to my mind, which so firmly convince one of the power and helpfulness of Spiritualism as the touching letter he sent me only two days before he was called hence. I reproduce it here: "It is plain to me now," he wrote, "that my time on this side is fast drawing to a close. To that I am quite resigned, and await the coming change with hope and confidence, knowing that my present weakness will give place to strength, and that once more I shall begin to lead an active, useful life, in which helping others and adding to their happiness will, I hope, take no small part. I see now that in my life here I have neglected many opportunities of doing good, but I am consoled by the thought that my time was not solely devoted to self. I am strengthened at this time by the faithful ones on the spirit side, who comfort and help me by their presence. You and I may never meet on this side again in the body, but if conditions are favourable I shall be no stranger in your family circle, and I shall wait patiently for the reunion with the old friends in my new home."

This earnest truthseeker and truthfinder, who had marched from Methodism to Unitarianism, found mental rest in the great religion of fact. As Browning says of the seeker for the great truth:

> He yearned to gain it, catching at mistake
> As midway help, till he reached fact indeed.

Spiritualism was his abiding resting-place for over twenty years. He gave himself up to it heart and soul, and is fully repaid for his devotion by the sweet reverence in which his memory is held.

The fact that he has come back many times to the old scenes is undoubted, for already his help has been extended to many. On a spirit photograph, which I have in my possession, he has been able to make himself visible, unmistakably true to life, by the side of a close and dear friend, Mr. John Dewar, who is well known amongst the Glasgow Spiritualists. It was through the powerful mediumship of Mr. Anderson that Mr. Dewar was convinced of the truth of Spiritualism.

In 1879 I was brought into touch with another heroic character whose life was sweet and noble, one who incessantly laboured to bring home to his fellows the glad tidings of spirit return. No name is better known or more highly reverenced in the Spiritualistic Cause than that of John Lamont, of Liverpool, who, at odd seasons, would drop into our Trongate Hall and charm us with his earnest speech and pious influence. John Lamont was a true type of robust Scottish character, one who, when he saw a truth, could not do otherwise than speak it forth bravely to the world. The old faiths had been extinguished by the bright light of Spiritualism which had come to him. He was a leader, a teacher, one on whom people naturally leant. His strong, common sense made the dark places bright and clear, and for years he was looked on in the light of a saint: not the saint of tradition and miracle, but of manliness, tenderness, and sincerity.

When I saw him for the first time, I was reading my first paper to the Glasgow Society, and at the close of the meeting he spoke some kindly words which buoyed me up and helped me onward. For years I was privileged to meet with him and to listen to his conversation, which was ever brimful of enthusiasm and wisdom. I feel all the richer that I knew and loved him. Since his promotion he has spoken through my own lips, and has been seen many times standing beside me. I have not yet lost the music of his presence, for while I pen these lines I am conscious of his nearness, and rejoice to feel that for him death was only a gateway to a new and truer life.

CHAPTER IX

GENUINE *VERSUS* COUNTERFEIT

At this time the work of Spiritualism in Glasgow was greatly helped by the presence amongst us of Mr. James Coates, a powerful mesmerist and a professional phrenologist, who had become acquainted with the spiritual facts in Liverpool. He it is to whom we are indebted for originating Sunday morning services. He himself was a good instrument for the transmission of messages from the spirits, and had commenced Sunday forenoon sittings at the house of Mr. James Bowman, where I was one of the sitters. As I listened to his controlling guides, "Dr. Warren" and "Pat," I felt that such treasures of wisdom as fell from their lips should not be kept to ourselves, but should be shared with others, and so the meetings were transferred to the Trongate Hall, and since then morning services have always been held. "Pat" was indeed a strongly marked character. He had been a dock labourer while on earth, and it was only after the change of death that his eyes had been opened to spiritual things. His control over the medium was perfect, and in him we had the typical Irishman, with his pointed and clear wit. He would gather up the threads of the most profound discourse, which perchance was proceeding on his entrance, and in a few words he would clearly explain it all to us. He believed that only by the effort of every individual Spiritualist to lead a nobler life would the true value of Spiritualism be made known to the world. "Let everyone sweep before his own door," he would say, "and the whole city will soon be clean."

James Coates was indeed liberal in the expending of his gifts, and his enthusiasm set aflame the spirit of earnestness in others. I have heard his spirit friends speaking through other lips than his, and they were always the same people whom I had first known through Mr. Coates. Ofttimes have I had the influence of these spirit friends poured upon me, and under their control my lips have been made to utter sentiments which were quite out of harmony with my own opinions. Dear old "Pat," I feel assured that your work for humanity is as valuable as that of the greatest earthly philosophers in advocating the useful life as the best preparation for eternity.

> *Of one thing we may be sure, conduct is prayer.*
> *And he is beyond misgiving who daily offers it up.*

Mr. Coates was secretary of our Society for a season, and brought Spiritualism more prominently before the public than it had ever been before. At his instigation a series of meetings were held in the Trades' Hall, Glassford Street, at which were present our most prominent workers. For many years Mr. Coates has resided at Rothesay, and he has issued many volumes on the subjects of mesmerism, thought-reading, and phrenology which have had a large circulation. His work on *Human Magnetism* is an authority. While in Chicago a few years ago, I was calling on an important bookseller in that city, and on my mentioning which part of the world I came from, he at once asked me about Mr. Coates, the author whose books he had studied and sold. He was astonished to learn that the man of whom he thought so much was not known and esteemed as a great writer in his own country. During all the years since his introduction to Spiritualism, Mr. Coates has been a frequent contributor to the Spiritual press, and in his own corner of the world has brought the claims of Spiritualism before scientific and literary societies. If he has left the ranks of public propagandists, his influence as a Spiritualist has been felt in many quarters. He has the consolation that in the days of struggle he helped to lay some of the stones of the temple of spirit revelation, into which none enter without finding some consolation. Through him the Cause has come more and more before the world, and obtained some measure of recognition as one of the religious movements of the day, potent with great possibilities for the future.

All great discoveries have had their hour of derision; have been called impious and ridiculous before they were accepted and their importance recognised, and in due season spiritual facts find a place and the world will wonder that mankind could ever have been so blind as not to recognise in Spiritualism one of God's choicest revelations to His children. Already there are glimpses of the dawn. Year by year the truth comes nearer men's hearts, and I know that mankind will welcome it as the solvent of doubt and dread, the messenger of infinite love to all the earth. In the words of Theodore Parker, "In spite of all the Herods in Jerusalem, a crown is got ready for him that is born king of the world. Wise men are always waiting for the star which goes before the newborn Son of God, and though that star stands still over a stable, they are ready on the spot with their myrrh, their frankincense and their gold. Society has its shepherds watching their flock and its angels to proclaim the joy to all mankind."

There is on record a letter from Galileo to his friend Kepler, which might be read today as an illustration of past blindness and intolerance. "How I wish," says Galileo, "we could have a good laugh together! Here at Padua the principal professor of philosophy, whom I have repeatedly and urgently requested to look at the moon and planets through my telescope, pertinaciously refuses to do so. Why, my dear Kepler, are you not here? What shouts of laughter we should have at all this solemn folly!" We think that we have escaped from this crass spirit of blindness, but the history of Modern Spiritualism makes clear to us that professors of philosophy today have not as yet outgrown the spirit of intolerance which actuated the opponents of Galileo. There are some things too far advanced for recognition from scholars, which are readily perceived by those who are by no means their intellectual equals.

He who speaks the thought and language of today gets the ready applause; but he who utters the thought of tomorrow is accounted a dreamer and a madman. Even the literary criticisms of a Jeffrey were wide of the mark! With all his erudition he saw not that which was true and enduring in poetry. Crabbe to him was greater than Wordsworth! He scarcely tolerated Carlyle, thought him a bit of a bore, and wrote to Mr. McVey Napier, his successor in the editorship of the *Edinburgh Review*: "I fear Carlyle will not do; that is, if you do not take the liberties and the pains with him that I did, by striking out freely and writing in occasionally." Readers of Pepys' Diary will marvel at that worthy's judgment on some of the works of Shakespeare. "August 20th, 1666," he writes, "To Deptford by water, reading *Othello, Moor of Venice*, which I have heretofore esteemed a mighty good play, but having lately read *The Adventures of Five Hours*, it seems a mean thing. Sept. 29th, 1662: To the King's Theatre, where we saw *A Midsummer Night's Dream*, which I had never seen before, nor shall ever see again, for it is the most insipid and ridiculous play that I ever saw in my life." Surely this is the criticism of an oyster on the song of a thrush!

Future generations will read with regret that enlightened minds of the nineteenth century acted as foolishly as did the contemporaries of Galileo. To acquire knowledge is what we are brought into this world for, and surely knowledge of that other world and its people who stand at the gates waiting for recognition is beyond aught else. We could never learn anything in this world if we kept asking the question: "Are such and such inquiries lawful and right?" If we were to follow the religion of those who went before us, we should still hold to primitive barbarism. Had this been done, there could have been no advance in thought. Those who have sought to deal the most crushing blow at Spiritualism have been neither religious nor what is considered bigoted, but rather opponents of religion in all forms. Bias and an innate prejudice against the possibility of demonstrating a future life so blinded them, that all the toleration they at other times preached was drowned and lost when considering the claims of Spiritualism. They thought that because certain ideas respecting the spirit which had been promulgated by creeds were irrational, there could be no spiritual world at all, forgetting that although the solar system which exists in fact is permanent, the theories of Thales and Ptolemy, of Copernicus and Descartes, regarding that system have but proved transient and imperfect approximations to the true expression.

This leads me to the record of certain incidents which occurred in 1878, and which dimmed the reputation of some great names in the eyes of those possessing the most ordinary insight. No Spiritualists were ever so far misled in their beliefs as the leading men of science have been in theirs. In February 1878 a crushing blow was thought to be given to Spiritualism, which would keep it from ever raising its head again. The story of the attack is one of which future generations will be much ashamed. No man was ever more liberal in speech and condemned intolerance with a louder voice than Professor Huxley, who certainly was one of the strongest forces of the age. Notwithstanding his clearheadedness, he became the dupe of a vulgar American showman, and for a time allowed prejudice to dominate his reasoning faculties. Though he had said that "No event is too extraordinary to be impossible," yet he would never open his mind to the possibility of spiritual phenomena being true. It was beyond the extraordinary. He had refused to investigate the subject when the Dialectical Society called for his presence, saying, "If it is true, it does not interest me." He had repeated the same sentiments to Alfred Russel Wallace; yet, when he heard there was a person in America who was prepared to expose the whole matter, he opened his arms wide to receive him. The clever American played his cards well—so well as to dupe the most intellectual man in the country. The story he fabricated was greedily accepted. He said he had had a dear friend who, while in a state of feeble health, had fallen into the hands of the Spiritualists and become insane. Roused by the wrongs done to this friend, his sole mission was to execute vengeance by exposing the arts by which the imposture was practised on the soft-headed and credulous portion of the American and British public. He had succeeded in discovering the vulgar but skilfully veiled secrets, and now stern virtue called upon him to lay bare to the world the full explanation of the frauds. Robert Dale Owen had been a credulous fool, Professor Crookes a weak-minded dupe, Professor de Morgan a person without brains, and Alfred Russel Wallace and Cromwell Varley were blinded and incapable observers. The great American high-souled gentleman of independent fortune was mightier than all the scientific and literary men who had attested the truths of spiritual phenomena. He had grappled with the mystery, and for humanity's sake alone had come out into the open with a clean soul to do the world a great service.

No one thought of asking for his credentials. So hateful was the word Spiritualism that they swallowed his story without questioning about the dear friend who had been caught in its toils, and the independent means of the high-souled and spirited exposer. The opponents of Spiritualism were only too overjoyed to find a missile to hurl at it and its supporters. Huxley was delighted, and patronised the arrant quack in London. Genuine phenomena could not interest him; the spurious claimed his attention at once.

The crafty American, who could not impose on the Spiritualists of America, found a fruitful field on English soil. Huxley wrote to some of the professors of the Glasgow and Edinburgh Universities, asking them to take this great champion of truth under their wing. How much the showman did to pull the strings himself is not known, but in February 1879 the Glasgow newspapers were flooded with long advertisements to the effect that Washington Irving Bishop, "B.A."—which I should read "Bold Adventurer"—had been invited by the prominent men of Glasgow to give a startling exposure of Spiritualism, an exposition by human means of all the startling manifestations claimed by Spiritualists to be done by the spirits of the dead. The man of ordinary capacity could scarcely have read the flaming announcements without seeing that here was a showman pure and simple, who knew his business, knew how to bring out telling headlines so as to draw the public.

In case all who were interested might not have a chance of seeing for themselves how feeble minds could be imposed upon, two nights were to be devoted to this noble attempt to save the world from credulity and folly. The prices of admission were 5s., 3s. 6d., 2s., and a few 1s. seats; but as money was far from the object in view, it was reiterated in every corner that the vindication of truth and the saving of the weak-minded was the sole aim this gentleman of independent means had in coming to Glasgow. All the proceeds were to be devoted to the Western Infirmary.

It will scarcely be credited that amongst the names of those who signed the requisite document which brought this adventurer into our midst were John Caird, the venerated Principal of the University, and his scholarly brother Edward, now Master of Balliol College, Oxford; Professor Berry, afterwards Sheriff of Lanarkshire; Professors Blackburn, Buchanan, Clelland, Cowan,

Dickson, Veitch, Grant, Jebb, Nicol, and Sir William Gardner, who had said clairvoyance came from a diseased condition of the faculty of wonder, whatever oracular meaning this might have. The most prominent advocate and supporter of the man Bishop, however, was Sir William Thomson, now Lord Kelvin. A few years later he acted even more ridiculously than that opponent of Galileo, the Professor of Philosophy at Padua, of whom I have spoken. Mr. Stead had asked Lord Kelvin to interest himself in borderland subjects, but he replied: "I have nothing to do with borderland. I believe that nearly everything in hypnotism and clairvoyance is imposture, and the rest bad observation." Mr. Stead very aptly says: "This oracular dictum will probably live in the history of the progress of mankind side by side with the equally positive assertions of the Lord Kelvins of their day in condemnation of Galvani and of Harvey, whose discovery of the circulation of the blood exposed him to the ridicule of the leading scientists of his time."

It was not the university professors alone who interested themselves in Irving Bishop's beneficent work of exploding what they considered—if they considered the matter at all—a hurtful fallacy, but all sections of the Church, the defenders of ancient superstitions, were determined that no new claimant should ever enter the field. So we had Archbishop Eyre and Father Munro, as representatives of that Church which has ever sought to stifle everything new. The Established Church had its representative in Dr. Burns, of the Cathedral, while the Free Church had its liberal Marcus Dods, Ross Taylor, and others. Episcopalians and United Presbyterians had also their share in the great honour of extending the invitation to the marvellous, self-sacrificing, and truth-devoted man of independent means who was to put an end to the existence of Spiritualism.

The night came when all the so-called spirit manifestations, which had for so long eluded the detection and imposed upon the credulity of men, would be laid bare. Lord Kelvin, who never, I suppose, attended a genuine spirit circle in his life, was in the chair, and helped the magician just as boys carry out the instructions of the showman at juggling and mesmeric entertainments. He had crowds of his educated colleagues with him, who seemed to enjoy what was presented. Those in the audience who had seen good conjuring thought it a most tame exhibition of legerdemain, but the prominent names on the committee carried it through. There was no exposition of clairvoyance, materialisation, or rapping, only an exposition of the folly of learned professors. The Spiritualists present laughed at the clumsy performance, and if it had been repeated for years it could not have affected the beliefs of a single Spiritualist. There had been many conjurers who, with the aid of machinery, had done some clever things which caused people to wonder; but Irving Bishop was a man who had not even well learned his business.

I wondered what the newspapers would say the next day, and for once I was ashamed of the Press. I recollect reading a leading article in the *Evening Times* of the period, and saying to myself, "This leader will be quoted someday as an example of the ignorant and bigoted spirit which prevailed." I recently took the trouble to hunt it up in the Mitchell Library, and there it was, as I had remembered it. In these days, when men like Sir Oliver Lodge, Professor Bichet, F.W.H. Myers, and others, have spoken out so clearly as to the objective reality of the phenomena, it looks as if it had been dug out of some ancient manuscript.

> *Maniacs, illusions, and impostures are difficult to kill. It is doubtful whether the startling exposure*

> *which Washington Irving Bishop is giving of the*
> *thing called Modern Spiritualism, the silliest*
> *delusion and wickedest imposture of our time,*
> *will be its death blow in Glasgow. With few*
> *exceptions, the immense audience assembled did*
> *not require to be convinced of the supreme*
> *humbug of Spiritualism. They went to see the*
> *bare-faced lie exposed by a clever man, who has*
> *sounded all its miserable shallows, pretty much*
> *as they would go to see an infamous scoundrel*
> *exposed in a court of law. Mr. Bishop is an*
> *American of independent means, whose dear*
> *friend, while in a state of feeble health, fell into*
> *the fangs of the Spiritualists, and became insane*
> *under their precious trickeries. He has*
> *succeeded in discovering their vulgar but skilfully*
> *veiled secrets, and is engaged in laying them bare*
> *to the world.*

Then we had a description of the tricks which had been the stock-in-trade of the regular conjurer for years. Lord Kelvin's appropriate remarks regarding the pernicious influence of the delusion are quoted, as being masterful and conclusive, and the leader concludes with these words: "A few presumably strong men have had their brains softened by seriously touching the imposture." (I suppose Sir Wm. Crookes, Wallace, and Varley were meant?) "Mr Bishop's crusade may help to clear the noxious vapours from the eyes and minds of a few."

There were two nights of the show, and at the conclusion the Western Infirmary naturally waited for the proceeds with which the benevolent American was to dower them; but professors and infirmary had alike been sold. Mr. Bishop was needy, and had made sure that his own people would draw the money, and that he would keep it, once it was drawn. He coolly pocketed the entire proceeds, several hundred pounds, less some £20 or so as their share of the spoil. All had been duped alike. It was a clever swindle. The professors and clergymen, and the potent assertion of independent means and avenging his dear friend's wrongs, had the desired effect with the public, and the modern Cagliostro rushed away with the "takings," leaving his silly dupes lamenting. It had been sufficient for Mr. Bishop to *seem* good and excellent, and although his credentials would not have stood any test, the eager desire on the part of the learned to believe anything unfavourable to Spiritualism made them liable to fall into the net which he had prepared.

The Press had little to say about the robbery when it was found out. The matter was never fully opened to public gaze, and was soon forgotten. Professor Huxley would be blamed, no doubt, for introducing such an arrant knave to respectable Glasgow society. What was it that these people wanted to crush out? The fact that there is a world beyond this: a world teeming with life, from which we can receive signals. These evidences which Spiritualism has helped to make plain have to be faced in some other way than by ridicule. To the earnest seeker the truth can be proven, and no exposure by conjurer or by the newspaper press can shake this knowledge when once established. "Seek and ye shall find, knock and it shall be opened unto you," is as applicable to modern as it was to ancient Spiritualism. Men seek to disprove the fact that the doors of the spirit realm are ever open for the return of the dead, but the messages keep on sounding, and those who have ears hear. The knowledge of spirit return when once attained is never lost, and though the Peters of the Cause may deny their Master, and the Judases at times betray, yet deep in their hearts is a feeling that they are betraying the truth.

CHAPTER X

THEORY AND PRACTICE

Spiritualism in 1879 was not troubled with the fanciful and speculative theories which afterwards invaded her domain. Madame Blavatsky was still a Spiritualist medium, producing wonderful phenomena and writing boldly in defence of the facts. However, as she sought to be a leader, and could not be one in Spiritualism, she entered new fields of thought, talked of the "astral plane," and coloured simple facts with an oriental tint. The mystical and confused thinkers of the movement who lacked clear perception may have found a home for a season amongst her books, *Isis Unveiled* and *The Secret Doctrine*, but their hearts would ofttimes seek to go back to the earlier times of Spiritualism, when they waited patiently to hear the voices of their arisen ones.

The Psychical Research Society had not yet set out on its long and toilsome journey to nowhere. The dwellers in the realm of "sub-consciousness" and "multiplex personality" have wandered in the wilderness, while the Spiritualist, who has fought his doubts and gathered strength, is revelling in the clear light of facts. The "Psychical Researchers" have discovered no new thing in all their wanderings. Telepathy and a deeper latent selfhood were recognised long ere they "discovered" them. Now, tired with their unsuccessful searchings, they are approaching the banner of angel ministry, as held aloft by the Spiritualists, and are falling into line with them, acknowledging at last that it is the living dead who are behind the phenomena round which they have circled, and for which they could find no other explanation.

It was the sneers of the Tyndalls and the Huxleys which made so many afraid to yield readily to what was plain from the first, and nothing is more certain than that the season of denying this great possibility of God's scheme—spirit return—as they did, is now at an end. We are coming to realise that God is—

> *Here by the little mind of man reduced*
> *To littleness that suits his faculty,*

and that we, with our little minds, cannot yet altogether comprehend Him in His greatness.

In 1879 Mr. E.W. Wallis came into the lecturing field in Glasgow, and his fine inspirations were the means of making many recognise the strong forces of light and wisdom which flowed from beyond the veil. Like so many of the workers who stand on Spiritualist platforms, he had been forced by the spirits to leave his ordinary labours to become a worker in the vineyard. When I consider the excessive energy which workers like Mr. Wallis have expended thus in going hither and thither to expound the truths of our Cause, I recognise what a great sacrifice it must involve of much that makes life dear. In modern days we look back upon the missionary efforts of St. Paul as something transcendent, but the courage and devotion which marked the work of the early Christian pioneers is not without its parallel amongst our workers of today. Men like Wallis and Morse, like Saul of Tarsus, have listened to the voices of the spirits, and, like him, have gone out into the world to teach, sustained by their unseen helpers. The voices have for long cried in the wilderness, not many hearing the sound, but the missionaries have held on their way, making the desert bring forth flowers.

Through Mr. E.W. Wallis I became acquainted with some rare souls of fine quality, who belong not to the realm of dreamland, but to that of real life. One of these, who gave the name of "Standard Bearer," had been a Quaker while in earth life, a personal follower of George Fox. He related the story of his translation to us in melodious periods, the charm of which I ofttimes recall. His eyes had been opened to see the spirits before he passed from the earth, so that he crossed without fear that much-dreaded chasm of death, and found himself among friends, who bore him to his new home. The desire to return to earth to describe the glories of the great beyond to those he had left behind came over him, and, acting upon this impulse, he revisited his old life, only to find that the earthly atmosphere made everything seem dark and dense to him. He found that there was emitted by the people of earth a light more or less brilliant according to their moral and spiritual qualities. The things of this earth now seemed vapoury and shadowy to his gaze. We can imagine how difficult it is to describe in earthly language the things of spirit life, but his feelings and experiences were easily comprehended. It was not a story of pearly streets and of the playing of harps he told us, but rather a description of a useful life of progression.

The "Standard Bearer" had found in Mr. Wallis an instrument capable of transmitting and interpreting the spirit vision, and for years many have heard from this source clear and rational views of life in the hereafter.[1] A wide gulf separated the Quaker preacher from another of Mr. Wallis's guides, who was most appropriately called "Lightheart." He was ever light and bright, shedding sunshine all around. He was a South American Indian, who had met his death by the attack of a wild animal. His was a sweet, loving personality, full of music and poetry, and he could extemporise charming little rhymes on any given subject. He would also describe the friends around the sitters in the most striking way, and if any article was placed in the hands of the

---

1. Some of "Standard-Bearer's" experiences, delivered in trance addresses, have been published by Mr. Wallis in a pamphlet entitled, *Death and the Beyond.*

medium, he could relate the history and character of the possessor. The first time I was in his presence he read me as if I had been an open book, and my closest friends said it was all marked with photographic accuracy. Dear gentle "Lightheart" was ever a bright companion, whose influence dispersed the darkest clouds, and brought us to the gate of the heavenly kingdom.

Another control was one "Tom Joyce," who had been a circus clown. He was full of quaint witticisms, and it was his great delight to ridicule some of those stories which the world calls sacred, but which to "Tom Joyce" were absurdities. "Lightheart" was, however, more heart than head. His sweet controlling power of love and gentleness helped to mould souls to get nearer the kingdom of righteousness and peace. In all the years I have known him, I have never heard him utter a cruel or unkind word. He gently scanned his brother man, and was ever ready to make allowances for those who see not the path of purity and right.

> *In men, whom men pronounce as ill,*
> *I find so much of goodness still;*
> *In men, whom men pronounce divine,*
> *I find so much of sin and blot;*
> *I hesitate to draw the line*
> *Between the two, when God has not.*

In our Glasgow Society we were not sustained and uplifted by those spirits alone of whom I have spoken, the guides of Mr. Wallis and Mr. Morse. These only visited us at intervals, but we had a fine instrument amongst ourselves in a young man, a fellow investigator, who, when entranced, became the mouthpiece of many of our own friends and relatives. What joy the touch of those vanished hands brought into our lives, and with what eagerness did we listen for the sound of the voice that had been still! We knew, indeed, that we were in the presence of our so-called dead, who spoke to us of the sad incidents of the past to make us realise their oneness with our lost ones, but who spoke also, with joyous feeling, of the delights of the immortal life. It used to seem to us that the music of heaven sounded in our ears, and each one felt that his communion was indeed beyond earthly valuation. The story the spirits told us of their life was clear, unmistakable evidence of their onward march towards perfection. The life there, as here, is progressive; erring steps taken here are retraced there, and by the awakening of the truer, inner life we as naturally reach out towards perfection as the plant turns towards the sun.

> *There lies in the centre of each man's heart*
>   *A longing and love for the good and pure;*
> *And if but an atom, or larger part,*
>   *I tell you this shall for aye endure;*
> *After the body has gone to decay,*
> *Yea, after the world has passed away.*

It is sometimes said that the evidences of personal identity received from spirits are most unsatisfactory; but in many cases those who receive these evidences, while knowing them to be to them all-sufficing, do not care to impart them to outsiders, who would but lend an unwilling and doubting ear. As the old proverb says, "Convince a man against his will, he's of the same opinion still." The world knows but little of the consolation of the family spirit circle; nothing of the light which has lifted the despairing heart out of its melancholy. Spiritualists, like other men, have all the faculties which enable them to be witnesses for and against truth. The earnest, simple, loving man can surely testify to what he sees as certainly as can the most profound philosopher. It is the heart which hallows the truth. The simple-minded man ofttimes sees it while the proud-minded shuts himself out from the light. The dead are not dead but alive.

"Tien Sien Tie" has, through Mr. Morse, scattered forth many golden gems of truth; has cleared away much of that which has blinded the eyes of man, and through the views presented by him of God and heaven, has established Spiritualism as a reasonable theory of life and of the life beyond. Stores of rich wisdom, almost encyclopaedic reviews of the world's growth and man's position therein, have assisted hungry souls to climb from darkness into light. It is not a blind force but a wise intelligence which has presented these things to our understanding, things gathered from all sources of knowledge. No one can listen to "Tien" without feeling that he is in the presence of a master-mind, in the presence of one who utters not platitudes, but true revelations of the inner life.

Through Mr. Morse's instrumentality also, we are brought into the presence of another spirit, one nearer the earth plane, and known as "The Strolling Player." This spirit passed through life amidst crosses that literally crushed him out of physical being, and entered that other state with senses blinded, and love a force which meant little. From this distressful state he was lifted by the unselfish love of "Tien Sien Tie," who, recognising the possibilities for good in him, helped with his kind sympathy to bring forth that generous nature that was lying dormant. "The Strolling Player" is a man of education, is keen and critical, and to some would appear cynical, but when once you get close to him, as I have done for years, you feel you are in touch with a warm, sympathetic heart. I know many will laugh at my talking of spirits as separate entities from the mediums, but so many of these spiritual beings have entered into my life, have helped and guided me for so long, that nothing in this universe is real to me if "The Strolling Player," whom I have known as a spirit, be not a human being who has but gone some steps onward. His words of truth and wisdom are stated in a jesting fashion, and they are easily comprehended. When I have done with this body I know I shall grasp his hand and participate even more than I do now in his loving friendship. These are only two of the great hearts that have pioneered this work.

The young medium of our Society, of whom I have spoken, was unconscious of all that took place while he was under the spirit control. The friends who came through him proved their identity unmistakably by all manner of personal characteristics, touches which had been familiar to us in the old times, and which could not be explained away by any theories of thought transference or mind-reading.

Our bodies provide, in some mysterious way, a substance which the spirits utilise for their manifestations. We know that the way from that other world is open to all classes of spirits, evil as well as good, and impure spirits have been known to revisit their old haunts here on earth, and to influence people for evil. But the pure in heart and sound in head are not likely to call to their presence those who have no love of good. The law of life is the same in both spheres; we get that for which we give the conditions. Tennyson realises how necessary this elevation of our thoughts is when he writes:

> *How pure in heart and sound in head,*
>   *With what divine affections bold,*
>   *Should be the man whose thoughts would hold*
> *An hour's communion with the dead.*

The world knows nothing of the hundreds of private gatherings to which those who have "gone on" have returned time after time to give unassailable evidence of their presence. Only those who have been present at these gatherings can testify to the value of the evidence given to them. When the same spirits return year after year, ever demonstrating the same characteristics that we knew so well on earth, we can no longer doubt: we know that Spiritualism is a great truth. So great and important are its claims that I do not wonder that many cannot believe them to be valid. They are so accustomed to speculation merely, about the future, that they fear to search for knowledge of it lest they lose what little faith still remains to them. Spiritualism robs religion of nothing; it puts new soul into it and satisfies reason, affection, and the deepest desires of our nature.

The young man who sat with us at the gatherings to which I have referred several times, showed wonderful clairvoyant gifts. So remarkable was his power that I began to think that the story of Jesus and the woman of Samaria might be no exaggeration after all. "Come, see a man which told me all things that ever I did!" It has been my privilege to witness many demonstrations of clairvoyance much more wonderful than that recorded in the 4th chapter of the Gospel of St. John. I have seen mediums lay bare a life's history so clearly and accurately that only the possession of the faculty of getting at the interior soul life could account for it. Having seen such mediumistic powers as Jesus' possessed by others, I consider him one of that great class of occult men and women who in all ages have been at the head of religion. Mediumship restores him to the race of human beings. Men's creeds are a disease of the intellect. They have shut the temple door of life, and have given us a fable to dwell upon instead of the facts our souls demand. To some it will seem blasphemy to try to compare the miracles of Jesus with incidents that happen in the world today, but if the world has to grow it must first free itself from the superstitions of the past. Everyone must think freely for himself, and not be content to quote some ancient saint or sage. We today are as near to God as any saint of any age ever was. Truly does Emerson say:

> If a man claims to know and speak of God, and
> carries you backward to the phraseology of some

old mouldered nation, believe him not. I have no
expectation that any man will read history aright
who thinks that what was done in a remote age by
men whose names have resounded far, has any
deeper sense than what he is doing today. Jesus
astonishes and overpowers sensual people. They
cannot unite him to history, nor reconcile him
with themselves. As they come to revere their
intentions and aspire to live holily, their own
piety explains every fact, every word.

From the lips of our young medium we had illuminating glimpses of olden times. An ancient Egyptian used to control him, whose lofty discourses were a proof of how we can learn much of ancient history through modern inspiration. No ancient Bible contains anything more worthy of having "Thus saith the Lord" put in front of it than the messages given us by this worthy spirit. We had him only at intervals, when purity of thought and harmony of mind let our inspirations flow towards him. Far removed he was from the earth sphere, yet he was not unconscious of the world's needs, and sought to promulgate a high and lofty ideal of spirit communion. The instrument of this Egyptian was all unconscious of the great wealth of wisdom which was behind him, and when told of it could scarcely believe that he was the mouthpiece of anything so profound. Those who heard his utterances while under the influence of this spirit control were charmed, and all thought he would become a great worker in our movement. Family calls, however, and perhaps fear of the world's sneers, drew him away from the standard. No doubt, at times, he feels the presence of his old masters on the spirit side and regrets somewhat that he has cast off the treasures of the spiritual kingdom.

I remember one young man, the keeper of the Secular Hall in King Street, Glasgow, whom the mediumship of our friend helped to bring out of the darkness of materialism into an assured knowledge of continued existence after death. When we started having sittings with him he was already far gone in consumption, and knew that death was not far off. However, before he passed away we had the pleasure of seeing him await, no longer with dread, but with joyful hope, the summons to go hence. The spiritual ranks are being filled all the time by those of agnostic tendencies who, freed from the shackles of the creeds, are eager to find some religion, some reasonable explanation of the puzzle of existence. To them it seems:

> 'Tis all a chequer-board of nights and days,
> Where destiny with men for pieces plays;
> Hither and thither moves and mates and slays,
> And one by one back in the closet lays.
>
> For in and out, above, about, below,
> 'Tis nothing but "a magic shadow-show";
> Played in a box whose candle is the sun,
> Round which we phantom figures come and go.

Their souls thirst after some new light, but they are held back by the fear of drifting anew into superstition.

Many years ago, while travelling in Ireland, I used to come into contact with a gentleman who had been in Glasgow, and who at one time had been chairman of the Glasgow Secularist Society. He and I had many conversations together, in hotels, at night, on various questions of science, more especially on the teachings of Tyndall and Huxley, of whom we were both ardent admirers. On most subjects we were at one, but when I would bring before him the evidences of spirit return I had met with, and the beauty of the spiritual philosophy so much in line with modern discoveries, he would turn a deaf ear, saying how pitiful it was that one who had shaken off the old superstitions should have become immersed in a new one. I could not influence him in the slightest, his ancient prejudice against anything that savoured of the supernatural being too strong. He insisted that my conversion to Spiritualism was simply a fragment of the old faith worship reasserting itself in a new direction. In reply, I could only ask him how he explained the powerful words, written in defence of Spiritualism, by Robert Dale Owen, at one time the high priest of materialism, and by him greatly admired. He could only say that he grudged such a man going to our ranks, but that with him also it was but a return to the old ideas in which he had been brought up.

It is hard to get the materialist to extend his vision and to recognise that the other life is just as natural as this, and is governed by the same forces as govern this. He will have it that when we talk of death being but the change from one room of the Father's mansion to another, that this must imply the acceptance of miracle. The realisation that the next life is but the natural sequence to this does not serve to illumine a moment merely, but to lighten our pathway all through life with its rays: the world then has quite another aspect, humanity a different face, and we imbibe a larger charity, which makes earth sweeter. It gives vitality to the soul, and helps us to be ever up and doing, helping others to bear their burdens, working to remove all causes of imperfection, and to prepare a way for the reign of harmony on earth.

> No curse is here from God, but only beauty;
> No curse is here for man, but only duty;
> God feels and blesses all, and faileth never,
> He works in light for life with love forever.

"The universe," Balzac has said, "belongs to him who wills, who knows, who prays; but he must will, he must know, he must pray with heart and will and mind. This is true worship."

The outside world, fed by the cheap sneers of the Press, will not give Spiritualists credit for having any religion. Even in this enlightened age some of our newspapers will not admit the notices of our Sunday services amongst the other church notices, the most motley of groups. The people who labour for the quickening of the soul, and who offer the very evidence which the churches need if they are to endure, find no acceptance. The ancient Spiritualism which was born of myth, and has only tradition for its mainstay, is honoured, while the living truth, borne witness to by the honourable of the present day, is scorned and despised. Perhaps it is to the advantage of our truth that its path is a thorny one; it will come forth all the stronger after having fought with difficulties.

> Then welcome each rebuff
> That turns earth's smoothness rough,
> Each sting that bids nor sit nor stand, but go!
> Be our joys three-parts pain,
> Strive, and hold cheap the strain;
> Learn, nor account the pang; dare, never grudge the throe!

Those who are on the side of truth are on the side of their own souls, which are as imperishable as God Himself. Many, when they have entered that other sphere, will regret that while on earth they condemned those who crucified the ancient Christ, while they at the same time helped to persecute the new Christ, who sought to cheer the mourning heart, and to reveal the infinite goodness of God. The work of Spiritualists is to declare the facts in their possession, to live the life which the spirit teachers point out, and to await patiently the harvest time, when the world will recognise its benefactors and thank God for His truest and best gift to man: Modern Spiritualism.

"May we not say," in the words of John Page Hopps, "that God is always on the side of the pioneers? It seldom looks like it, but that is because we look in the wrong direction for the signs of God's presence. We take the world's standard for His standard;

and that is altogether wrong. We think of what the world calls 'success' of happiness, of the sunny side of the great highway. But the inexorable God calls His chosen ones to make paths in the desert. His is 'the voice of one that crieth in the wilderness, Prepare ye the way of the Lord; make level in the desert a highway for our God'; and that means solitude, and hard work, and hunger, and thorns. The truth is that God is the mysterious Time-Spirit which unceasingly urges His world onward, and the strong, the animated, and the noble spirits best respond to His call."

CHAPTER XI

RATIONAL SPIRITUALISM

Thomas Paine named his great work, which stirred up so much thought at the end of the seventeenth century, *The Age of Reason*. It appeared at a time of upheaval, when reason did not triumph, when turbulence and rebellion were in the air, and men were more interested in physical than in spiritual problems.

It was a rational work, however, which appealed calmly to man's reason, and though the German critics have followed in the same field, and the higher critics of our own country have done likewise, they have only done in kid-glove fashion what the brave reformer accomplished in his own strong way. What Paine saw at a glance, and laid bare with a pick-axe, as it were, has been arrived at by others after a long course of halting and hesitation. Paine was an epoch-making man, with an eye to see through falsities, and the courage to lay them bare at a stroke.

Our modern theological critics are careful not to use words which will be offensive to orthodox ears. The arguments balance each other so nicely that the reader is in doubt whether there be any heresy behind the writer after all. When some acute observer points to something which can only bear the interpretation of a departure from the old thought, the writer can readily prove the contrary, and when the words are looked at again, really they can be read either way. In all that is said there is a double sense, a blowing hot and cold, which is not the spirit which should characterise the reformer. Luther worked in open, blunt fashion, while Erasmus coquetted with both sides, though at heart he had progressed much further on the path of spiritual freedom than Luther.

> *Let a man contend to the uttermost*
> *For his life's set prize, be it what it will.*

He was a trimmer, not a hero, like his more ignorant contemporary. Time has been on the side of Luther, whose brave words, as Richter says, were "half battles," and today the world recognises that of the two only the heroic Luther was worthy of the admiration of mankind.

You will ask, What has the foregoing to do with Spiritualism? It conveys to my mind the position of the Society for Psychical Research, which has been the Erasmus, while Spiritualism has been the Luther. Erasmus would have continually stayed the hand of Luther. Psychical researchers have made desperate efforts to place obstacles in the path of Spiritualism. The facts which Spiritualism has sought to demonstrate are that spirits, by utilising the forces at their command, have been able through the tiltings of a table, or rappings on a solid surface, to convey messages to the earth dwellers. When other conditions are presented, they can use the organism of the person in the body to tell out their story—a story so complete and authentic that only those whose mentality is befogged can read in it anything else than spirit action.

In 1881 Spiritualism had asserted itself so strongly that certain very clever people felt that the subject was moving on too fast, and began to say that Spiritualists in general lacked culture and intelligence, and also required to be guarded from credulity. They said that all the stories which were afloat could not be true, and it only needed that the scientific mind should dissect them, for them to fall to the ground. For this purpose was formed the Society for Psychical Research, which at first was welcomed by Spiritualists, as they were most eager that such knowledge as they possessed should be attested by men of attainment and worth. Spirit return, however, was the last thing they would give in to.

Though dealing with what to them was a new and subtle force, they demanded their own conditions, as if the forces of nature were at their beck and call. Nature says to everyone, Learn my modes, get at my secret, but psychical research metaphorically suffocated the body, and still demanded a revelation of consciousness.

Spiritualism, with its facts rationally observed, brought conviction to the minds of Crookes, Wallace, and Varley, Robert Chambers, S.C. Hall, Elizabeth Barrett Browning, Mrs. Stowe, and hosts of other thinkers, that the people at the other end of the line are human, and at times may be disinclined, or unable under the conditions presented, to make manifest their powers. But psychical research after years of labour has only been able to demonstrate that telepathy is real, that thought can be transmitted from mind to mind. Telepathy does not feed the hunger of the soul, nor brighten the lives of the multitude. When the Psychical Research Society did come into touch with intermediaries whom the spirits could utilise under ordinary circumstances, these workers were frozen by the chilling conditions, and little of value was obtained. There is a relation between the physical forces and those forces by which the spirits produce phenomena, but this fact was largely ignored. If the Researchers wanted to create a science, they have miserably failed. Myers, it is true, ended his career with the clear pronouncement that he had found that human personality survived bodily death, but this conviction was reached when away from research methods. I have followed all their work for a quarter of a century, and I find they have not yet come near to the ground which Crookes, Wallace, and Zöllner covered so long ago. It has been a case of seeking to milk the barren heifer: profitless. Spiritual truths are not to be toyed and trifled with by those who lack spiritual insight, and who wander amongst the tombs looking for the blessed light of immortality. I pass on to the work of one who had the true spirit of research which the followers of truth require. Business took me frequently in the early eighties to Newcastle-on-Tyne, where I came into touch with several mediums of power, and also with capable observers who had investigated the phenomena in a most careful manner. The most prominent of these was Alderman Barkas, a public man, and yet a courageous and outspoken Spiritualist. Mr. Barkas had for long known that the facts were real; not the work of the subliminal consciousness of the mediums, but the work of people in the after-death other sphere of being. Belief for him was not sufficient on any subject; he wanted knowledge. He was a student of the sciences, who took nothing on trust, but experimented for himself. He was not the type of person to hear of Spiritualism and to pass it idly by. To get proof palpable of a life hereafter was to him worth much effort, and so for many years he had tested the matter for himself in London and in Newcastle, and gained an assurance which could not be broken down.

Newcastle had caught hold of Spiritualism with firmer grip than almost any town in the kingdom. All the notable lecturers filled its platform, and the Society had developed several remarkable mediums for materialisation. Mr. Barkas got through the mediums, Miss Kate Wood and Miss Fairlamb, the most conclusive evidence that spirit people could clothe themselves with matter, and present to the observer the form and features of earth. He had casts taken in wax of hands and feet which could not have belonged to embodied human beings. A careful student, he kept notes of all that took place, which notes he reproduced in lectures and papers contributed to the Press. I met nearly all the mediums in whom he had been interested, and had sittings with them. Miss Kate Wood had certainly one of the finest organisms for the production of full-formed materialisations. She had been engaged, she told me, by Professor Sidgwick to give séances at

Cambridge University, and at the house of Mr. Arthur Balfour, the late Prime Minister; F.W.H. Myers and Edmund Gurney, the originators of the Society for Psychical Research, being amongst the investigators. Corroboration of her statements has recently been furnished by Dr. Alfred Russel Wallace in the Spiritualistic experiences set down in *My Life*, published by Chapman & Hall at the end of 1905. He there states that Mr. Myers showed him several MS. books full of notes of these séances, of which he was the reporter, and drew Dr. Wallace's attention to some, which he read through. He described to Dr. Wallace the strict precautions which were taken in order to make certain that the phenomena were not produced by the mediums. At this period the mediums were but girls, and could not have dreamt of imposing on clever university professors. Mr. Myers described to Dr. Wallace some of the tests which were applied. A curtain, which was hung across a corner of the room, formed a cabinet. In this was placed a mattress and pillow on the bare floor. The wrists of the mediums were tied securely with tapes, leaving two ends a foot or more long. These ends were tacked down to the floor, then covered with sealing wax and sealed. Under these circumstances one or more forms came out from behind the curtains, sometimes to a considerable distance, and touched each one present. The light was sufficient to see the figures, which were at times those of children, at others adults. Afterwards the mediums were found either awake or still entranced, with the tapes, knots, and seals all apparently untouched. Such evidence would seem sufficient to the great majority of mortals. It could only bear the one inter-pretation, that, in the presence of these girls, forms appeared which were not of this earth, but belonged to some other sphere of existence.

But it was not sufficient for these Sadducees, who afterwards toiled on the same lines in the Society for Psychical Research. No amount of outward evidence will ever be conclusive to men of this stamp. There must arise within their own souls the instinct to recognise truth when it is presented. Men of science do not keep an open mind on all subjects. All the tests which they could conceive of were not considered sufficient to exclude the possibility of imposture. The mediums might have provided themselves with tape, tacks, wax, and a copy of the seal, and, by practice and ingenuity, might have been able to restore things to their original state after coming out and impersonating the figures. To render this impossible (or, as Dr. Wallace reports, much less probable), at each séance these rare observers had the width, quality, or colour of the tape different, the sealing wax of another colour, or seal of another pattern. Yet still the same phenomena went on recurring. To secure assurance that they were not being imposed upon, still other tests were suggested.

Hammocks were procured for the girls to lie in, and these hammocks were connected, by means of pulleys, with a weighing machine, so that the mediums could not possibly leave them without instant detection. Yet still the phenomena were produced, and the mediums were found afterwards comfortably lying in the hammocks. Dr. Wallace says that when Mr. Myers talked with him about these wonderful séances, he laid great stress upon the rigid precautions that were taken against the possibility of imposture, and conveyed the impression that he was quite convinced of the genuineness of the phenomena at the whole series of séances.

Mr Myers, however, like so many others, did not publish these remarkable experiences. He kept them stored in his own heart, and fed a hungering world with telepathy, phantasms of the living, and simpler physical phenomena with which Spiritualists have been long familiar. I have heard often, from men who were in close touch with Mr. Myers, that he in practice was a pronounced

Spiritualist, but when I looked at the *Proceedings of the Society for Psychical Research*, I found little to corroborate this. There never was a hint of the phenomenon of the materialisation of the human form or its parts. In Mr. Myers' work, *Human Personality and Its Survival of Bodily Death*, there is at last a halting confession that the dead really come back. He no longer discusses the subliminal self and its marvellous powers as being the cause of the phenomena, but says, "It is some enfranchised soul, some soul like George Eliot, which has penetrated the old world secret, and has piloted the unnavigable way." But the Society, since his death, has not marched forward on his lines; the publications have become more retrograde, devoting space to phenomena which are worthless.

Dr. Alfred Russel Wallace very naturally says that "if these records of the whole series of séances by Mr. Myers are still in existence and can be obtained, it is the duty of the Society for Psychical Research, in justice to the mediums (one of whom, my old friend, Mrs. Mellon-Gleave, is now living), and in the interests of science, to make the entire series public. Such an inquiry, long continued, must elucidate a mine of invaluable facts." We are not, however, likely ever to see them. Had they been hurtful to the subject, the world would have been familiar with them long ago. A like fate met the writings of Robert Chambers, of Edinburgh, whose brother, Wm. Chambers, in the autobiography of the brothers, says, "Robert left a considerable bundle of manuscripts dealing with the subject of Spiritualism." Evenhanded justice has not yet been meted out to the Cause, but it triumphs over all obstacles, and in due season finds recognition. I have wandered, however, from Alderman Barkas and his work for Spiritualism. Perhaps the most valuable instrument with whom he investigated the subject was a young woman, who has since become famous; a woman, noble and pure, who has met with tribulation through the ignorance and blindness of mortals; a true woman, spiritual and refined, who has been made sweet and saintly through the ministrations of her spirit friends. She had, like so many spiritual exponents, no educational advantages. Ill health kept her from scholastic duties, yet she instinctively drank in knowledge. When Mr. Barkas met her she was a young woman of twenty-six, the wife of an outdoor foreman. She was but a working woman, who, in her small house, did all the work thereof. Yet within that modest home there gathered scholarly souls from the higher realms who sought to declare the message needed more than aught else to bless and charm the world. Through this woman, who had no taste for scientific studies, and who never attended a scientific lecture nor read a scientific book, were penned treatises on the most abstruse subjects. Her hand was controlled by invisible intelligences to tell out their story and to make replies to the questions which were submitted. These communications were written by, or at the dictation of, several different spirit personalities, who ever maintained a separate individuality which could not be mistaken. They were poets, philosophers, scientists, who had gained vast stores of knowledge on the many subjects which were submitted to them. This knowledge they gave forth through this woman's hand. Mr. Barkas prepared the MS. books in which these extraordinary manifestations of intelligence were set down. These volumes I have had the pleasure of perusing. No remuneration was given for the mediumistic services. They were quite gratuitous, as has been the case with so many of our notable workers. Great gifts are not meant to be hidden, nor sold to the highest bidder, but to be shared by all. Robert Burns poured out his celestial melodies, sent them freely to those engaged in the subject of Scottish song, without ever asking a fee, and few more priceless gifts have been given to the world. The instrument was not in a trance or mesmeric sleep, but in her normal condition, and took part in the conversation with the others who sat round the table. The only abnormal sensation she had was that of her hand being invisibly directed, but she had not any consciousness of what was being written. When Mr. Barkas read the answers, she did not understand the meaning of many of the words. There were generally from six to ten persons present. Mr. Barkas, who sat next the medium, wrote the questions in the MS. book as they were asked, and turned the book to the medium, who instantly wrote the replies to the questions. The theory of thought-reading gives no solution of the problem presented, as the answers to the questions were in the majority of cases beyond the knowledge of all present. The intelligences were outside and apart from the physical sitters. The questions covered the largest field of inquiry, embracing music, acoustics, musical instruments, the condition of the future life, musical composers and their works, heat, light, optics, biology, botany, astronomy, physiology, the brain, the eye, the ear, the circulation of the blood, the nervous system, chemistry, metaphysics, electricity, magnetism, history, clairvoyance, mesmerism, etc. The authors of the answers gave their names, and told their life's histories. There was a departed German student, Humnur Stafford; an American student, Walter Tracy; a German lady, an English physician, and a doctor of the Alexandrian School. All were essentially human in character, and showed great individuality. Sometimes when a question would be put, the controlling intelligence of the hand would write, "Stafford knows," or, "the anatomist will answer." To detail the matter presented would be too much to set down here. The properties of light, reflection, refraction, velocity, polarisation, retinal impressions, stereoscopic vision, the structure of the eye, the coating of the brain, etc., are for technical works. The great matter, however, is that here was a manifestation, which occurs in so many instances in the history of Spiritualism, of an uneducated woman becoming an instrument for the expression of ideas far beyond her normal capacity. Not even a person with the most severe scientific training could have answered all the questions which this woman did. The area was so extensive that no one living man or woman could have faced them. Only spirit intelligences in association can give a solution of such great intellectual power. Prejudice against the possibility of such things taking place is so strong that few will take the trouble to probe their genuineness: like the Levite, they pass by on the other side. When the Society for Psychical Research was originated, Mr. Barkas offered to submit the entire matter to them, but it was too strong for them to tackle at a first start: he was never called up. Trifles of little moment engrossed the Researchers; they thought it wise to wander in the wilderness for forty years rather than enter into the promised land, which could have been reached by brushing aside the shrubbery which covered that land from their sight. Neither Mrs. Britten, Mr. J.J. Morse, Mr. E.W. Wallis, nor any prominent Spiritualist advocate, was ever asked to enter their sanctuary to give them the experience which they had gained through contact with spirit people.

The medium with whom Mr. Barkas sat developed many other gifts besides that of automatic writing; her clairvoyance was of the most lucid nature. She could diagnose the diseases of the body, as well as describe the spirit surroundings of the sitters, and also cause the spirits to be recognised by means of sketches which she made of them in total darkness. Then began materialisation, when the spirit friends, "Walter Tracy" and "Humnur Stafford," appeared in the form of the portraits sketched by her. "Yolande," an Arab girl, was also amongst the spirit visitors, and marvels almost unbelievable were forthcoming. One incident, vouched for by Mr. Wm. Oxley, is clearly set down by that gentleman, and in all his experiences nothing more striking ever came within his sphere of observation. Mr. Oxley and his friend, Christian Reimers, sat in front of the cabinet, which was a plain wooden box, with a gauze division in the centre. In a little time the figure of "Yolande," draped in white, came out from the empty compartment, a figure quite different in size and outline from that of the medium, who was heard breathing all the time. "Yolande" asked Mr. Reimers to get a glass water-bottle, and some sand and water, which he mixed and put into the bottle. "Yolande" then made a few passes over the bottle, and sat down on the floor. Presently the sitters saw, for there was sufficient light to distinguish the operation, the gauze veil gradually rising, as if there was something moving it upwards. In two minutes "Yolande" went to the bottle, from which she removed the covering, when lo! there was a plant, with green leaves, grown out of the bottle, with its roots in the sand, but with no flower. "Yolande" took it up, bottle and all, and placed it in Mr. Oxley's hands. She then went into the cabinet. After the company had inspected the plant, Mr. Oxley put it at his feet, and waited for what would come next. In a few minutes he was requested by the spirit to look at his plant, and, on taking it up, he found not only had it grown considerably in size, but there was a beautiful flower about four inches in diameter on it. This was produced while it was between his feet. Mr. Oxley was no credulous person, as I have before remarked. He was a most careful observer, who on no single matter could lend himself to exaggeration. Mr. Oxley took it to his hotel, and had it photographed, afterwards taking it home and placing it in his conservatory under his gardeners care, where it lived for three months, and afterwards shrivelled up. The name of the plant was *Ixora Crocata*. The singular thing was that he had been promised at some other circle a specimen of this particular plant, and his object in going to the séance had been to obtain it.

The next night "Yolande" gave Mr. Oxley a small rosebud on a short stalk, with not more than two leaves on it. This he put in his bosom, and kept it there while the séance lasted. He felt some motion while the séance was going on; when it was over he drew forth the rosebud, and found that it had developed into a bunch of three large full-blown roses, with a bud as well! I know that to chronicle these things will only cause laughter in many quarters, but they are quite in harmony with many similar events which I have witnessed; they are, moreover, as well attested as thousands of facts, the truth of which we would not question. Mr. Oxley, as I have said, was careful in his observations, and was as capable an observer as any student of psychical research.

The instrument for these remarkable phenomena has been long known in the spiritual ranks as Madame d'Espérance. My friend, and her close and true friend, Mr. Matthews Fidler, on his visits to Glasgow, has frequently detailed the many wonderful phases of her mediumship. Zöllner, the German scientist, found in her one who gave strength to his convictions, and more than one university professor was led through her to accept the gospel of gladness. She has told her life's story in a volume entitled *Shadowland*: a book that breathes the spirit of a true and saintly woman. Her gifts have been indeed priceless, as many in our own country and on the Continent can testify, and her spirit friends have rounded out a nature that was ever rich. Like so many mediumistic benefactors, Madame d'Esperance has had her season of martyrdom. Hostile and unspiritual influences entered the chamber which should have been recognised as holy, and caused her much pain and suffering. How few recognise when the bringer of good tidings comes forth! Many since the days of travail have looked into her face and paid reverence to this apostle of pure and undefiled Spiritualism. Her integrity has been established wherever Spiritualism is named. She has consecrated herself to bring the kingdom of consolation to mortals: an exemplar of the religion of sacrifice. The light of the new day is shining all around us because she has lived and helped to open the way by which ministering spirits can bring to us the highest revelations of human blessedness.

CHAPTER XII

IN VARIOUS FIELDS

Newcastle in the late seventies was, as I have said, the great centre for spiritual work, and many who visited it to learn of the new science and religion had much of refreshing cheer. I ever met with the utmost kindness in every quarter for several years, during which I visited it every other week. The Newcastle press, no doubt from the influential position of many local Spiritualists, had no hesitancy about publishing reports of séances, of Alderman Barkas's lectures, and giving considerable space for correspondence on the subject. Many doors were open to me, and I witnessed many phenomena. Groups of Spiritualists would assemble round the bookstall of Mr. W.H. Robinson, then, as now, an enthusiastic labourer in the ranks. Here I have seen Joseph Skipsey, the Northumbrian poet, himself a notable psychometric medium, who edited the life of William Blake for the Walter Scott issue of the poets, and who afterwards was the custodian of Shakespeare's birthplace at Stratford-on-Avon. To me there was much of inspiration in coming into touch with the living, throbbing workers of Newcastle. Mr. H.A. Kersey, who is still to the fore in our movement, gave me much of helpful kindness.

It was in 1881, at the house of Mrs. Hammerborn, afterwards Mrs. Kersey, who has recently passed on, that I first came into touch with one of the most striking figures in the movement, Emma Hardinge Britten, whose voice had been sounded in all continents, and who stood forth as one of the most cultured and eloquent exponents of our Cause. Her career had been a long series of triumphs. Originally an actress, she had gone to New York to fulfil an engagement, when she heard of spirits making their presence known to some of her friends. She ridiculed the idea, and laughed to scorn the message which was given her at a séance, that she was a great medium, who would devote herself to Spiritualistic work. She resisted for long the strong spiritual power which was brought to bear upon her, but ultimately became one of the most powerful of inspired advocates. The story of her life, the brave struggles she made, the fearless spirit with which she preached the new gospel, are all set down in her interesting biography, edited by her devoted sister, Mrs. Margaret Wilkinson. When once she heard the spirits' message, no circumstance was strong enough to hold her back.

On her first visit to London, after her conversion, she stirred all hearts. Literary persons like William Howitt were amazed at the sweet grace of diction, the continual flow of lofty and inspiring thought given forth without preparation or effort. Alfred Russel Wallace gives quotations from one of her addresses in *Miracles and Modern Spiritualism*, calling attention to their high eloquence and moral beauty, and asking whether the philosopher or the man of science could picture a more perfect ideal than she portrays as to a future state. Gerald Massey, who had taken the chair at one of her meetings, amongst other fine utterances, said: "All hail and all honour to her who has so chivalrously devoted herself to the service of others in fulfilment of the Father's bidding. If she has not found her kingdom, she will have helped to found one—the kingdom of freer thought and clearer light, and sweeter charities and nobler life." She has penned histories of *American Spiritualism* and of *Nineteenth Century Miracles*, also a valuable volume, *Faiths, Facts, and Frauds of Religious History*. What a delight it was to me to come into contact with such a great figure, about whom I had read so much! What rich stores of wisdom she poured out! What graphic pictures she gave of Victor Hugo, the French poet, and Sardou, the dramatist, Andrew

Jackson Davis, and others, whom she knew well. Dr. Elliotson, the friend of Thackeray, to whom he dedicated *Pendennis*, and who is the Dr. Goodenough of his novels, met her when she came to London, and welcomed her as a warm and devoted Spiritualist.

Mrs. Britten was certainly one of the most brilliant women I have ever met. A storehouse of rich knowledge came to her from her friends in the unseen. She gave us some graphic pictures of a visit to Monte Carlo, which showed how real was obsession even in our day, and which made the stories in the New Testament of such occurrences look like actual facts. With her clairvoyant vision she had seen the ghosts of those who had gone out of life standing by the victims of gambling, luring them on. So dramatic was her speech that one could almost see the scene as it occurred. Spirit photography was also first brought to my notice at this interview. She had a large collection of pictures of great interest, each of which had a story of spirit identity. She had known Abraham Lincoln intimately, and had a portrait which his widow had obtained when she went unknown and disguised to a spirit photographer, a real portrait of the murdered President, differing from any that had ever been taken. Her own ex-periences of this phase of spirit phenomena had been most varied. She told the story of how, in the early days of her mediumship, Beethoven, the composer, had come to her, and as she doubted the reality of his presence, he told her he would give her three tests. One came to pass the next day about a musical criticism she was writing; another at the house of S.C. Hall, the aged *littérateur*, where one of Beethoven's symphonies was played by spirit hands; and the third when, with a friend, she went to a photographer in Boston, herself having no intention of sitting. The photographer, however, insisted on taking her picture without payment, and there appeared upon the plate, beside her, the form of Beethoven, with a lyre formed of flowers.

The man or woman who reads statements like these for the first time will naturally say, "Nonsense; such things cannot be, or the great ones of earth would have testified to their reality," and yet, in spite of such speech, they are scientific realities, if science be an accumulation of facts which have been verified. As Gerald Massey has said, "Spiritualism fears no truth that can be dug out of the earth or drawn down from the heavens." Truths fall into place quite naturally, just as Darwin's *Origin of Species* fitted into the universal law of evolution of which Herbert Spencer had already caught a glimpse.

Wide was the field of thought which I traversed with Mrs. Britten. The Salvation Army, and the value of Colonel Ingersoll's writings were amongst the many topics we discussed. It was after midnight when I left her presence, excited at the many strange experiences she told me of, and at the almost encyclopaedic knowledge of which she was the repository.

The next day I was at a séance which Miss Kate Wood gave in the Spiritualists' Hall. I had been at several before, but the conditions presented at these promiscuous gatherings were not such as enabled me to speak with that certainty which statements regarding materialisation should possess. Now, however, the conditions were all that could be desired. In Newcastle the Society had been furnished with a cabinet, from which there could be no possible egress on the part of the medium. Of this I was convinced as need be. It was a cold winter morning, and we had shut out the light, the only gleam coming from a little stove which stood in the middle of the floor. Before Miss Wood was screwed up in the cabinet we had her weighed on the machine which stood in the room, her weight being 105 lbs. Soon we had different forms coming out, enveloped in drapery. Each of these forms in turn placed itself upon the scales, and on a light being struck we found that some of the forms registered 23 lbs. weight, others more, the heaviest being 54 lbs. There was no doubt about the forms being of different sizes and weights. All this was most satisfactory, but I could not manage to see the faces clearly, they being covered with drapery. Another little form came out whom I had met before, and whose photograph I had seen standing beside her medium. This was "Pocha," the little Indian control, with whom all were familiar. She chatted for a long time, spoke about Glasgow friends, and asked me to leave the circle and stand beside her. I had to go down on my knees, and she put a sweet into my mouth, and threw her tiny arms around my neck, toying for some little time. She rattled the knob of the little stove, and from the gleam of light which came therefrom I saw the little black face. There could be no mistake that this was a little girl, with a body in which there was a real being. She talked freely all the time, and my whole heart knew for all time that here was the physical evidence that the dead can come back and manifest themselves to the living.

Very striking physical phenomena abounded in the Newcastle district. I loved, however, to listen to the wise words which fell from the controls of Mr. Lambelle and others. It was in Newcastle that I got close in spirit to "The Strolling Player," with whom a friendship was established, which has endured all these years. No friend of earth has been more to me than this companion in the spirit, and I am convinced when the change comes, the further step in my evolution, he will be the friend who will teach me the secrets of my new habitation.

The newspaper, *Light*, made its appearance in 1881, and supplied a want, which had long been felt, for a cultured exponent of the movement. Scholarly and literary, it helped to forward the truth. Its contributors have been amongst the ablest, and its pages will carry to future generations the great efforts which were made to give the world carefully attested facts, as well as sublime philosophical disquisitions. Its earliest editor was E. Dawson Rogers, a thorough man of letters, who was followed by one whose name has become endeared to all Spiritualists, Wm. Stainton Moses, also known as "M.A. (Oxon.)." His "Notes by the Way" were for long amongst the most valuable contributions to spiritual literature. After the decease of Mr. Moses, Mr. Rogers resumed the editorship of *Light*, which he conducted with increasing success for many years.

I moved all over the country at this time, and participated in many rich spiritual feasts. Mr. Alex. Duguid in Kirkcaldy was ever a wise teacher, as well as a fine physical medium. During 1881 I was often in his company. At one séance I assisted him to hang up the curtain in a corner of the room, behind which he retired when the company had assembled. The old familiar friends of years were there to greet me—"Sabo," "David Brown," and others, who seemed to be able to read me through and through. Soon we had great, clear, striking flames of light which were seen at the opening of the curtain. A little Indian girl like Miss Wood's "Pocha" came out and walked about the room, while Mr. Duguid, entranced, now sat outside the curtains. The "flames" shown were almost sufficient to light the apartment. As he sat entranced by the old friend, "David," a female form came from a corner and pushed the curtain back. I looked again and again, and the figure became quite distinct. While this was going on I never lost sight of the medium, who was sitting in the chair talking away and using both his hands in the expressive way he had when under this influence. One of those present asked the materialised form to kiss old "David," controlling Mr. Duguid, and the figure moved round and placed its head over the face, which obscured him from sight for the moment. I assisted in taking down the curtain, at the close of the meeting, with the feeling that I was a privileged man to have had this great certainty of materialisation.

Spiritualism did not deaden my interest in general literature, but rather quickened it in many directions. When I would read such books as the life of Edward Irving, I knew I had the key to the gift of tongues and other phenomena which had distracted that great soul.

Carlyle was still for me a great spiritual teacher, though he had passed by the pearl of great price. Francis William Newman, W.R. Greig, and Robertson of Brighton, were still for me spiritual teachers who had a message for the world. Through many avenues the new thought was being expressed. Tradition was giving place to a freer atmosphere, through which men would get beyond creeds, and recognise reason and observation as better than ancient myths.

> *Wait, my faith is large in time,*
> *And that which shapes it to some perfect end.*

I had begun during 1880 to keep a diary, in which were recorded the many séances I attended, and my thoughts regarding men and books, so that my recollections have been quickened by the perusal of these jottings, written when the events were fresh in my memory. Some portions of this diary were printed after many years in *The Two Worlds* newspaper, in which were set down some of the breathings of my inner life. At no season has my interest slackened in the Cause, or the conviction been dimmed that this revelation is beyond all else that has ever blessed humanity. I know the battle will be long and arduous, that many voices will cry out before the world is awakened to the treasure which is at their doorstep, yet I know that one day its acceptance will make the whole world glad. As Gerald Massey has written, "This despised Spiritualism will put a light into the one hand and a sword into the other, that have to be flashed in on many dark places and many a dungeon grating of humankind, in spite of the birds of night that may hoot at the light and blaspheme against its brilliance." It has come to quicken a keener conscience in the human race, to set up a loftier ideal of life and a nobler standard of appeal than fear of punishment or hope of reward. "The life he lived, And not the death he died, was first in judgment It is the writing on the folded scroll Death sends, and not the seal, that God will judge."

CHAPTER XIII

DEEPER ASPECTS OF SPIRITUALISM

Buckle has said, "The doctrine of immortality is the doctrine of doctrines, a truth compared with which it is indifferent whether anything else be true!"

It may be asked where confirmation can be had as to its reality? All the preaching that the world has listened to for centuries has seldom brought conviction to the doubter's mind. These doubts cannot be set at rest by Bibles nor churches. Spiritualism alone offers the means of establishing immortality as a fact, and it alone has dissipated much of the materialism which was rampant. Now that the worst of fears has been overcome, there is foothold given us for crossing the gulf of death. All the observations devoted to Spiritualism by those who were not at all friendly to its claims have been on the way towards acceptance of the facts. Telepathy, which Psychical Research has established as a fact beyond cavil, points to the transmission of thought across a gulf greater than any space of earth and ocean: it bridges the space between the visible and invisible worlds. We have prayed for the descent of the Holy Spirit with our lips, but have never believed in our hearts that holy, unselfish souls were ready to minister, and did minister, whether we were conscious of the fact or not. We have thus shut out from our sight a great working influence which has been in operation all the time. There are few human souls who, in their hour of agony, have not been lifted out of their depression as if by some angel voice whispering a message of cheer. This power works in us and through us, and we are continually replenished from the world of spirit. Spiritualism seeks to bring these emotions, these inner feelings, out from the vague into the realm of reality. As Huxley says, "We should not say we know or believe anything which we have no scientific grounds for professing to know and believe." Spiritualism, when properly comprehended, will bring a new life into the world. When we recognise that the so-called "dead" can look us through and through, a desire will leap up in our souls to walk wisely and justly in the sight of angels and men.

Present facts are of more value to us than ancient statements which have become weak and obscure after their long march. The ancient stories can only be of value when we can verify them by something which is taking place in the present. The world must have reality, and will not be satisfied with the narcotics of the Church: these have played their part, and have to give way to demonstration. This is an age which tests everything, and will not be stilled by hearsays. Spiritualism asks all to drink at its fountain without money or price, and from this fountain can be drawn the sole possible, palpable, natural evidence of a future life. That so much of blessing should be at our doorstep is almost too good news to be true, hence the mistrust with which the news has been received. But the world will awake from its sleep of death, and voice its regrets that for so long it refused its true redeemer. Once the claims are looked squarely in the face, then the day of redemption has come. During all the past half century all those who have seen and believed have never retreated, nor sought, like Peter of old, to deny the Master. In the words of Lowell:

> Get but the truth once uttered, and 'tis like
> A star new-born that drops into its place,
> And which, once circling in its placid round,
> Not all the tumult of the world can shake.

When men like Alfred Russel Wallace, Dr. Hodgson, and Professor Hyslop, tell us that materialism chained them till they met the spiritual phenomena which gave them the proof palpable that human existence continued after death, the world cannot sneer at the subject. These are keen men of scientific attitude, who followed the dictum of Huxley when he said, "Sit down before a fact as a little child, be prepared to give up every preconceived notion, follow humbly wherever and to whatever abysses nature leads, or you shall learn nothing." It is to be regretted that Huxley did not sit down like a little child before the facts of Spiritualism, like the friend he held in such honour, Dr. Wallace. It appeared too contemptible in his eyes; as he said, even if it were true, he had no interest in it. The canon of criticism which he lays down in his *Life of Hume* regarding the acceptance of new and strange events is so rational that every Spiritualist would accept it as a tolerant setting. He says, "No event is too extraordinary to be impossible," but there was not even suspension of judgment in his case; he condemned the whole matter in ruthless fashion. But all the sledgehammer efforts to beat it down have never affected its onward march. The Spiritualist who is a daily witness of the spirit's action and love can afford to pity the philosopher.

Elizabeth Barrett Browning saw deeper than Huxley did in this special realm, and wondered how people could receive the striking facts so adversely. "I do not know," she wrote, "how people can keep up their prejudices against Spiritualism; how they are not, at least, thrown on the wish that it may be true"; because of "that abrupt shutting in their faces of the door of death, which shuts them out from the sight of their beloved." Many brave and clear-headed women have spoken out in similar terms to Mrs. Browning.

Mrs. Harriet Beecher Stowe ever affirmed her entire belief in the manifestations from the unseen, and gave reasons for her faith, which was assured. When writing her stories she was clairvoyant and saw how they must be written. One of her letters to her friend Mrs. Fields, the wife of the well-known Boston publisher, has these words: "When the spirits will help I can write, otherwise I can only wait humbly at their gates, watching at the post of their doors."

The influence of woman has indeed been most powerful in the furtherance of our truth. The most prominent workers who have stood upon the platform have been women. Mrs. Britten I have already named, and Mrs. Richmond, for forty years, has been pouring out the most luminous and comprehensive addresses on the most varied points. This lady paid a visit to Glasgow during 1882, and charmed many with the melody of her speech and the profound thoughts of the spirit people. She has been the mouthpiece of illustrious souls, like "Lloyd Garrison," "Theodore Parker," and many others, and the student of Parker's writings can have little difficulty in recognising the idioms of speech of that great religious reformer. Thousands of remarkable addresses have been given in private circles of which the outside world never hears. It is because so many are nourished from such storehouses that the work goes on in spite of opposition.

Mr. Edward T. Bennett, who for twenty years was secretary of the Society for Psychical Research, has published some records of a private circle, at which addresses were given through a lady, which breathe the loftiest spirit of piety and wisdom. One, entitled, "God is a Spirit," purporting to be inspired by "Robertson of Brighton," surpasses in power anything I ever read from his pen. Were such gems of spiritual literature issued apart from the word Spiritualism, many would find in them a solace far beyond the ordinary sermon which is printed.

It is the public workers, however, who have kept the lamp burning. I have already mentioned my introduction to Mrs. Wallis in 1878, when she was without thought of becoming a public worker. I listened in my own house to many effusions which stirred the life of the soul; but I cannot forget her gifts as a test medium. Personal friends made their presence known to us, and with many unsought bits of evidence made their individuality a certainty. A brother-in-law of mine, who had been accidentally drowned a few years before, came back with all the old memories, and wrote his name plainly on my wife's hand. It was the result of a private circle, at which Mrs. Britten heard her speak, that drew Mrs. Wallis forth into the public work. Such gifts, Mrs. Britten said, should not be hidden, and so she timidly stepped forth, and has for many years refreshed and strengthened many by her clairvoyant gifts, as well as by her philosophic setting forth of the problems of life and man's destiny in the hereafter.

In 1882 Glasgow had a visit from Miss Lottie Fowler, one of the most valued spirit mediums, who had been known pretty well all over the world as a clear seer of spirit people. Before I saw her I had met many persons who had told me that but for her they might have lived in the darkness. Stainton Moses, M.A., has declared in his book, *Spirit Identity*, that what he witnessed in her presence made him a Spiritualist. His story is a most interesting one. Some friend had shown him the present Earl of Dunraven's book of records of séances with D.D. Home, but this seemed to him only the dreariest twaddle. Later on his friend put into his hands one of Robert Dale Owen's books, which interested him more, and he felt impelled to use every means to find out all about the alleged phenomena. Although he was a clergyman of the Church of England, he required the external evidences of immortality: such facts as appeal to all man's faculties. He heard about Lottie Fowler, and went to one of her séances. Much which was at first presented did not appeal to him. He wanted tests of spirit identity; something clear on which he could rest as a stable piece of evidence. The spirit controlling the medium seemed to him frivolous, and he desired that she should go away, and send someone who was more serious. After a time the voice came again, the voice this time of a man, very calm and unimpassioned.

"You want me?"

"Yes. What is your name?"

"I'd rather not tell you. You can ask me any questions."

"Tell me what you see, or describe anyone whom you see near me."

"I will answer 'yes' or 'no'; no more."

"I see a man; very old, tall, with a long white beard and long hair."

"Yes."

"He has a very high, broad forehead, and his eyes are drawn down. Why, he's blind!"

"Yes."

"And his face is black and blue. Oh! what's that in his mouth? It's like slime—and mud—and—oh! blood."

"Yes."

"And—it's dark. I can't see."

"Go on. How is he dressed?"

"He has on a long blue coat. No, not exactly a coat—something long. I can't see his feet."

"Where does he stand?"

"Right opposite, close by you."

"Can you see his name?"

"No. He seems in trouble. I think it's money. He looks so horrible. Let me go. Why do you keep me here?"

"Go, then. Do you know me?"

"No."

I have copied this from Stainton Moses' writings,[2] as he set it down at the time, and as the scene was photographed on his mind. Everyone at the circle was petrified and astonished. "They would have been more so," he says, "had they known with what accuracy a scene in my own private experience was being re-enacted before my eyes. It was, I am sure, absolutely unknown to every person in the room, as unknown as I was myself. It was a scene that passed in a very distant part of Great Britain, and it was reproduced with a realistic power that bore down before it all doubt and hesitation. I felt that the man was there before me himself, reproducing the story of his death for my conviction." This incident gave Stainton Moses, who afterwards became a wonderful instrument himself for spirit teachings, a faith and a knowledge which nothing was able to shake.

Readers of Florence Marryat's work, *There is no Death*, will remember many striking prophecies which were given her by Lottie Fowler, all of which were fulfilled to the letter. It was a marvellous gift she possessed of looking before and after. There seemed to be no cloud in her vision, all so penetrative and exact. The woman herself did not seem to possess any specially lofty view of life. She was a simple-minded, chattering woman: an instrument purely for the bringing to light of the great fact that discarnate souls could work through her.

On looking over my diary, written during the time of her visit in 1883, I am surprised at reading many prophecies regarding myself, all of which have come true. There were no sustained addresses, only spirit messages and tests of identity. In her presence I felt that the dead were looking me through and through. She opened to my mind many conjectures as to how far spirits could see, and to what extent our lives were mapped out and directed to a certain course. The fact was there, whatever

---

2. *Spirit Identity*, Appendix V.

might be the philosophy of it. She had sustained this role of seer for many years. There could be no gainsaying the evidence she had given to high and low—for she had friends amongst many of the Royal families in Europe, whom she had often visited. A perfect stranger to us all, at once she got into our surroundings, and few secrets but were laid bare. Her principal control was named "Annie," a German girl in earth life, who often blurted out matters which should have been hidden. There was no revelation of wisdom through "Annie," only the seeing of certain facts that had occurred in the lives of those before her, and foreseeing the outcome of events. At moments when she seemed to be treading on dangerous ground another control, named the "Doctor," would step in to put matters right. He was a person of judgment as well as insight. It seemed incongruous that two personalities so utterly unlike should work in the same sphere. The spirit people, however, have a mission to perform, to give healing to a mourning world, and have to work with what tools are at their hand. Florence Marryat and Stainton Moses were persons of culture, and could not have been hoodwinked in any way. Florence Marryat said of Lottie Fowler that she had one of the most grateful, affectionate, and generous natures possible, and half starved herself for the sake of others. She had seen her under sickness, poverty, and trouble, and considered her one of the kindest-hearted and best women living. Money she did not seem to care for, except to give away, and she would as readily have sat for nothing, if she was likely to be a consoling influence, as for a fee. I had many opportunities of seeing this aspect of her character in the after years. Many persons of note consulted her, who would not have their names mentioned in public. It is said she was largely consulted by physicians of the first rank to diagnose disease, and at the time of the present King's dangerous illness she predicted his recovery from the commencement.

It was through her mediumship that the body of the late Lord Lindsay, of Balcarres, which was stolen from the family vault, was eventually recovered, and the present Earl of Crawford, who at one period showed great interest in the subject of Spiritualism, gave her a beautiful watch, enamelled, and set in diamonds. I attended, I think, all the séances Miss Fowler held in Glasgow, except private interviews, and at every gathering some striking incident came out. Unfortunately most of these related to persons who gave me no authority to make them public, but they were amongst the most realistic bits of evidence of spirit return that I have yet known.

One prophecy relating to a relative of my own, which seemed most improbable, has made an impression which will last as long as physical life. It is on the lines of one recorded by Florence Marryat, which hung over her head for many months as this one did, only to be at length realised. When "Annie" gave it out, the other spirits seemed to draw her back, and sought to soften the harsh message she had given, as if they would rather she had said nothing; but time proved that "Annie's" vision had been accurate. It is perhaps better at times to live in the dark rather than the light. Foretelling the future has its dangers in some directions. We have to be grateful for the darkness as well as for light. When "Annie" blurted out information which had been better kept hidden, she but revealed the faulty human nature that is not changed by death. She was not over-wise in this respect, but outside this her marvellous gift of vision made clear to many that immortality was a great fact in nature, and that contact with this earth of ours after death was a natural circumstance, which, would we but open the windows of faith wider, might be made plain to all the world.

CHAPTER XIV

THE OWENS

The old meeting-place in Trongate, which had housed the Glasgow Society so long, was vacated in 1883, when the meetings were transferred to Carlton Place. The growth of the movement did not seem to be rapid. At times it seemed to possess little of vitality externally, but the living power was ever at work. There was no retreating; those who had been in the charmed circle of spirit communion knew that the hour of triumph must come.

> *With aching hand and bleeding feet*
> *We dig and heap, lay stone on stone;*
> *We bear the burden and the heat*
> *Of the long day, and wish 'twere done.*
> *Not till the hours of light return*
> *All we have built do we discern.*

Mr Morse and Mr. Wallis were regular visitors who helped to keep the flame alive.

Mr Walter Howell had joined the movement only shortly before visiting Glasgow in 1882. He had been a preacher amongst the Methodists since he was sixteen years of age. Then, the brethren thought his eloquence so wonderful that they deemed he was under the special guidance and inspiration of the Holy Ghost. But the words which sometimes fell from his lips were too broad for Methodism, and so he had to leave that body as a heretic. Like many a preacher of power, he knew not the source of the fervent thoughts which quickened his own being— he was but an instrument. Once he dropped into a spiritual meeting-place by seeming accident, and there being no speaker present, under the influence of his spirit friends he was taken to the rostrum and gave forth an address embodying the great spiritual gospel, and so became an ardent Spiritualist. Like all philosophic speakers, he had a familiar friend who came close to all—"Dick," a Lancashire pitman, who used to tell the story of his earthly carousals, and how, when he got out of the body, he did not understand his condition, saw his own funeral, and could not understand how it was he was not heard when speaking. Mr. Howell has now become a normal speaker; while spirit agency has quickened his own perceptions, the inspiration which marked his early utterances is still most evident, and thoughts, new to himself, are prompted by those guides and guardians who have watched over his life.

I have already set down how much the character of Robert Owen had impressed me. To me he seemed a modern saint, ever loving himself last. All my old fervour was quickened anew when I heard that a daughter of the race had arrived in England as an advocate of Spiritualism. She had been favourably received. George Jacob Holyoake, her father's old follower, had written a laudatory notice of her in the freethought journals, and the Rev. John Page Hopps had taken the chair at one of her meetings. She arrived amongst us in the summer of 1884, and was my guest for two weeks. She had been reared a Spiritualist, and the reality and beauty of the truth were part of her life. There were few places she had such a longing to visit as Glasgow and New Lanark, the stories of which, associated with her grandfather's and father's life, had long been familiar to her. Robert Dale Owen, her father, whom Hepworth Dixon had called the Privy Councillor of America, had been born here. Her great grandfather, David Dale, was one of Glasgow's most eminent citizens, a man still held in the highest honour, not only for his piety and benevolence, but also for being the pioneer of the cotton industry. He it was who, with Sir Richard Arkwright, had set going the New Lanark Mills, which were subsequently sold to

Robert Owen, who married his daughter. The name of David Dale has still a sweet fragrance. When Carlyle was writing on the formation of a national exhibition of Scottish portraits of historical characters, he said, "I would take in, and eagerly, David Dale of the cotton manufacture." His death in 1806 was mourned as a public calamity, every shop in Glasgow being closed on the occasion. Robert Owen said of him, "He was the most liberal, conscientious, and kind-hearted man I have met with through life." A street on the south side of the river and another in the east end of the city still bear his honoured name.

The story of Robert Owen's attempt to form a new Eden in America is a most interesting one, and has not yet been fully told. Mr. Frank Podmore, of the Society for Psychical Research, who once wrote me that Owen was amongst his saints, has recently issued a life of this great soul, which should kindle much of reverence for the man who was too far in front of the world for its comprehension. Robert Dale Owen was as enthusiastic as his father in the attempt to redeem the world, but the paradise they planned was never realised. Human nature has yet to expand and ripen before such experiments as were planned at New Harmony will bear fruit. It was casting seed into the ground which may one day blossom. "He who goes through a land and scatters blown roses may be tracked next day by their withering petals that strew the ground; but he who goes through it and scatters rose seed, a hundred years after leaves behind him a land full of fragrance and beauty for his monument and as a heritage for the race." These men sought to translate the great ideas which were given them into institutions, to yoke men together, and, by the yoking, secure the liberty of all and the welfare of each. Poetry of a lofty form must have dwelt in their souls; faith that might remove mountains they had, but to harness fittingly men and women animated by divergent natures and interests was not then possible.

"Earth is earth, and not heaven, and ne'er will be. Man's work is to labour, and leaven, As best he may, earth here with heaven."

I heard much from Miss Owen of the New Harmony effort. She had lived on the spot after the community had broken up, and still retained a portion of the land which had been purchased. Of her father's connection with Spiritualism I learned much. She told me how affected her father was when he came to London in 1854, en route for Naples, where he had been appointed American Minister, on hearing that his father had taken up with the superstition of Spiritualism. He could only feel that dotage and decay had sapped his mental faculties, and yet within a short time the clouds lifted, and he too knew for all time that the dead are in our midst and working with us continually. The old past dropped away, the ripening period had come. He got evidence that dispelled the materialism of a lifetime. Miss Owen was a cultured speaker. She was not entranced, nor did she claim to be a medium, but she had a wealth of experience. "Man's Spiritual Possibilities," which was the title of her first address, gave one a feeling of elevation: that the world did not seem so poor, and that heaven was nearer than ever before. Her face was lit up at times with trust and hope, like some of the Madonnas of the old masters. Another lecture was on the characters of her mother and father. She had been cradled amongst virtue and intelligence, though what is called creedal religion had been outside their family. The church they laboured in was the church of right-doing, where conscience and reverence for all that was lofty and pure were inculcated.

> So many gods, so many creeds,
>   So many paths that wind and wind,
>   When just the art of being kind
> Is all the sad world needs.

Another lecture was entitled "What the Spirits Have Taught Me," wherein she set forth the dignity and power of the living truth. She moulded hearts by the rich thoughts which she uttered, and she made the most glowing appeals for a righteous Spiritualism: to help us to lead the life of godliness, to work continually for betterment, to search how the highest human blessedness could be accomplished, was above all things the mission of Spiritualism.

The birthplace of her father, an old mansion house in Charlotte Street, at one time the town house of David Dale, was still in existence, little changed interiorly. It was one of the few places which had not been affected by the changes in the city. Not a room had been structurally altered since Robert Owen was married within the walls. We mentioned to the occupants that an Owen, whose father had been born there, would like to see the old rooms. The people in charge had been there for many years. They had received traditions of the house from their predecessors. The rooms were little changed since David Dale's day, the ceilings and grates being in their original state. Here was David Dale's study, there the library, there the dining-room, where the marriage of Robert Owen and Caroline Dale took place.

Of deeper interest perhaps was the visit to New Lanark Mills, which were meant by Robert Owen to spin not only cotton, but virtue, wisdom, and noble characters. Here, isolated from and yet so close to the world, he saw a choice spot on which to work out the thought which ruled his life: that man was the creature of circumstances, therefore it was needful that his environment should be of the choicest pattern. The spiritual philosophy which he caught in his later years revealed to him something more of human nature, yet there was a mighty truth in his ruling thought. The daughter of a race who had done so much for humanity entered New Lanark without trumpets and banners. We did not feel that the name of Robert Owen was even a living memory, but on this point we were mistaken, as on sending in our names and stating that a grand-daughter of Robert Owen would like to see the mills associated with her ancestor, we were most cordially received. We soon found that the memory of the pure old man was full and fresh. Everyone seemed to know the story of the wondrous past.

We visited what had been the infant schools, passing down the walk, now covered with grass, along which the children went each day. The larger schools, the erection of which so disturbed his partners, who were, they said, manufacturers and not philanthropists, were still standing, long unused, but still containing the huge revolving globe, by which the children were taught their geography. Other relics of his educational processes had disappeared. Old people were still alive in the village who had worked there when the mastermind ruled, and were full of what to them had been the golden age. These old people, who had a thrill of emotion at a real Owen being in New Lanark after all these years, gathered round. "There, there she is," we heard one saying to another as we drove on. We came to Braxfield, the estate where Robert Owen had entertained the great ones of earth. Here emperors and kings had been his guests after witnessing his model works at New Lanark. In this dining room had been discussed those essays on the "formation of character" which made such a deep stir in their day. Few persons have ever had so many admirers in their lifetime as he, in spite of his heresies, for in his famous speech at the London Tavern in 1817 he had boldly declared that it had been the gross errors embodied in all religions taught that had hindered the progress and happiness of humanity. Lord Brougham, who met him the next day, when all sectarianism had been roused by the bold statement, said to him: "How could you say what you did yesterday? If any of us (meaning the Liberal party) had said half as much we should have been burned alive," a suggestive comment on the times. The late Queen Victoria's father, the Duke of Kent, was Owen's closest friend to the last day of his life, and had it not been for his sudden death, he would have spent three months at Braxfield, as arranged, along with his Duchess and the Princess, afterwards Queen Victoria. A brother of the Duke of Kent, the Duke of Sussex, was an equally warm admirer of Owen's schemes. In the after years, when the old hero had touched the spiritual verities, he was often visited, he said, by the spirit of the Duke of Kent, who uniformly expressed for him the same kindness, confidence, and affection he had shown during his earth life.

"I have," he says in his autobiography, "the best evidence of my senses to know that spirits do exist, and that they communicate, in the best manner that their new state will admit, with the friends they have left on earth. From the highly gratifying communications which I have had from time to time from the spirit of His Royal Highness, I have reason to believe that he has had a fatherly, watchful care over his daughter and her family." Braxfield, which is beautifully situated, stands close to the Clyde. All this comfort and luxury he gave up when he sought to found the community at New Harmony.

During Miss Owen's visit I introduced her to Mr. James Murray Templeton, son of one of Glasgow's most eminent merchants. He was a young man of high ideals—artistic, poetic, and spiritual. He was seeking the evidence of spirit return, and Miss Owen's strong speech and varied experience, followed by some sittings in London, brought about in him the desired conviction. I had many letters from him in which he detailed his progress and where he stood in relation to the subject. Mr. Templeton was often resident in Paris, where he studied art, and became the associate of Laurence Oliphant, with whom he talked much about Miss Owen and her spiritual views, which, in some respects, were akin to his own. Oliphant was attracted by the personality so lovingly described by his friend, and crossed the sea to visit her.

This is not the place to speak fully of the remarkable life of Laurence Oliphant, so crowded with incident and adventure, so blended with affairs of State and spiritual mysticism. Where had he not been? Out with Garibaldi, secretary to Lord Elgin when the British Legation was attacked in Japan, and engaged in many bits of diplomatic work in America and Europe. He was a clever, keen man of the world, who might have risen to the highest position in the State. M.P. for the Stirling Burghs, a brilliant writer, the friend of everyone in position, the world was startled one morning to hear that he had thrown all over to become a follower of Thomas Lake Harris, who for years had been a spiritual medium in America, labouring earnestly for the propagation of the cause, but who had now caught some ideas of the Messiahship. All London, when he visited it, was startled by Harris's burning words. A friend of mine has told me that he saw the tears running down Thackeray's cheeks as he listened to him. Oliphant, at least, was captivated. To him Harris was the greatest figure on earth, a messenger from the Infinite with teachings that would redeem the world. *Piccadilly*, a work which he had evidently begun before he met with Harris, introduces that mystic before the close, talks of him as the one exponent and interpreter of God's mysteries, and calls him "the greatest poet of the age yet unknown to fame." A strange figure is Oliphant in human history—a bright and beautiful soul with a tendency to over-hasty and headlong belief. In a few years the halo departed from Harris's brow, to Oliphant's vision, and he drew a graphic picture of the man in his novel *Masollam: a problem of the period,* published by Blackwood in three volumes. Long before his meeting with Miss Owen he had withdrawn himself from the thraldom of Harris, though, according to Mrs. Oliphant's *Life*, he seemed to fear him to the end.

Influenced by Mr. Templeton's speech, Oliphant made a pilgrimage of 1100 miles from New York to see the woman whose thoughts were akin to his own. With the marvellous so strongly manifested in him, he read Divine interposition in it. He found that Miss Owen had arrived at all he had set down in his *Scientific Religion,* and he arranged that they should be married, and she should join him in his work amongst the Druses at Haifa. She became the medium through whom his ascended wife "Alice" could still speak to him. He said: "She realises 'Alice' most intensely, and brings her closer to me than ever I felt her." A few days after the marriage, when they had returned to England, Oliphant was seized with a serious illness, the doctors giving no hope. His wife's magnetic powers and the help of the unseen friends lifted him up for a time, and for weeks there seemed to be hope that the old buoyant spirit would again be permitted to roam over the world of matter and speculation. He accepted an invitation to the home of his old friend, Sir Mountstuart Grant Duff, at Twickenham, but disease held him firmly in its grip. For one hundred and twenty-six days his wife carefully nursed him, and with her magnetism eased his pains; then the end came peacefully, and he joined the friends gone before.

There is almost a touch of sadness in the thought of the incompleteness of Oliphant's life: the darling of society, the brilliant wit and *littérateur,* the brave traveller, he gave up all for what he believed to be the work of God. Amid his adventures and his gaiety there was, deep down within him, the desire to find the true religion, and in his groping he followed many a will-o'-

the-wisp. After his death in 1888 I had a visit from his widow. The sweet, pensive face looked older and the hair greyer. She spoke much of the brilliant man she had lost, wishing that I had known him. She told me of the twelve weeks during which she had continuously sat beside him, listening to his thoughtful, witty speech, his aims, his visions, and his aspirations. He had slept peacefully away, and she was aware of his presence as a spirit within four hours of the change. She had gathered from him during his illness much about his relations with Harris, of the hardships he had endured under his despotic sway. Though he had seen beyond the tinsel and recognised the weak and commonplace mortal, he bore with him for a period of ten years, as he felt he needed to get the vanity "knocked out of him." She dwelt largely on how she was guarded and guided by her husband in mundane affairs; how she was instructed regarding the work he wished her to carry on at Mount Carmel amongst the Druses. She had got a small company to go out with her to the East, amongst these being Mr. James Murray Templeton, who echoed her sentiments and seemed to see in the work a realisation of some of his ideals. I had letters from them in which they told me of their marriage and of the joy which ran through their lives. But the bond was of short duration. He, one of the choicest souls I had ever met, was transplanted. Reared in luxury, he sought to live for others. He seemed to be a denizen of some other sphere, who had been given to us but for a season.

Mrs. Oliphant Templeton has long resided in the East, but was lately in London bringing out a new mystical work. Thomas Lake Harris was visiting in Glasgow during 1903, when he promised to give an address to the Glasgow Spiritualists, but failed to do so. He passed away in March 1906.

CHAPTER XV

THE RELIGION OF SPIRITUALISM

The Spiritualism which has soothed so many does not run into the realm of the mystical. The rational Spiritualist looks with clear, open eyes at what is presented, and holds firm grasp of what is revealed, not seeking to make it harmonise with some churchal idea which he does not like to give up. The ancient thought ascribes to all religions the miraculous and infallible, and so when phenomena are witnessed which bear some resemblance to what is set down in books called sacred, some think this is clear evidence of the truths of Christianity. But Spiritualism has no miracles. Conscious communion with spirit Intelligences is a fact in nature, but a physical resurrection of the dead is not. We have had a religion based on belief—on "belief in a God who cared an infinite deal more for a few apples," as Gerald Massey says, "than for the eternal damnation of myriads of immortal souls." We have to get done with a "word of God" that is in opposition to his truth as manifested in nature. Man has no power to lose his own soul, or damn himself for all eternity. Man is immortal by nature, though, as spiritual evidences have shown, he may retard his development by limiting his life to the lower self, which may be a hell for him to struggle out of hereafter.

> Both heaven and hell are from the human race,
> And every soul projects its future place;
> Long shadows of ourselves are thrown before
> To wait our coming on the eternal shore:
> These either clothe us with eclipse and night,
> Or, as we enter them, are lost in light.

The man, or woman, who puts the new wine of spiritual natural facts into the old bottles of myth and tradition will never touch the free spirit which free-minded religious observation gives. Forever will he wander in unrest, groping for something which has no existence, as Oliphant did. Jesus is still too potent a figure for the world to look at him rationally. God-men belong to the fabulous, and have no relationship to life. Spiritualism will never bolster up Christianity, though it can throw much of light on what is behind all religions. Religion is not a set of precepts or a given mode of worship. That our earth deeds affect our future life is what all returning spirits keep telling us. Creeds do not count in the eternal court; it is not what we believe, or profess, but what we are: nothing avails there but the life lived. Day by day broad men in all churches are preaching this doctrine, having forgotten the creeds they once professed and promised to preach.

We have had a religion without knowledge—now comes a religion based on a common experience. That religion which is based on knowledge need not be the subject of diversity and contention. Human souls have come back to us who have gone through the furnace of purification, hence we know that life is progressive over there, and many who may blindly have missed their chance here will yet find it in the beyond, and work out their salvation with fear and trembling. Gerald Massey has said: "The phenomena which so many can vouch for go to prove that we have found the bridge that crosses the unfathomable gulf between the dead and the not dead—the organic and the inorganic— between mind and matter—which science has sought elsewhere, but never yet found. The cable is laid between the two worlds, and the communications prove that there are intelligent operators at the other end of the line who can send us messages in human language." Let all who know these things as genuine facts rejoice and be glad, knowing that the hour is almost at hand when the true salvation will come to all the people who have wandered in darkness.

What volumes have been written on the immortality of the soul! Each generation of writers has furnished a fresh crop, without giving much of actual life. At best it has been but an inference drawn from some vague words which had relationship to a physical resurrection. It is a topic which has exercised the minds of profound thinkers as much as of theologians. When Carlyle and Emerson first met in Dumfriesshire their speech was on the immortality of the soul. It is a subject which all men have pondered over. To some of the ancients it was a real belief. Socrates said, "As soon as I have taken poison I shall stay no longer with you, but depart from hence and enjoy the felicity of the blessed." Socrates perhaps went further and saw clearer than the many who founded their belief on some ancient statements. He was a medium who had his familiar spirit that guided him in his earthly career. He had the inner vision, a sight of the soul's capacity to know the truth. Cicero, the wise Roman, was, like Socrates, spiritual in his thoughts and not materialistic, as so many Christian workers are. "Oh, glorious day," he said, "when I shall go to that divine company and assembly of spirits!"

Let men laud Christianity as they may, it has never shed the least new light on this question which concerns all. There has been nothing relating the subject to nature. It is all vague and afar off, and Christian apologists have not brought the solution nearer to us. The story of the rich man and Lazarus does not help us to get any glimpse of the real future life; neither do the revelations of St. John. These are only the kind of things to be expected to happen in some miracle play before a Shakespeare's mighty genius transformed the stage. What can the world make out of the rich man being tormented in the flame, or of the other character in the drama, lying in Abraham's bosom? Of course we are told it is a parable, but even parables have some relation to truth, and if this one does not convey any thought out of which we can get guidance, then we had better let it go to keep company with the childish things which satisfied us in infancy.

I may be wrong, however, in saying there is no lesson to be gained from the story of the rich man and Lazarus. There is the potent fact revealed that sympathy and humanity had not quite died out in hell. The rich man asked Abraham to let someone go and tell his brethren, so that they might be saved from his torment. He was evidently a much better man in hell than he had ever been on earth; by thoughtfulness, self-knowledge, and repentance, giving evidence that progress in goodness does show forth after death. It was evidently only in hell that this divine characteristic of being concerned for others showed itself, as Abraham seems to have been innocent of any sympathy. He told the unfortunate one that there was no road to earth, and that the words of Moses and the prophets were sufficient to guide and warn. We can only think that Abraham was ignorant on many points, more particularly about the open door to earth. The spiritual facts of today alone make clear that in all ages and amongst all peoples the dead have manifested themselves to the living. Dr. Johnson has said that this opinion could only have become universal by its truth, and Lord Byron in expressing the same sentiments says:

> I merely mean to say what Johnson said,
> That in the course of some six thousand years
> All nations have believed that from the dead
> A visitant at intervals appears.

Abraham, in his remarks to the rich man, was claiming too much for the writings of Moses and the prophets. If there is any light shown there, it is microscopic, and it is doubtful whether immortality concerned the Jews to any extent. At all events, today we find it extremely difficult to extract even the doctrine of a future life from the Old Testament. There is no allusion to the destiny of the spirit, and nothing but the vaguest glimpse of spirit agency. Those who did come back in dramatic fashion were never our brothers and sisters, but angels and archangels, who were not much in touch with our common humanity. To many who have been reared in the atmosphere of Christian dogma it has largely been a matter of speculation as to whether or not there is a future life. All the preaching and Bible circulating have never touched the sceptical mind.

> *Is there beyond the silent night*
> *An endless day?*
> *Is death a door that leads to light?*
> *We cannot say.*
> *The tongueless secret locked in fate*
> *We do not know; we hope and wait.*

To cry out that Jesus arose from the dead was scarcely sufficient, in view of the fact that it was claimed for him that he was more than an ordinary mortal. The veil between the two worlds could not be lifted, we were told, and it was impious to seek to peer through it. Spiritualists have not of themselves lifted any veil. The curtain which hid that other world from view has been drawn aside by the spirits' own hands, and we have been asked to look at and consider what has been presented in a religious, earnest, and truth-loving spirit. The light which struggled to show itself with fitful and refracted rays now becomes clearer, and the question of immortality is removed from the domain of speculation into that of actual fact.

The day for laughter and ridicule has gone past. The person is merely ignorant who denies the reality of spiritual phenomena. The imposture theory has played its part, and largely because of the assumed impossibility of the phenomena asserted. Those who say that these things cannot be true are quite in line with those who maintained that the earth could not be round because, as they said, the people on the other side must tumble off. This cry of imposture is often raised without thought or reflection by unreasonable and prejudiced persons. The mass of evidence which learned and unlearned have set down during sixty years cannot be affected by any parrot cry. The people who say that they are "perfectly convinced that they have seen and heard, in a manner which should make un belief impossible, things called spiritual, which cannot be taken by a rational being to be capable of imposture, coincidence, or mistake," to quote the words of Professor de Morgan, the great mathematician, cannot be cried down. Sir William Crookes, thirty years after the publication of his *Researches into the Phenomena of Spiritualism*, was bold enough to say, when President of the British Association, that he had nothing to retract, but very much to add thereto. It is certain that objective realities, as well as a recognition of the subjective, have given Spiritualists real grounds for the faith that is in them. Veritable facts have had to be faced, which bear only one interpretation, that at last the great secret has been revealed. An assurance is now possible as to another life after death. Explanations as to the phenomena, advanced by those who would not investigate, have all been grappled with, only to bring us back for a true explanation to the unseen spirit world and its dwellers, who have ever claimed to be behind all so-called spirit manifestations.

The fight to obtain recognition of this revelation of nature has been a hard and long one. Men of science readily believe all the new discoveries in astronomy, chemistry, and biology, but when the more important discovery of a spirit world acting on the plane of matter is proclaimed, and valid evidences offered, we hear of credulity, and superstition, and want of due observation. The most conclusive tests are sneered at. In the language of Scripture, these men have eyes, but see not, ears but hear not; they are ever learning, but never coming nearer to a knowledge of the truth. What is there improbable in what Spiritualism claims to make clear? We recognise that the phenomena occur in harmony with natural law, and we feel that recognition of this fact would throw light on all the religions of the world, and so reconcile religion and sound philosophy. Religionists at least acknowledge that there is a spirit in man, and that this spirit will survive in some other sphere of existence. Is there anything unlikely in the idea that the being who parts from so many who are dear on earth should desire to make signals of his presence, and send such messages of love and hope as can be interpreted? Many will say that this is true, only they do not seek to prove it, but let it rest in the vague and shadowy form in which we have for so long regarded it. However, there has been implanted in the mind of man the feeling that nothing should be passed over as outside the realm of human investigation. As John Page Hopps has written when speaking of his own experiences of Spiritualism, "Is not everything hidden until man presses on to the discovery?" The expression "beyond the veil" does not apply to the future life alone: and we never know what God intends us to find until we seek. The finding will demonstrate that God willed us to find. "Seek, and ye shall find," is written everywhere by the merciful Father's hand, and His method of revelation is manifested in man's longing to know. We may be sure that if there is a path of communication between the seen and the unseen, it must be a necessary part of the perfect order of the universe.

When Spiritualism had only begun to be heard of in this country, so clear-headed and penetrative a man as Dr. Robert Chambers could write of it as already redeeming multitudes from hardened materialism and atheism. It had done so in his own case. According to his friend, S.C. Hall, who had been with him at a spiritualist sitting, Chambers told him that his opinions and views had been entirely changed as to immortality and the here-after, and that he had burned a manuscript, *A History of Superstition*, on which he had been occupied for some years. Even a person of his lofty intellect needed the positive demonstration that there is another world, and, having obtained it, he believed many things at which he would have scoffed when writing *The Natural History of the Vestiges of Creation*.

I do not forget that many of the things I have seen and heard are not made visible to the sight and hearing of those who read my testimony, but I do say that such evidences as have come to me can be obtained by all who will look for them patiently and with an open mind.

It was my great privilege during 1884 to get to know a young lady who had but barely heard that there was such a thing as spiritual evidence. She had just come from a little town in the west of Ireland, and was deeply imbued with the teachings of the Episcopal Church. The fact of her strong churchal leanings was one of the reasons given by the friend at whose house we sat for not bringing her into the room where our sittings were held. Getting familiarised with our talk on the subject, she was induced to become one of the sitters, and almost at once revealed powerful mediumistic gifts. She not only saw and described with marvellous accuracy the forms of many spirits whom we had known when in earth life, but we heard their raps and were soon able to recognise the presence of each spirit by the raps alone, as each one had its own special characteristic. These sounds would be heard on the table round which we sat, under our chairs, on the pictures in the room, and each series of raps would spell out some communication when the alphabet was gone over. They were distinct sounds which it would be difficult to describe; at times they were as if done with the finger nails, at others like a sharp concussion, but each spirit ever maintained through its rap

141

an individuality of its own. At times the rappings would be heard all over the room, as if a crowd of operators were at work. No one could listen to them without being convinced that the person of the medium had not been used to produce them.

You asked for a response to a question to be made in some given place, under your own hand it might be, or on the wall, and it was at once forthcoming. Bright and melodious to us were these messages telegraphed from another sphere of being, while we knew from the descriptions clairvoyantly given who the operators were. The lady seemed to be quite plastic in the hands of the unseen friends; the force or spiritual aura emitted by her enabling our visitors to act on the most ponderous substances. When she had only one hand on a large dining room table it would move several feet away from her, and tilt up several degrees. Many times, when in the most observant attitude, and weighing up all that was presented in careful scientific fashion, I have witnessed a large table suspended in mid-air without the least contact with the medium, her hands being simply held above it. At these times I would notice that the blood had seemingly left her hands, they becoming like marble. This alone would be simply the manifestation of an unseen force which might be called blind, but intelligence ruled even here. We knew the spirit people who co-operated through the medium to produce these striking results. Nothing could be more wonderful than the motions of the heavy dining room table, lifting itself almost upright and wriggling backwards and forwards while this woman's tiny hand was laid at one corner. The table seemed to be pulsating with life. There was a creaking at first, and then a thrill, which seemed as if human muscles were at work. Such manifestations as I have sought to describe are called by Spiritualists "physical" phenomena.

Our sensitive developed other gifts of a mental nature. She became readily entranced and was used as the mouthpiece of several spirits, many of them our own personal friends who had passed away. The parted links of long ago, with all their sad memories, were once more rejoined. The empty place was again filled, and a joy like no other took possession of our hearts. Life to life, spirit to spirit was knit. It was no delusive dream, but heaven really come to us on earth. Sometimes spirits whom we had known, through other mediums, would make their appearance amongst us. One of these was "Pat," an Irishman, whom we had known first through Mr. Coates, the mesmerist. Though naturally timid and retiring, the medium, when this spirit obtained control, would be made to throw off her bracelets and show forth all the characteristics of the boisterous "Pat." She did not specially care for his presence, but frequently he had a word for myself, and at times he would speak through my own lips. Though I never lost consciousness, I would be made to assume his attitude and speak the brogue, often giving expression to sentiments regarding individuals which were scarcely in harmony with my own. I could not mistake the personality of "Pat," my friend for years, any more than I could those of men and women with whom I came in contact in the physical life. The rapping phenomena with this lady ceased after a time, more fully developed clairvoyance and trance taking their place.

It is thought by some that these more sensuous or physical phenomena are not on the same elevated plane as the spirit's action in the form of speech by entrancement, but I regard the rap as one of the most valuable forms of spirit manifestation. It is needed to come before the philosophical setting of the spirit's message. It is a demonstration of the continued presence of the immortals which cannot be doubted, and which can stir men's minds when moral platitudes fail to touch them. Unconscious cerebration, or the subliminal self, may get credit for being the origin of mental phenomena, but all the theories of psychical research cannot account for those audible and intelligent sounds, nor for the movements of furniture, either with or without an intelligent aim. The thought of some who have been reared amongst Ecclesiasticism, painted windows and lawn sleeves, is that the spirit world would employ something more dignified than electrical sounds. Those on the spirit side who developed this mode of telegraphy were wise, and practical. They knew that interior or mental communion might soothe some few minds, but that more palpable evidence was needed if all the world was to listen. It followed the magnetic telegraph, which was a herald of the better day, when messages would be sent from realms unseen by physical eyes. That it was what the world needed is evidenced from the fact that the earth's inhabitants did listen, investigated to discover whence the sounds proceeded, and so advanced in wisdom, knowledge and truth. The sceptical intellect of man could scarcely have been reached more forcibly than through the material senses. Materialistic as these means might seem, they have thrilled many a heart with a joyous sensation, and many powerful minds have been affected by the raps and truly called from death to life.

It was the rappings through the Fox sisters in 1848 which first startled the world and brought forth such brave and powerful advocates as Judge Edmonds, Professor Hare, and Robert Dale Owen. The first medium who came to this country was Mrs. Haydon, and the raps which were produced in her presence brought to Robert Owen the crowning light which blessed his life. It was these rappings which caused Professor de Morgan to write the clear preface to his wife's volume, *From Matter to Spirit*, wherein he states that he "had heard and seen things called spiritual which could not be explained by imposture, coincidence, or mistake." Though so many persons went to Mrs. Haydon with the conviction that they would only find some new trick, or the manifestation of some hitherto unrecognised physical force, the majority had to bend before the clear fact that intelligences were present who did not belong to the physical life. However elementary seemed the idea, the spirits commanded attention and recognition. Those close friends, Drs. Elliotson and Ashburner, who had stood together bravely for the facts of mesmerism, differed from one another for a time as to the spirit origin of the raps. Dr. Ashburner was convinced and converted, after a few years. Dr. Elliotson followed in his wake, and humbly expressed his regret at having fought against the truth. There is no doubt that the presence of Mrs. Haydon set aflame in this country a light which time can never put out: a light more powerful than Luther kindled, because more valuable to humanity, touching the heart-strings of mortals, and giving them a priceless heritage.

CHAPTER XVI

SCIENTIFIC TESTIMONY

Professor Barrett, of Dublin University (whose paper, read before the British Association at Glasgow in 1876, caused so much commotion), in a paper which he read before the Society for Psychical Research, makes some references to sittings he had with a Mr. Lauder, a well known photographer in Dublin. It was my privilege to come into contact with this gentleman during several visits I paid to that city.

Mr Lauder and his niece were wonderful mediums for rapping phenomena. They were alone in their Spiritualism in Dublin, where such a subject is not likely to make headway. Along with another friend, a Spiritualist, I spent an entire Sunday in the Lauders' company. "We lunched with them at their place of business, and had many messages through the raps. After spending the afternoon in the Phoenix Park, we repaired to their house on the outskirts of the city. I do not know whether it was Mr. Lauder or his niece who gave forth the conditions through which the spirits were able to manifest. I suppose, being alone with an unpopular subject, their forces had so blended as to produce a most powerful battery. While sitting at tea we heard raps. Questions were put, and smart responses were given. The furniture thrilled and moved, and we had the feeling that we were surrounded with a great cloud of witnesses and helpers.

Afterwards, in a well-lighted room, we were treated to something more marvellous than had yet occurred. Mr. Lauder and his niece stood up, and, holding a sheet of white paper, each taking an end with both their hands, there were rapped out on it answers to our questions. Not only were the sounds clearly heard, but each time the raps came upon the paper it was seen to vibrate, as if it had been struck with a pellet. My evidence as to the reality of this phenomenon should be as valuable as if it had been vouched for by the most learned on earth. My friend and self were in full possession of our faculties. We both saw alike, and could have attested the fact anywhere. It was a case of simple observation. The same friends who signalled their responses on the table and the teacups were able to produce the sounds on the stretched sheet of paper. Though this special form of spirit manifestation is rare, it is not more wonderful than hundreds of other forms which have been chronicled in spiritual literature.

In the early days of the spiritual movement the present Earl of Crawford and Balcarres was frequently in evidence as supporting its claims to recognition. When the Committee of the Dialectical Society was formed in 1870 to inquire into the subject of Spiritualism, the Earl tendered some very strong testimony as to the reality of the phenomena which took place in the presence of D.D. Home, and on being asked if he ever obtained any information which could not have been known to the medium or to anyone present, he vouched for the following facts, which I give in his own words:

> A friend of mine was very anxious to discover the will of his grandmother, who had been dead forty years, but he could not even find the certificate of her death. I went with him to the Marshalls (well-known rapping mediums, who had brought conviction to many inquirers), and we had a séance. We sat at a table, and soon the raps came. My friend then asked his questions mentally. He went over the alphabet himself, or sometimes I did so, not knowing the question.
>
> We were told that the will had been drawn by a man named William Walker, who lived in Whitechapel. The name of the street and the number of the house

were given. We went to Whitechapel, found the man, and subsequently through his aid obtained a copy of the draft. He was quite unknown to us, and had not always lived in that locality, for he had once seen better days.

The medium could not possibly have known anything about the matter, and, even if she had, her knowledge would have been of no avail, as all the questions were mental ones.

This is a clear piece of evidence, and shows that spiritual beings can and do take an interest in the concerns of mortals. The Earl of Crawford, apart from his position as a landed magnate, is a person of scientific attainments, being recognised as an astronomer of note, a gentleman whose veracity would be questioned by no one.

In 1874 the Earl was engaged at Cape Town observing the transit of Venus over the sun's disc, with other astronomers, and Rear-Admiral Usborne Moore has told me that at that time he sought to bring the subject of Spiritualism under the Admiral's notice, with some measure of success, for of late years the latter has entered upon investigation, and has boldly proclaimed with voice and pen the evidences he has gathered. There is another piece of evidence which was laid before the Dialectical Society by a man of acknowledged scientific worth, the late Cromwell Varley, F.K.S., which helps to show the value of the spirits' work to earth dwellers. Varley was amongst the first electricians of his time, and was the colleague of Lord Kelvin in the laying of the first Atlantic cable. He had been convinced of the reality of mesmeric phenomena before he came into contact with Spiritualism. Knowing the therapeutic value of mesmerism, he had mesmerised his wife, who was afflicted with a very aggravated form of chest disease, and was supposed to be suffering from consumption. It was stated to him by medical men that she could not live for three months. One night she became entranced, or mesmerised, as he thought, and he was surprised to hear her speak in the third person, saying to him, "If you are not careful you will lose her."

"Lose whom?" he exclaimed.

Her voice replied, "Her—your wife."

"Who is speaking?"

The reply was the one ever given through every form of spiritual phenomena; not that it was a secondary self of the speaker, nor any of the complex explanations offered by psychical researchers, but the clear and simple statement: "We are spirits, not one, but several. We can cure her, if you will observe what we tell you."

And then was given to him the information, full of details, as to her condition, and as to what would take place. First the spirits told him that three ulcers would form on her chest, and that the first would break in ten days at thirty-six minutes past five o'clock. It would be necessary, they said, that he should have certain remedies at hand. No one was to be with him for fear of causing excitement, and he was warned to tell his wife nothing of the communications made to him, as the chances were that the shock of knowing about her state might kill her.

On the tenth day he went home early. He had set his watch by Greenwich time, and exactly at 5:36 his wife screamed out. That happened which had been predicted. He applied the remedies as directed, and she was relieved.

The second crisis was foretold three weeks, and the third a fortnight, before they actually occurred. He had promised at the time of the third crisis to take her to Peterborough to see an eclipse, but he found that the ulcer was to break at a time when she would be in the train. The spirits said, however, that it would not do to disappoint her, and she went, he taking the remedies with him in his pocket. Half an hour before the appointed time she became ill, and precisely at the hour named the ulcer broke. He produced the remedies, to her surprise, for she knew nothing of the prediction which had come out of her own mouth. By acting on the instructions he received from the spirits she was restored to health, and afterwards bore him a family.

The literature of Spiritualism contains records of many such occurrences. It is as the result of similar experiences that so many persons eminent in science and literature have been attracted to the movement, and have given forth testimony, much of which has been overlooked. It was facts, not theories, that made Robert Chambers, William and Mary Howitt, Mr. and Mrs. S.C. Hall, and so many others devoted Spiritualists.

If the dead are not dead, but alive, how natural it is that they should hover over those they love and seek to minister to them. The darkness, which has overhung all that relates to an existence after this life, has prevented the right track being entered on. Evidence which was capable of blessing had been rudely thrust aside as of no value. An honest inquiry would have shown how harmonious and rational is all that is presented, linking the phenomena on to other realms of nature, and giving to humanity the greatest blessing that can be conceived. It has been realities coming into the lives of Spiritualists that have given them the strength and confidence which make the outside world wonder. Incidents as marvellous as those recorded by the Earl of Crawford and Cromwell Varley are continually being met with, and the daily lives of many thousands are coloured with the evidences of spirit ministry.

Before I received the spiritual evidences, it had not been my lot to observe anything of an occult kind, being convinced pretty strongly that such occurrences belonged to the realm of fancy.

Yet, once I had started on the round of knowledge, I was literally flooded with proofs which could not be set aside as coincidences or fancies.

One striking incident which came to me in 1883 has ever held a place in my mind as being conclusive and satisfactory. In the days of my boyhood I was closely attached to a family, being considered almost as one of themselves. The mother's kindness to me was ever marked, and when she crossed the bourne, while comparatively a young woman of forty-three, my grief was great. As the years rolled on, the eldest son rose to a position of affluence, and became a pillar of the Church. He had not over much regard for me, as already I had begun to manifest free-thinking tendencies, but this did not affect my relations with the other members of the family. After some years, I heard, in a distant kind of way, that the son had met with financial misfortunes, and that he was comparatively a poor man. He was so far removed from my sphere that I did not know for a fact how much of truth there was in the story of fallen fortune. It was a thing which did not concern me closely.

In September 1883 I had been journeying in the Leeds district, and at the weekend I went up to Middlesborough, having made an appointment to meet a friend, Mr. Burton, who had arranged to speak for the Spiritualists of that town on the following day, Sunday. In the evening, when walking through the marketplace with Mr. Burton and another friend, there suddenly came upon me the words, "Send £25 to James Scott," the gentleman whose riches I had faintly heard had taken wings. Whether it was an objective voice I heard or an impression made on my mentality, I know not, but I was literally thrilled with the strange feeling. It simply put aside all other thoughts.

I said to myself, "Well, I can do nothing in such a matter at this hour. I will see if more comes to me." I went to my hotel strangely moved, and in the morning, at breakfast, I sought to analyse the feeling which had come over me the previous night, but there was no return of the message.

I went in the forenoon to the Spiritualists' meeting-place, and after dinner, along with the friends who had been with me the previous evening, set out for a walk in the public park. We were chatting away, when the same sudden impulse or message again overpowered me: "Send £25 to James Scott." I said to myself, or rather to the influence, "This is Sunday, and I cannot well look after money matters today," but I resolved that the next day I would do something. After this all was quite calm with me, and I suppose had there been nothing more I would have let the incident slip out of my memory, particularly as £25 was a considerable amount to me at the time. I had arranged to go to Saltburn-on-the-Sea on the Monday morning on business, while my friend Mr. Burton was to return to Newcastle. At the railway station, however, he changed his mind, saying he would wait my return from Saltburn, so that we might travel to Newcastle together. No sooner had I got seated in the train than there came to me a return of the old feeling, and a repetition of the demand to send the £25. The message was so imperative, that I took out my pencil and wrote to my wife at Glasgow, asking her to call and offer the £25, telling her how the prompting had come to me. When I had posted the letter at Saltburn I felt at peace, having obeyed the spirit message.

When I got back to Middlesborough I found my friend waiting for me at the station, but instead of going direct to Newcastle, he suggested that I should go round with him to a town called Spennymoor, where there was a friend whom he was anxious to visit while in the neighbourhood. I readily acquiesced, especially as I had a customer there with whom I might do some business. On arriving at Spennymoor my friend entered a boot shop, telling me to call for him there when I got through with my own business. I did so, and was ushered into a parlour at the back of the shop, and introduced to a Mr. and Mrs. Scott, who had for years been devoted spiritualists, Mrs. Scott being a valuable instrument for spirit control. After tea we had a séance, the front shop having been closed. A strong spiritual influence was in the apartment, and Mrs. Scott was entranced. I felt strangely moved, could not get rest on the sofa where I was sitting, and was forced to go over and lay my head in the lady's lap. I was told all about my home surroundings, and my past life seemed to be read as from the pages of a book. Then was described to me a lady, about forty-five years of age. Each feature was clearly limned, and I had no difficulty in recognising at once the mother whom I had known in the past, and whose son I had been asked to help. The spirit spoke of my generosity to her son, and addressed me by the old familiar name by which she had called me when I was a lad. I saw unmistakably that it had been a mother's love which had been at work, prompting me to do a kindness.

The sequel to this story is, that this exact amount of £25 was required in a special manner to avoid what would have been a great financial calamity. When I saw the recipient of my gift a few days after, he thanked me for my kindness, and said my wife's visit seemed like that of an Angel of Providence. I told him it was not me he had to thank so much as his ascended mother, whose promptings alone had forced me to carry out her request. Whatever sceptics may make out of this incident in my life, it must ever live in my memory as a clear case of spiritual guardianship, and no outsider can grasp to the full how real it all was to me.

A few weeks later I had a dream, while asleep in my own home in Glasgow, which, although it does not deal with pearly streets or angelic beings, gives a glimpse of the occult possibilities of our human nature. It was the only dream I ever had which penetrated the external consciousness and touched the realm of fact. At the period in question I was responsible for the conduct of the Howe Machine Company's business in Scotland and Ireland. I had returned on the Saturday night from a tour in Ireland, and between the Sunday night and Monday morning I dreamt I had sold fifty sewing machines to the firm of Alexander Mathieson and Sons, of the Saracen Tool Works, Glasgow. Some years previously I had done a considerable business with the firm named, but at the period in question all this had ceased, so that I laughed at the idea, when I awoke, as being amongst the most unlikely of incidents to take place.

On going over to the Howe Company's premises in Buchanan Street, amongst the letters which were lying there for me to open was one bearing the name of Alexander Mathieson and Sons on the outside of the envelope. I literally shook at the name and its connection with my dream, and before opening it thought about telling the incidents of the night to the cashier, but as my Spiritualism was pretty well laughed at by those associated with me in business, and it might be there was no connection between the communication before me and my dream, I nervously opened the envelope, to find enclosed a memorandum asking for a quotation for fifty sewing machines, the exact number I had sold when asleep. I went out to the firm during the day and concluded the sale. The circumstances made such an impression on me that I wrote them down in my diary at the time, and, of course, told many of my friends of the accuracy of my dream.

To read of such occurrences is one thing; to have them coming into your own life is quite another. I had not before this met with anything of an occult nature from dreamland, and I puzzled myself a good deal as to how the knowledge of such a transaction had penetrated my external consciousness. There is no need for bringing spirit intervention into the matter, though this might be one solution. At the moment of my dream Messrs. Mathieson's letter would be lying in Buchanan Street. What more likely than that my own spirit during the sleep state wandered there and read the communication, the contents of which filtered through to the external consciousness? We have lived so long on the material plane of thought that though we speak of the spiritual possibilities of man while encased in flesh, we have little or no belief in them. We are but emerging from the animal, and know not the powers within us which are waiting for further evolution. Man is a spirit now as much as he ever will be, and it is these modern revelations which are throwing a world of light on man's spiritual possibilities.

CHAPTER XVII

THE BATTLE OF IDEAS

What great ideas have been stifled in the past from the fear that their expression might bring about pain and trouble! Opinions relating to the physical world were held under because natural science had to harmonise with what had been erected by priests from a study of the Bible. Angry passion was raised against all who were bold enough to declare that they saw something in nature which did not quite coincide with current ideas. But the battle of physical science has been almost won, and our Lyalls and Darwins had not to face the trouble which met Galileo, Bruno, and Copernicus. A crowd of disciples like Huxley and Tyndall stood by the side of the new discoverers, and laboured to make clear the great truths of geology and evolution expressed by their masters. The creeds which cramped the minds of men had to be expanded, and with a measure of inconsistency, to find some place for the new revealments.

It has not been so, however, with regard to things pertaining to the spiritual side of man's nature. The battle is still being waged, and for a season yet many people will resist with all their might the introduction of ideas which point to the spirit in man and his conscious relationship with those who have done with the battle of life and now inhabit another world. No matter what facts may be accumulated, the world acts as if it either did not hear or did not comprehend. The crowd of scientific and literary men who in this realm have sought and found evidence which sustains the view that the so-called dead can come into contact with the living, are ignored when they speak. Spiritualism, which covers a rational philosophy of being, which fears no. truth that can be found in nature's realms, is continually spoken of with contempt, as if it were not worth the trouble of even so much as an investigation or a regard. Elizabeth Barrett Browning wondered why people could shut out the wish that it might be true. Dr. Alfred Russel Wallace, after forty years' face to face acquaintanceship with the subject, still asserts that the facts which sustain the Spiritualists are as well proved as any other scientific data which the world credits; but blind ignorance and open contempt still go on, no matter how much evidence is forthcoming. The world of matter is still the all in all.

Mesmeric phenomena, which are, after all, a link in the chain which leads the searcher to spiritual things, had the same battle to fight. Reputations were shattered because the ignorant, without any searching, made up their minds that what was declared had no basis in fact. Dr. Elliotson was almost hounded from his great practice because he affirmed that there were powers in man which could be brought forth to reveal a higher order than the normal. Harriet Martineau, because she was saved from death by mesmeric operations, had a tremendous fight with those who would credit no such factor as mesmerism amongst mortals. The modern miracle, so clearly proved, was laughed at, while the ancient miracles of healing, which were not proved, were held in honour. The scientific mind, instead of seeing a relationship between past and present, and catching hold of the law which operated in all such marvels, shut its eyes, and hoped all such things would be ignored. The story of Harriet Martineau being given up by all the eminent medical men summoned to her presence, and her recovery through mesmeric agency after five years of helplessness, is one of the best attested pieces of evidence to be found. New life and being, which enabled her to work so well for so many years after, was the outcome of a force which science ignored. Hallam, the historian, has placed on record that having, with Samuel Rogers, the poet, come into contact with a mesmeric clairvoyant in Paris, they were startled by the reality of his clairvoyant vision, and came back to London to affirm what they had seen and heard. When they told their story, they were met by such insult and ridicule that they were compelled to be silent, or quarrel with some of their most intimate friends. A great natural fact like mesmerism was ridiculed in every magazine and newspaper for a long season, till gradually the medical school admitted some of the facts, though never with a good grace. Still, today there is scarcely a person of repute who would venture really to assail the facts, as was common sixty years ago. "Time is a strange thing. It is a whimsical tyrant," as Goethe says, "which in every century has a different face for all that one says and does." A few years before spirit manifestations were heard of, Hallam seems to have caught the prophetic instinct, and looking down the corridors of time saw something more in the newly-discovered force than the great crowd who had no toleration for anything that looked mystical, for he said: "I have no doubt that mesmerism—and some other things which are not mesmerism, properly so-called" [no doubt referring to the faculty of clairvoyance] "are fragmentary parts of some great law of the human frame, which we are on the verge of discovering."

To read some of those slashing articles of the past, condemning the possibility of mesmerism having any thing in it beyond trickery, would fill the present gene ration with pity and wonder at such ignorant reception of so pregnant a truth. So noble a man as Robertson, of Brighton, outspoken and brave on so many points, had eyes, but saw not the possibilities and realities of this new wonder. The same clairvoyant, Alexis, who had brought a measure of conviction to Hallam and Rogers, was looked upon by Robertson as a charlatan. When he met him, as is told in Stopford Brooke's *Life*, he had great delight in the fact that no specific revelations were made to him. "The want of faith or strong opposition," said the clairvoyant, "had dimmed the mesmeric vision," but the great preacher said, "My close observation confused the charlatan." With a different spirit he might have found through Alexis an answer to many of the seemingly unfathomable questions which crowded round him. Had he but thought how it was said of Jesus that he did not many mighty works in certain places on account of the prevailing unbelief, there might have been given him a key to understand the position better; or had he but entered fully into the spirit of his master Tennyson, on whose *In Memoriam* he thought he had thrown light in his dissection of that spiritual poem, he might have come close to truth. But so many seekers after truth are biassed with the feeling that truth is not to be encountered by the wayside, but must come forth from exalted places, or it is valueless. The popular preacher might laugh at the clairvoyant and think him a vulgar cheat, but he was witnessing an exhibition of the same faculty which enabled the Galilean teacher of old to tell the woman of Samaria so many facts regarding her past life.

Spiritual manifestations are, however, of colossal importance beyond aught else that has come to man. They give to all those who examine them something more than the hope which flashed at times before the gaze of the mesmerists. They open the door yet wider and reveal real people who have passed through the change of death, still mingling their thoughts and affections with those on earth; not in some vague sort of dream, but in familiar face to face communion, which cannot be mistaken. That other world, about which no ancient church ever gave us any clear light, gets quite close to us, and we are lifted up to a realm where our foothold is secure for ever.

The strength of this feeling has ever kept Spiritualism alive. It could not be weakened by any amount of controversy or ridicule.

Each Spiritualist, though he stand alone, is conscious that he holds a truth about which there is no mistake, for he can check his experiences day by day, and has not to depend on memory or tradition. And thus the Spiritualists of Glasgow never wavered in their attachment to the truth. They looked along the corridors of time, and saw that which was rejected by one generation becoming the chief corner stone in the temple of a new vital religion.

A greater reformation than ever Luther dreamed of was in sight: a religion which would solve problems of politics and sociology, as well as give peace to the souls of men. The religious faculty is the strongest spiritual faculty in the constitution of man, but it can only be kept truly alive when we open our hearts to the inspiration which ever flows from another realm of being. The religious faith which seeks sustenance from ancient books must wither and become a mere form, ending in doubt and scepticism; but the religion which is kept alive by the ministrations of those who have walked earth's pathway, and who have reached a spiritual state, keeps aflame the divine spark implanted in man. So it was with the Glasgow Spiritualists; each day numbers were added to the household of faith, few of whom ever retreated, but kept noising the truth abroad. It flashed from mind to mind, till there was gathered together a body of men and women who grew strong in the companionship of the unseen, who felt the season was ripe for calling into their midst, as permanent teachers, workers who had received their credentials from the spirit side of life.

Mr and Mrs. Wallis, who had for years been visiting us at intervals, accepted the invitation which was offered, and in September 1884 took up their residence in our midst. The choice was indeed a wise one, as both were not only accomplished speakers whose addresses abounded with the treasures of the spirit, but each had phenomenal gifts, capable of bringing home the truth of spirit intervention. On Sundays large gatherings were held, and many who came out of curiosity were charmed with a gospel of nature and reason, and so remained with us. Many found their ideals strengthened by realities, which faded not away. A new world had opened; a key was given which unlocked the religions of every age. Present-day inspiration is as rich as any in the past. God has not withdrawn into silence, but today, as of old, is breath ing love and hope to mortals. The scales fell from many eyes at the presentation of a religion of feeling and action, instead of words and faith merely. Such rich treasures of the spirit were poured out from an ocean which needed no replenishing.

Private gatherings were held during the weeknights at the home of Mr. and Mrs. Wallis, which brought many into close personal touch with those who had lived the earth life, and who, from their enlarged experience, were capable of giving light and guidance to mortals. The dear "Lightheart," so full of gentle ness, entered closely into the surroundings, and replenished the heart with living waters. "Morambo," earnest and clear, became for the time an earth-dweller, and with his breadth of view satisfied the intellectual questionings which ever arose. The memory of these more private gatherings has left on the hearts of many a fragrance which will ever help to brighten life and warm the religious emotions. So great were the crowds which gathered at the Sunday services, that soon it became necessary to look out for larger quarters, and a church in West Campbell Street was rented, but the old warmth was not found in the new quarters. The atmosphere of the old theology seemed to linger in the building, and we were glad, after a few years' occupancy, to get rid of our burden.

Mr and Mrs. Wallis were now called upon to enter into work at Manchester, where Mr. Wallis was soon engaged in the starting of a new Spiritualist journal, called *The Two Worlds*. The Glasgow Society, after giving up the burden of the church, returned once more to the South Side, where the work was vigorously carried on.

CHAPTER XVIII

GERALD MASSEY

The year 1885 brought me into close touch with one who had done a noble battle for the reality of Spiritualism—Gerald Massey, the poet and seer, who came amongst us to deliver a series of lectures on those subjects which had been claiming his attention for many years: "The Historical Jewish Jesus," "The Devil of Darkness," "The Coming Religion," etc., all of which were freely impregnated with the spiritual facts.

Massey's name had been for me one held in reverence from my earliest recollection. I had heard him ranked amongst the great masters of song whose lyrics of freedom have elevated and warmed many hearts. It might be said of him, as he has said of Thomas Hood, in the beautiful poem he wrote on his death:

> *Ever the blind world*
> *Knows not its Angels of Deliverance*
> *Till they stand glorified 'twixt earth and heaven.*
> *It stones the Martyr; then, with praying hands,*
> *Sees the God mount his chariot of fire,*
> *And calls sweet names, and worships what it spurned.*
> *To those who walk beside them, great men seem*
> *Mere common earth; but distance makes them stars.*

His story is that of many men of genius, born in poverty and reared in the school of difficulty. He "learned in suffering what he taught in song." His education was of the scantiest, and he had to toil from his earliest years at whatever his hand found to do. At the age of seven he worked in a silk factory, from six in the morning till half-past six in the evening. No wonder John Ruskin spoke of his life as having been dreadful! All the wages he received in the silk factory was ninepence per week, Then he was at straw plaiting. At the age of fourteen he found himself in London as an errand boy in a draper's shop, and in two or three years was advanced to stand behind the counter. While engaged thus he began to write his wild red republican rhymes, full of the fire and fury which dwelt in his own bosom. In the year 1848, when twenty-one years of age, he joined the Chartist agitation, singing his songs of liberty and freedom.

In 1850 he published *Voices of Freedom* and *Lyrics of Love*, which gave evidence that a real poet was in the world once more. Frederick Maurice and Charles Kingsley, who, with great hearts flowing out towards the social amelioration of the people, founded their Christian Socialism, were attracted to the youth who had sung the sorrows of his class, and brought him forth as a labourer in the vineyard. For several years he was one of the secretaries of the movement which to him seemed so full of promise. His story made a deep impression on Kingsley, who has used his characteristics in his *Alton Locke, Tailor and Poet*, who is the figure of Gerald Massey. Now he was fairly embarked on the sea of literature, associating himself with the Radical cause. The fierce storms that beat within him were poured out through his fluent pen. Soon he got to be known as a bold and intrepid writer, and he became for a time the London correspondent to the *New York Tribune*. With Italian independence and the aims of "The Spiritual-minded Mazzini" he was closely associated. Such a soul as the great Italian, whose writings and himself were prescribed in every country but our own, must have had a charm for the young Radical poet At twenty-four years of age he was married to the daughter of a clergyman, and her wonderful clairvoyant powers opened out to his gaze that other world "not made with hands," the inhabitants of which come into contact with the world of matter, and seek to usher in the kingdom of righteousness and peace. In 1854, two years after his marriage, when he was twenty -six years of age, he issued the volume called *The Ballad of Babe Christabel*, which at once made him famous. It was a revelation of soul, pure, bright, and tender, expressing in lines of beauty the divinest emotions of the human heart.

> *But Nature on the darling smiled,*
> *And with her beauty's blessing crowned;*
> *Love brooded o'er the hallowed ground,*
> *And there were angels with the child.*

Hepworth Dixon, the editor of the Athenaeum, who was then a strong power in literature, saw the book, and so keen was his appreciation that he showed it to Douglas Jerrold Dixon himself wrote seven columns about it in the *Athenaeum*, and Douglas Jerrold wrote a strongly appreciative article in *Lloyd's Newspaper*, which procured for the book immediate popularity. A new light in the firmament of letters had appeared, and reviews of the most eulogistic kind appeared in every quarter. The success was great, but as each edition had to be reprinted afresh the financial profit to him was little. To his wife he would say, all through her life:

> *We are poor in this world's wealth, but rich in love,*
> *And they who love feel rich in everything.*

In 1855 he went to reside in Edinburgh, where he edited the *Edinburgh News* for a time, and was also engaged on some of the leading quarterlies. Here he came into close touch with that genial scholar, John Stuart Blackie, the Professor of Greek in the Edinburgh University; Russel, the editor of the *Scotsman*; and Hugh Miller, the Cromarty stonemason, whose works on geology, *The Old Bed Sandstone*, *Footprints of the Creator*, and *My Schools and Schoolmasters*, were read everywhere. Hugh Miller edited a Church paper called the *Witness*, which had many contributions from the pen of Massey. The whole country was stirred one morning when the news was flashed out that

Hugh Miller had committed suicide, that the great brain had given way. A student of natural science, he had sought to understand the movement of progress all around him, and it is thought that when he found that *The Testimony of the Rocks* (one of his volumes) did not harmonise with the creeds which he had so long vindicated, the shock caused him to lose his reason.

Sectarianism and science could not run together for long; nature's revelation is larger and fuller than that of any bible, and the investigator must let reason play its part beyond aught else. Massey had the deepest love for Hugh Miller, and felt deeply the shock of his sudden death. In the beautiful poem he wrote, entitled "Hugh Miller's Grave," he sought to drop a few poor flowers on the resting-place of the great man whom he had loved while living, and mourned with a full heart:

> *Low lies the grandest head in all Scotland.*
> *We'll miss him when there's noble work to do!*
> *His tall head holding up a lonely lamp*
> *Of steadfast thought still-burning in his eyes;*
> *His eyes, that rather dreamed than saw, deep set*
> *In the brow's shadow, looking forward, fixed*
> *On something we divined not, solemn, strange!*
> *He was a Hero, true as ever stepped*
> *In the forlorn hope of a warring world.*

It is altogether a poem of the heart, speaking gently of the "iron will" that hewed a path from "stone quarries to the heights of fame." "Never doubt," he said, referring to the tragic nature of Miller's death:

> *God's children find their home,*
> *By dark as well as day. The life he lived,*
> *And not the death he died, was first in judgment.*
> *It is the writing on the folded scroll*
> *Death sends, and not the seal, that God will judge.*

He hoped that the spirit of Cowper might clasp Miller's hands in the spiritual kingdom, and whisper his first welcome to the heavens. Massey at this period of his life had not grown to the fullest realisation of the message of Spiritualism, but what he knew had enlarged his vision and given him glimpses of a world larger and brighter than that viewed by the devotees of creeds.

When in Edinburgh, two of his children were removed by death, a blow which shook his nature to the depths. "The Mother's Idol Broken" is one of the tenderest poems ever penned. Every emotion is touched and the heart laid bare.

O, ye who say, "We have a child in heaven,"
And know how far away that heaven may seem,
Who have felt the desolate isolation sharp
Defined in Death's own face, who have stood beside
The Silent River, and stretched out pleading hands
For some sweet babe upon the other bank,
That went forth where no human hand might lead,
And left the shut house with no light, no sound,
No answer, when the mourners wail without!
What we have known, ye know, ye only know.

He was able to say, in after years:

The patient calm that comes with years,
Hath made us cease to fret,
Though sometimes in the sudden tears
Dumb hearts will quiver yet,
And each one turns the face and tries
To hide who looks through parent eyes.

After he left Edinburgh in 1858 he took to the lecture platform, where his services were in great demand. Such subjects as Burns, Shelley, Shakespeare, Hood were treated as only a true poet could handle them. He caught the secrets of these inspired singers, and flashed forth views which the multitude had failed to recognise. No man had ever a keener appreciation of his subjects than the man who wrote the secret of Shakespeare's sonnets, or who penned those noble eulogies on Robert Burns and Thomas Hood, passages from which are often quoted, and are yet to be found in poetic selections. Young Men's Christian Associations all over the country had the name of Gerald Massey on their lecture syllabuses, he having as many as seventy or eighty winter engagements of this kind. His poetry was then accepted by the world as particularly pious. Had he not written many sweet hymns, "Jerusalem the Golden," "At Eventide," and others, which had found their way into the Church Hymnal? All this, however, was now to end; a new chapter in his life had opened. Truths stared him in the face which were in advance of an unadvancing Church.

In 1869 he published a volume of poetry, entitled, *A Tale of Eternity*, which was founded on a personal experience of a haunted house. Even as Robert Owen, by his outspoken speech at the London Tavern, in which he denounced all religions as hindering the welfare of humanity, lost caste and influence for his social schemes, so did Massey lose popularity by this *Tale of Eternity*. The lecture platform, except here and there, did not want a person who preached Spiritualism as a natural fact. So long as it was given forth as a vague and obscure sentiment, well and good, but to talk of it as an actual fact in human life was going too far. All had to admit that this was a powerful poem, but, they said, the writer should not have introduced his ideas as facts. Editors spoke of him as having gone clean over to the Spiritualists, which was enough to damn the reputation of a saint. Massey was not only a poet but a patriot, a hero, a philosopher, and a theologian, who had kept the doors and windows of his mind open for the reception of whatever light might come. When someone asks, "Is it not wrong to seek to have dealings with the dead?" he utters:

> I believe that God is Master, still. He reigneth;
> He whose lightest breath can thrill
> The universe of worlds, like drops of dew,
> And if the spirit world hath broken through,
> It cannot be unknown, unseen by Him;
> It must be with His will, not their mere whim.

He is careful and bold enough to say, "For the truth's sake I ought to explain that the Spiritualism to be found in my poetry is no delusive idealism, derived from hereditary belief in a resurrection of the dead." It was through close touch with mediumship that he was able to bring the relation between matter and spirit into clearer view, by words like these:

> What you call matter is but as the sheath,
> Shaped, even as bubbles are, by spirit breath.
> The mountains are but firmer clouds of earth
> Still changing to the breath that gave them birth.
> Spirit aye shapeth matter into view,
> As music wears the forms it passes through.
> Spirit is lord of substance, matter's sole
> First cause, formative power, and final goal.

It is pleasant to feel that a man of this rich quality is in no doubt about the reality of the two worlds being knit by close ties. The fact is as real to him as any other fact in nature, and he reiterates, in language about which there can be no mistake, that he is making no new attempt to cheat the ignorant by false pretences of knowledge. "My faith in our future life," he says, "is founded upon facts in nature and realities of my own personal experience. These facts have been more or less known to me personally during forty years of familiar face-to-face acquaintanceship, therefore my certitude is not premature; they have given me the proof palpable that our very own human identity and intelligence do persist after the blind of darkness has been drawn down in death."

It was through knowing of spirit realities that he could present graphic pictures of what the world might often see were its spirit sight opened. He tells the story of a man who, with the spirit vision, walks through a low neighbourhood in London, and sees a woman in rags, holding a cherub child. Her beseeching eyes draw the man to her:

> For the babe's sake, he thrust a coin of gold
> Into her hand; but it fell through, and rolled,
> Ringing along the stones; he followed, found
> It, brought it back, and looked around—
> There was no woman waiting with her hand
> Outstretched, no child where he had seen them stand.
> The beggar was a spirit, doomed to plead
> With hurrying wayfarers, who took no heed,
> But passed her by, indifferent as the dead,
> Till one should hear her voice and turn the head;
> Doomed to stand there and beg for bread, in tears,
> To feed her child that had been dead for years.
> This was the very spot where she had spent
> Its life for drink, and this the punishment.
> She felt she had let it slip into the grave,
> And now would give eternal life to save:
> Heartless and deaf and blind, the world went by,
> Until this dreamer came, with seeing eye;
> The good Samaritan of souls had given,
> And wrought the change that was to her as heaven.

It is pleasant to know that the world has been blest with fearless investigators, with souls sufficiently strong and independent of prevailing dogmas to venture into new paths of inquiry. Massey has never feared to speak out all he learned through spirit communion. He could not think the pity of God was less than his own, and so he sung out in clarion tones:

I think heaven will not shut for evermore,
Without a knocker left upon the door,
Lest some belated wanderer should come,
Heart-broken, asking just to die at home,
So that the Father will at last forgive,
And looking on His face that soul shall live.

More rational than the effete theology is his presentation of heaven and hell. Calvin and Jonathan Edwards would have sent him to the flames, but the reasoning souls of men today feel that he expresses what must be true when he says:

Both heaven and hell are from the human race,
And every soul projects its future place;
Long shadows of ourselves are thrown before,
To wait our coming on the eternal shore:
These either clothe us with eclipse and night,
Or, as we enter them, are lost in light.

These poems by Massey have done welcome work in helping to destroy the tyranny of death. The voice is angelic which sounds forth in lines like these:

The angels, singing in their heaven above,
Feel when ye strike the unison of love,
The prayers of heaven fall in a blessed rain
On souls that parch in purgatorial pain.

They could only have been written by one who could speak with a certain knowledge—a knowledge which has never weakened with the years. In these days of half beliefs and drifting views it is worth pages of Scripture to come into touch with a living soul who in tones of assurance can say, as he has done:

*The Spiritualist who has plumbed the void of
death as I have, and touched this solid ground of
fact, has established a faith that can neither be
undermined nor overthrown. He has done with
the poetry of desolation and despair, the sighs of
unavailing regret, and all the passionate wailing of
unfruitful pain. He cannot be bereaved in soul.*

In 1872 a meeting was held in London to bid farewell to Mrs.
Emma Hardinge, who had been charming so many with her rich
presentation of the spiritual gospel. Gerald Massey was in the
chair, and delivered an address pregnant with great thoughts, as
melodious as his verses. The address was afterwards printed, with
some additions, in a little volume, entitled *Concerning Spiritualism*. It seems a pity that such a rich gem should not be
reprinted, as many would prize it, not only as a joy, but as a sweet
consoler. It is a perfect mine of good things, radiant with love for
the greatest of revealments.

One passage I have often quoted as showing forth the great
beauty and force of Spiritualism:

*It has been for me such a lifting of the mental
horizon, and letting in of the heavens, such a
formation of faith into facts, that I can only
compare life without it to sailing on board
ship with hatches battened down, and being
kept a prisoner, living by the light of a candle,
and then suddenly, on some splendid starry
night, allowed to go on deck for the first time
to see the stupendous mechanism of the
heavens all aglow with the glory of God.*

There must surely be something transcendent in the message
of Spiritualism when it warms the soul to speak in such uplifting
strains. All his poetry is saturated with the same rich expression

of spiritual light. Thomas Carlyle, who was not given to praise poetry, has spoken of Massey's "In Memoriam" as being heroic:

> Why should we weep, when death is but a mask,
> Through which we know the face of Life beyond?
>
> Why should we weep? We do not bury love;
> The dust of earth but claims its kindred dust.
> We do not drop our jewels in the grave,
> And have no need to seek our treasures there.
>
> Why do we shrink so from eternity?
> We are in eternity from birth, not death I
> Eternity is not beyond the stars—
> Some far hereafter—it is here and now.
> The kingdom of heaven is within, so near
> We do not see it, save by spirit sight;
> We shut our eyes in prayer, and we are there
> In thought, and thoughts are spirit things—
> Realities upon the other side.
>
> In death we close our eyelids once for all,
> To pass for ever, and seem far away!
> And yet the distance does not lie in death;
> No distance, save in dissimilitude.
> Death's not the only door of spirit world,
> Nor visibility sole presence-sign:
> The near or far is in our depth of love
> And height of life; we look without to learn
> Our lost ones are beyond all human reach:
> We feel within, and find them nestling near.

"It is no wonder," the *London Review* said, "it is no vain speculation, to suppose that such a poet will be come a household word amongst millions. This has not been realised as yet, however, but it is hoped will yet be. His love poetry is pure and sweet, worthy of being ranked with the most genuine strains of

Burns." *The Tale of Eternity*, besides conveying the truths of spirit association, is full of scientific allusions; Wheatstone's electric experiments and Humboldt's earthquake experience, Darwin's theories and Huxley's protoplasm, the structure of Saturn's rings, all furnish material for beautiful similes; as also the phenomena of the spectrum, of complementary colours, and the velocity of light.

When I first came into personal association with Gerald Massey, in 1885, his singing on the old lines had ceased, as no one lived by poetry but Tennyson; but outside this he had ceased to look upon poetry as the special work of his literary life. He had dropped out of the world's sight for some years, and many thought, when they came across his name in quotations, that he had ceased to be. Another realm of thought had engrossed him, on which he had been patiently working. He had always been an evolutionist, recognising in Darwin and Wallace revealers of the laws of the Most High, and so the creeds of Christendom had been long displaced from his serious thinking. The origin of things, apart from the fabulous, engrossed his being, and so for years he had been seeking to trace the origin of language and the symbols which men had incorporated into religion and named in their varied tongues "The Word of God." Egypt he found had been the fruitful mother of much, which, with differing details, had become the religions of the world. He had produced, as the outcome of his long silence, two volumes, entitled The Book of the Beginnings, which he called "an attempt to recover and reconstitute the lost origins of myths and mysteries, types and symbols, religion and language." He had gone over the ground many times, with the result that to him Africa was the birthplace and Egypt the mouthpiece of religion. His researches had proved to him the Egyptian origin of those Hebrew legends and Christian doctrines which had only reappeared with a new face. He found that four thousand years before there was any Christianity the Egyptians taught the fatherhood of God, who was revealed to men by His own Son, who had said of His Father, "I utter His words to the men of the present generation (i.e., the living), and I repeat His words to the dead." These Egyptians had the Christian doctrine of the Trinity, with Osiris as the Father, Horus as the Son, and Ra as the Holy Spirit, which three were one in essence and threefold in identifiable phenomena. They had their Christ or Anointed, who rose from the dead, and altogether there was forced on Mr. Massey the strong conviction that ancient words and ideas had been used as if they were original with reference to the life work of the more modern Jesus of Nazareth.

It was clear to him that the documents from which the gospels were written had been more or less taken from a copy of the Egyptian Ritual, and the explanation of the great difference between the tone of St. John and that of the Synoptics was that this gospel retained more of the original matter. He found the sayings of Jesus, one after another, paralleled in The Book of the Dead. The man who all his life had stood forward for truth, who had declared his Spiritualism when it cost something to do so, could scarcely be expected to keep his conclusions in his own bosom.

He compiled a series of lectures embodying his thoughts, and once more occupied the public platform and gave them utterance. These lectures bore the titles of "The Historical (Jewish) Jesus and the Mythical (Egyptian) Christ," "Paul as a Gnostic Opponent, not the Apostle of Historic Christianity," "The Logia of the Lord, or the Pre-Christian Sayings ascribed to Jesus the Christ," "The Devil of Darkness, or Evil in the Light of Evolution," and several others, in all of which was embodied his thought that the Christian religion was largely the outcome of ancient myths. He had been to America and Australia before coming to Glasgow, and his fame as one of the world's poets had brought him a generous reception, though the enunciation of his views on the creeds had not always commanded acquiescence. I had the great pleasure of being his chairman at one of the Sunday meetings, when questions were allowed, but though there were several clergymen pre sent no one took it upon himself to combat the views expressed.

One of the lectures was on "The Coming Religion," one of the most brilliant bits of word painting ever uttered. It was brimful of great truths, which the world will one day take up with reverence and apply to daily life. "The religion of the future," he said, "has got to include Spiritualism. It has to be a sincerity of life, in place of pretended belief; a religion of science in place of superstition; of man's ascent instead of his fall; a religion of fact in the present, and not of mere faith in the future; a religion in which the temple reared to God will be in human form, instead of being built of brick or stone; a religion of work rather than of worship; and in place of the deathly creeds, a religion of life—life actual, life here, life now, as well as the promise of life everlasting."

It was my privilege at this time to meet with him day after day, and to walk out with him, conversing, in some of our public parks. I learned much of his noble life, and of the men of note who had entered into it. Scarcely a man of commanding position in the world of letters but the genial poet had something to tell of him. Walter Savage Landor, who was said to be more addicted to the ancients than the moderns, had said of his poetry, that there were thoughts and expressions in it which reminded him of Shakespeare in the best of his sonnets, such poetry as Tennyson would read with approbation. John Ruskin was amongst his greatest admirers, and took the most special interest in him. Once he wrote him, "Your education was a terrible one, but mine was far worse." Ruskin never knew adversity, which would deprive him of one powerful chord which vibrates through literature. Adversity, the sternest of teachers, without which we could never have had those stirring strains by Robert Burns, or those wild heart throbbings of Massey, had nothing to teach him. He never knew the companionship of want, nor the necessity of acquiring for oneself breathing room in the world. Ruskin further said, "I rejoice in acknowledging my own debt of gratitude for many an encouraging and noble thought, and my conviction that your poems in the mass have been a helpful and precious gift to the working classes."

Of Thackeray he was deeply enamoured. He had sung of him in rich strains:

> We never told our love! He would have thought
> We prattled prettily, amused the while,
> And held us at a distance with his smile,
> Until we hid the presents we had brought.

o   o   o   o   o   o   o

> Large-hearted, brave, sincere, compassionate;
> We could not guess cue half the angels see;
> They found you out, old friend, ere we did! We
> But reach the nobler justice all too late.

Massey knew of Thackeray's deep interest in Spiritualism, and how he braved his publishers by inserting in the *Cornhill Magazine*, of which he was editor, the article describing a séance with Mr. D.D. Home, "Stranger than Fiction." He told me that he had been informed by Mr. George Smith, of Smith and Elder, the publishers of *Cornhill*, that the circulation of that periodical went down 20,000 copies in consequence of printing this article, and thereby inflicted an injury from which it is doubtful if it ever recovered. Of the Tennyson family he had much to tell. Frederick Tennyson was a devoted Spiritualist, and contributed articles to the Spiritualist papers. He was a poet of mark, but his fame was dimmed by that of his great brother, the Laureate. Having seen in print a letter from Alfred Tennyson, in which he said that he had read Mr. Massey's book more than once, and would like to hear him lecture, I asked Mr. Massey, at one of our interviews, "Does this refer to your *Book of the Beginnings?*" "No," he replied, "it is my little book *Concerning Spiritualism.* Don't you know that all the Tennysons are Spiritualists?" We can scarcely read the Laureate's poetry without feeling that he was a man through whom the spirit world voiced many lofty truths. We catch again and again sentiments which voice many of the truths laid bare by modern Spiritualism, especially the great facts of spirit control, as when he speaks of the dead man, word by word and line by line, flashing his living soul into that of the poet, or when he sets forth the conditions which should rule at the spirit circle:

> *How pure in heart and sound in head,*
> *With what divine affections bold*
> *Should be the man whose thought would hold*
> *An hour's communion with the dead.*

Robert Browning and his great-souled wife had been amongst Massey's friends. He had reviewed the poems of the former in the pages of the *Quarterly*, and several times in the *Athenaeum*. Mrs. Browning was a devoted Spiritualist, who had for years in every society spoken out her beliefs, which are referred to by all her friends and contemporaries. She had instinctively grasped the power and beauty of Spiritualism, while her husband had no ear for it. Once after Mrs. Browning's death Mr. Massey asked the poet if he had never heard his wife's "rap"; but death had not made Browning more receptive to the phenomenal facts of Spiritualism, which had been so much prized by his gifted wife. You cannot furnish arguments which will convert the blind to a sense of colours. Massey ever realised the need for what

Spiritualists call physical manifestations. These he did not look upon as an end in themselves, but as a means to an end, an incentive to growth in spiritual life. As he said: "Where the phenomena tend to lead the soul into the inner presence-chamber of God and enrich the spiritual life, the lowliest means may be sanctified; but where the meal is everything, and the miracle goes for nothing except to evoke an encore of the miracle for the sake of another meal, then it is degrading, and of the earth earthy." These are wise words, which, if pondered over, might help to counteract the materialism of some Spiritualists. With what a large eye the poet saw the meaning of Spiritualism! He pointed out that at a time when physical science was too much for the old creeds, Spiritualism came into view with its message: "Just when the scientific report is that the deeper we dive the further off is the supposed heart-beat of the eternal life, in breaks this revelation from the unknown, and, as was assumed, unknowable, which is destined to put a new soul into belief and usher in a resurrection day." He was the prophet of the golden day:

> 'Tis coming up the steep of Time,
>   And this old world is growing brighter!
> We may not see its dawn sublime,
>   Yet high hopes make the heart throb lighter!
> There's a divinity within
>   That makes men great if they but will it,
> God works with all who dare to win,
>   And the time cometh to reveal it.
>
> This world is full of beauty, as other worlds above,
> And if we did our duty it might be as full of love.
> Were truth our uttered language, spirits might talk with men,
> And God-illumined earth should see the Golden Age again.

Every brave man or woman who has stood forth for the right has ever brought out some sympathetic strain. Massey cared little about creeds or lack of creeds, so long as people stood forth for freedom. When W.T. Stead went to prison for his efforts to let the light in on a great sin, Massey cried out in indignation at the press for their treatment of him :—

> Stead struck his blow and failed and fell, you say.
> Such was their failure who have paved a way
> With their dead bodies for our feet today.
> Honour to him, we cry, who sought to save
> The girls dragged down our gutters to the grave!
> For him our plaudits ring, our welcomes wave.
> Though not in the Salvation Army's van,
> Nor of the shut-eyed Faith, some of us can
> Respect a worker, recognise a man.

When Mrs. Besant was making her brave fight for the girl matchmakers, standing forth as the champion of the oppressed, duty her only religion before a spirit world had dawned on her sight, Massey sent forth his hearty greeting, while pointing her to the knowledge of spirit life which was his :—

> Annie Besant, brave and dear,
> May some message uttered here
> Beach you, ringing golden-clear.
>
> Though we stand not side by side
> In the front of battle wide,
> Oft I think of you with pride.
>
> Fellow-soldier in the fight!
> Oft I see you flash by night,
> Fiery-hearted for the Right!

You for others sow the grain;
Yours the tears of ripening rain,
Theirs the smiling harvest-gain.

Fellow-workers! we shall be
Workers for eternity;
Such my faith. And you shall see

Life's no bubble blown of breath
To delude the sight till death,
Whatsoe'er the un-seeing saith.

Love that closes dying eyes,
Wakes them, too, in glad surprise;
Love that makes for ever wise.

Soul—whilst murmuring "'There's no soul"—
Shall upspring like flame from coal:
Death is not Life's final goal.

Bruno lives! Such spirits come,
Swords immortal-tempered, from
Fire and forge of martyrdom.

You have soul enough for seven;
Life enough our earth to leaven;
Love enough to create heaven.

One of God's own faithful few,
Whilst unknowing it, are you,
Annie Besant, bravely true.

All honour and gratitude to Massey, who gave him self for the truth, who proclaimed the great spiritual facts, while so many who know them have been silent, or have hidden the knowledge amidst a mass of verbiage, giving stones when the world needed bread. He was a worker for humanity, who cared but little for the applause of men, one whose sole ambition was to plant hope in the hearts of the despairing, and bring the world to a knowledge of the true God, not the sham figure of theologies. Although out of the body, he has not gone to the silence, but, a throbbing, actual presence, he still moves and lives and works with and for men. One day, surely, the whole world will recognise how a great soul with a message from the Infinite lived amongst us, and with all his powers pointed to the celestial verities, the knowledge of which is capable of quickening and redeeming the world.

CHAPTER XIX

REMARKABLE COMMUNICATIONS

I think that of all the many eventful years which have passed since the world of spirit became to me a reality, 1887 and 1888 are the most memorable, bring ing me into contact, as they did, with many worthy people and incidents of much importance. The seed which had been sown by Mr. and Mrs. Wallis had taken root, and the movement grew in numbers and importance. Many earnest men and women were attracted, and bore their share of the burdens which the pioneers of unpopular opinions have to carry. New workers, normal and abnormal, came into view, capable of giving forth such evidence as the materialism of the times required.

Amongst those who were of the highest service, and who, with Mr. David Anderson, helped to make the local platform a power for good, was Mr. William Ritchie, a good trance speaker, clairvoyant, and psychometrist. As a rule, instruments through whom the spirits can manifest develop slowly, the faint glimmerings of psychic power growing brighter by degrees, until the spirit people can use them with purpose. With Mr. Ritchie it was otherwise. He came to the meetings, attended sittings, and at once showed through his mediumship that the marvellous powers which D.D. Home and other great mediums had manifested were not so rare, but might spring forth in many quarters, were only the necessary conditions forthcoming. Mr. Ritchie was not by any means a person of culture or education, nor did the pious spirit dwell in him to any great extent. He was the roughest of diamonds, happy-go-lucky in every way, and did not seem to trouble about spiritual matters. He was an instrument, how ever, who possessed that psychic aura by means of which it seemed easy for the departed to make their presence known.

He had been in the army for a year or two, in the cavalry, and had been discharged through meeting with an accident to his foot. The normal man and the same person under spirit control were as wide apart as the poles. There seemed no point of similarity between them. He would ascend the platform and give forth an invocation breathing the sweetest thoughts, and deliver an address which was marked by intelligence and profound knowledge. The normal man made no pretence at speaking grammatically, whereas, under the spirits' influence, he spoke in quite scholarly language. Spiritualists have no room for miracles, and do not credit that a Shakespeare could come forth from a nation of savages; neither do they set forth that a medium can give forth anything beyond his own mental possibilities. But the question is: What are these possibilities? What may not situation and cultivation do to set in motion powers not dreamed of? And so a medium like Ritchie had, in more than germ, a phren-ological possibility which was capable of being developed, and this possibility, being seen by clearer, larger eyes than ours, was utilised to give forth the spirits' message. A man of little mind can only take in the contents of his primer, but men with minds ungrown abound, who are utterly unconscious of their own possibilities, and who are only set aflame when some Prometheus comes down with the spark of light in his hand. Few things look more like miracles than those marvellous writings of Andrew Jackson Davis in *Nature's Divine Revelations*, and *The Great Sarmonia*, that series of the most profound books which were ever penned; yet Davis as a youth was only asleep till touched with the power that unlocked his spiritual faculties.

Mr Ritchie could not be called reverential nor devotional, yet there were moments when, under inspiration, he spoke forth thoughts pertaining to the highest. He had a whole group of inspirers, each distinct from the others, and all widely separated from the man himself. The chief platform control was one "Abou," who claimed to have been a personal follower of Mahomet. There was much of Eastern colouring in his mode of speech, and a wonderful acquaintance with the Koran, but he also touched on all matters of life and being, and ever dwelt largely on the great truth that spirit people had found an entrance into the earth sphere which would be utilised in the providence of God for the uplifting of the race. That the intelligence was an Arab, and familiar with many phases of Eastern life, seemed very clear. A friend of mine, and a warm appreciator of Mr. Ritchie's gifts, Mr. G.W. Walrond, who had been an officer in the British army and fought at Tel-el-Kebir, brought to one of our sittings a prayer book in Arabic which had been taken from the person of a slain Arab, and this being placed in the hands of the medium, he read it with fluency. "John Edgar," however, was the spirit who came most close to us when we sat in séance. He was one of ourselves, belonging to Beith, Ayrshire, and had the most un-bounded appreciation for Burns, whom he quoted with marked fervour. "John" could, himself, at times, pour forth pretty little poems, and tell in rhyme many a story of his earth life. It all came forth with ease; never any waiting for a word, and ever the most perfect rhythm.

It was not one phase of mediumship only that Mr. Ritchie was gifted with; the spirit people made their presence a reality through varied ways. Tables would move and raps be produced on all parts of the room in answer to questions put. Numbers of people who had gone out of my life were recalled, and their forms and characters painted in the clearest way. Some came to me, whom I did not then know to have already crossed the river of death. They gave their messages, and indented on me the great fact that, were our spiritual eyes open, our view of life would be entirely different. Milton was repeating but fact when he said, "Millions of spiritual creatures walk the earth"; only the world persists in taking all such statements as poetic language merely.

One old friend, whose description was given, I could not recognise for some time. I seemed to know the face, but could not locate him in my life, even after the initials "J.L." were given. I was still at sea, when the medium said, "I see him playing billiards, and I now get the name John Logan." Nothing could have been more graphically descriptive of the man of that name I had known in former years. Logan had been a quiet, decent fellow when resident in Glasgow, taking a considerable interest in church work, yet with a strong inclination for playing billiards at every possible opportunity. He had been connected with a working men's club for a long time, and billiards had become for him a great fascination. I sent him over to Dublin to work, but while there he had gone downhill. One Sunday evening when I had hunted him up, on my arrival in Dublin, I was surprised and pained to find the one-time office holder in a Christian church sitting playing cards, surrounded with bottles of liquor. It was a terrible lapse from the old life, and showed how much environment will do to change a person's mode of living. I mourned the declension in his life, followed his career for some few years, when he became lost to me, until the hour when he was described to me at the séance, and sent the message: "Billiards were my ruin."

This is not by any means a solitary instance of Mr. Ritchie's clairvoyance. I have listened to hundreds of such instances, where not only accurate descriptions were given, but also Christian and surname. Once he described to me, giving the name, "Kate Wood," the materialising medium of Newcastle, to whom I have previously referred as the instrument who sat at the home of A.J.

Balfour, the ex-Prime Minister, along with Professor Sidgwick and F.W.H. Myers. The records of these séances, as I have already said, have never been published, though they were read over on one occasion by Mr. Myers to Dr. Alfred Russel Wallace.

If I at any time put a letter from a correspondent into Mr. Ritchie's hands, he would place it on his fore head and give a word photograph of the writer, with all hie traits of character. Sometimes he would prophesy events which would arise in the future, not in any vague fashion, but as directly and as clearly as could be wished. He seemed to be an instrument capable of reading what was going on in distant parts, and giving it expression. I made notes of many things relating to myself, which I was told would come about, and these I have shown to friends before the events were fulfilled. It is not for me to enter here into the question as to how such things are possible; but that they are within the domain of natural law I have no doubt. In days of stress and storm, when clouds were many, this man peered through the mists and vapours, and with some encouraging message lifted away the load that oppressed me and others.

Of the many instruments I have met these thirty years few have surpassed Ritchie in clearness of vision and accuracy of statement. It was a grief to me, after some years of close association, when he left for America with Mr. James Bowman in 1888. I have not heard for many years past whether the spirit controls helped to endow him with the moral fibre which would sustain him in the rough life he entered upon in the western world.

That he was a great medium, with rare gifts, is un doubted, though few outside the Glasgow circle ever heard his name. Such a man would have been prized in many circles of society, capable as he was of settling the great question, "If a man die, shall he live again?" Where the cathedrals and pulpits were of little value in arresting materialism, this happy-go-lucky, thoughtless soul brought the certainty of a future state of existence to the minds of many doubting and troubled ones.

Men, however, see not the profound which is at their doors. The mass of men receive new ideas with difficulty, except such as lie in the track of their own know ledge. Is not every new discovery a slur on the sagacity of those who have overlooked it? Can we wonder, therefore, that professional theologians and the great dull world, who swallow all that has been handed down to them, ignore or defame the opening of the spiritual kingdom through these modern phenomena?

My sitting in circle with Ritchie and David Anderson so often was instrumental in developing my own mediumistic powers. I had for several years been acted upon by Indian spirits, and would repeat a string of words which were almost forced through me, of the meaning or purport of which I could make nothing. It seemed purely automatic or muscular. I had no feeling specially in giving utterance to this seemingly foreign speech, nor could I say that the words uttered were those of a foreign tongue. In the presence of other mediums, however, who were controlled by Indian spirits, these latter kept up a conversation with the power that ex pressed itself through my lips. I am doubtful if ever I should have got the length of speaking in my own language to express the spirits' thoughts had I not been impelled to open the way with this torrent of foreign jabbering. I knew that I could not of my normal self manufacture those strange words, and I felt that the antics which accompanied them were not the result of any personal volition. I was never rendered unconscious. Whatever sentences fell from my lips, my own mentality was entirely wakeful.

A circle of friends was drawn together, and soon all manner of persons began to tell out their story through me, or sought to stimulate the sitters to a noble life. All the time I was speaking I would find myself criticising the utterances and saying to myself, "Are you not manufacturing this?" It seemed so difficult to analyse my sensations, the words seemed to be in the atmosphere and to drop, as it were, into my mouth. Persons came who gave their names, and each had a different characteristic which was readily recognised by the sitters. Yet amid it all this sceptical feeling would come in, "Am I not deceiving myself as well as others?" When Ritchie had gone to America some of his guides with whom I had been familiar would use my lips, and the idiom of speech would bear a strong resemblance to the original utterances. Yet, amidst it all, though the words would roll out with marvellous fluency, the sceptical part of me would keep saying, "You are but imitating Ritchie."

We had amongst our sitters a Lady Hall, who said the spirits had sent her to me. She was a lady of much culture, full of the spirit of real religion, pure and aspiring. She had lost a daughter some years before while resident in Italy, and this dear one's departure had taken away much out of the mother's life. I knew nothing of her family relationships at the time. One evening a sweet and elevated vein of thought seemed to fill my being, and I began to speak to Lady Hall, words the meaning of which I could not grasp, but which she said were clearly understood by her. They were the words of the lost daughter. Again and again this influence came to me, and I would speak in quite poetic strains, which was a surprise to myself. I was filled with deep feeling and affection, and yet all the time I would ask myself, "Is not Lady Hall reading more into what I say than is warranted?" I find that I noted in my diary, at this period, my thoughts on these "controls." What a wonderful thing is ordinary penmanship. One writes with very little of volition, or, at all events, the will is almost unconscious. "May not this 'control' be automatic, like writing? Is 'John Hutcheson' really beside me while I give out what purport to be his thoughts? What can I do to be sure? Am I not self-deceived?" And then my pen was made to act as my lips had previously done, and these words were rapidly written: "My life in the spirit is real, and my presence beside you is as real. I am able to come close to your mentality, and, as a person would touch the keys of an instrument, so I touch your keys, and you reflect pretty much what I would like to say. You say, 'There is no evidence in this'; but there is all the evidence you want. I say that I am here, and you write this down because there is something which impels you to do it. I do not say it is impossible for you to resist it; but you are carried on, and it is down before you realise whether it is yourself or another. Be not deceived by your own doubting nature; rather, listen to what is said as to the reality of these 'controls.' We can come to you now more readily than before, because certain barriers have been broken down, and there is a path way for our utterances to be flashed down. Wait and weigh, and you will mark the progress that is made. All will become clear, James," and here the writing rushes on so quickly as to be almost indecipherable. "Wait, we say, and see. The spirit communion which you have talked about so much should be of real help to you, and so it will. Since I made the change I have thought of how you could be helped, and once I get in close contact with you, my presence will be as real and continuous as the hand that has touched you so often"—referring to the touch on my forehead, which I have experienced for many years.

There then follows much more of a personal nature, all bearing on my life and its circumstances. John Hutcheson "was my father-in-law, who in life had not much sympathy with my Spiritualism. Before the death change came to him, however, I had sought to point his thoughts to the reality of the after-life, and he has ofttimes said since that my words were of value, and that he found there was much truth in what I had said.

My diaries are made up of many similar writings, some persons, of whom I had never heard, writing out their life's story when I would be alone and in a passive mood Many letters were written by me, purporting to be inspired by spirit friends, which I was asked to send to those who were named, but my scepticism and timidity, as also the fact that I was conscious of what was being written in the majority of cases, kept me from fulfilling such behests.

"Our doubts are traitors, and make us lose The good we oft might win, by fearing to attempt." To one old friend and devoted Spiritualist, Mrs. Urquhart, who passed to the higher life in 1906, I did send communications which came through my pen. These she used to prize as veritable communications from her husband. The thoughts were his thoughts, and even the penmanship had a great similarity to that of the departed. With a few such friends my doubts did not act as a barrier. I knew they were truth-seekers like myself, and so with this feeling uppermost I could give more free play to the unseen intelligence, and, throwing myself in the background, allow the friends to come near. With Mrs. Urquhart and other close friends I was the instrument of giving many tests of spirit identity, though through it all my own scepticism in relation to my own mediumship was never entirely dissipated.

One afternoon, at the Lyceum service for children, Mr. Ritchie was describing certain forms, which he saw beside the young people who were there. He had got to a daughter of Mrs. Urquhart, and began to describe a child, a sister, he said, with peculiar eyes and other traits of form. While he was doing so my hand automatically wrote on the air the name "Amy," no less than four times. I did not pay much attention to this, particularly as the mother's face, who was present, did not seem to give forth any mark of recognition of the portrait drawn by the seer. Mr. Ritchie went on to say that the spirit had been on the other side for some ten years, he thought; when my finger again wrote in the air, as before, sixteen years. I felt there was nothing said by Mr. Ritchie sufficient to bring any conviction. At the close of the meeting, however, Mrs. Urquhart came over to Mr. Ritchie and said to him, "Those eyes you described were most accurate." I then said, "Did you call the child 'Amy'?" She at once answered, "That was the name." I told her how I had got it through my hand, and that I thought she had been in spirit life more than ten years, that my finger had written sixteen years. The next day she sent me an excerpt from the family Bible, giving the name "Amy" and the date of passing over, sixteen years and a few months before. Some persons seem to provide the conditions which enable the spirit people to give such full details regard ing themselves as to make conviction positive, and almost from her first connection with the subject Mrs. Urquhart got tests innumerable. Before I knew her well-balanced critical mind I used to think she was only credulous, but later I became certain that her open mind, and sweet harmonious nature, as well as her natural psychic power, made transmission of messages, and reception on her part, an easy matter. Men and women of notable names, for several years, seemed to come into my atmosphere. I do not know that information was conveyed which would be of a test nature, but I would be lifted out of myself and, with a fluency of speech widely removed from the normal, enter on profound questions which I would not have dared of myself to handle. Ofttimes the sitters were persons of intelligence, well read and capable, and these felt the power and comprehension of the talk, and esteemed it more highly than I did myself. So long as the influence dwelt with me there was an exaltation of spirit and a reverence for all that was noble and true, which ever left a moral impetus which was helpful to me in the struggle of life. At some moments I heard myself expressing ideas which were foreign to my opinions, and yet amidst it all I had the thought that much of the material I had imbibed from books was given out in the addresses. I wanted to be honest with myself and others, and the spirit of criticising would be carried on by my mind while speaking.

"Harriet Martineau," about whom I knew very little at the time, was a name that was often given. Her addresses were all of a lofty tone and breathed the spirit of true piety. My own impressions of the woman were very different from the idea conveyed by her speech. Then, I did not know what a noble, elevated soul she had been on earth, in spite of her agnosticism. "Robert Dale Owen" used to write, or I wrote, rather lengthened paragraphs, which at the end were signed "R.D.O." I was, of course, much in sympathy with the Owens, and knew much of Robert Dale Owen and his life's work through my association with his daughter, Rosamond, afterwards the wife of Laurence Oliphant. Pages were filled with practical observations on many social themes, and the power of Spiritualism to throw light on these. The mode of expression differed in every way from the other influences. With Owen it was ever to get at the practical, and never trouble about fine phrases. "Let the world know the true meaning of Spiritualism, and how its knowledge can affect the growth of man." I copy from an old note book one of these messages which flowed from my pen without thought on my part, and many parts of which were far removed from my thoughts at the time. I omit portions which have personal relation to myself, and I think I can honestly say that neither the thoughts nor the expression are my own:

A Message from Robert Dale Owen

*My own dear Friend,—My own life on earth was
once bright and sunny, then it became clouded,
because I saw only an enemy in the world—nature
violent, and mankind bruised on every hand. I
looked to Matter as the only God, and I thought that
man might some day get at the secret and subdue
this power. Let the old theologies die, I said. They
have made men slaves; let the new light shine. We
are more than the gods, we are conquerors. My
father, I thought, was a blind man in many of his
views, for he saw in God the friend of man: I only
saw in man no need of any God. I waited for the
development of better communistic systems; then I
lost faith in human nature for a time, but I still came
back to feel that beautiful circumstances had much
to do with the happiness of mankind. All my life I
wished to make my fellows happy. Each day I was
willing to sacrifice myself, if by so doing I could ease
the lot of others. I became doubtful and sceptical of
human nature; I thought at moments man was
villainous and, when chance was given, would seek
to override his fellows. One part had faith in virtue,
the other part had no respect for goodness. Slavery I
thought a great evil, and yet I had my doubts but that
it was unwise to root it out. I would have moved
slower than the whirl of events brought about. I
would have had no Revolution, only a preparation
of men and women for the new order of things. But
wisdom higher than mine overruled the question,
and I did not hesitate to welcome the situation.
America was my country and I loved it with all my*

heart, though I often went back in thought to the joyous days I had spent in Scotland before Reform claimed me as a worker. All my life I laboured at any new idea that had within it the possibility of making changes for the better, but darkness overhead was my lot.

Bible, God, Jesus were playthings for children. Men had nothing to do with these. No glimpse of heaven had ever been seen on earth. No divine word was ever spoken, other than the word of man. No message had ever come from man once he had closed the eye of physical life. Not a tree proclaimed the truth; not a man nor a woman, that there was a life beyond or a God ruling even here. Was not my intellect one of the best? Had I not communed with the greatest souls of my time, and did any one of them give me a sense of evidence? Not one! It was all dark, and I was satisfied it should be so.

One day I awoke to a new knowledge. The breath of the God I had despised came faintly over me, and a sensation I had not felt from childhood was mine. I touched and knew there was an Infinite God, Maker and Moulder of these worlds, and the loving Father of every child. Oh! so strange was it all. What welcome did I give the thought so new and strange? Step by step I retraced my life's history; saw the rocks on which I had gone astray from the safe waters where anchorage might have been had. I saw my own life (which I thought brilliant) had been clouded and shut out from what little children saw. I did not despise myself. I was content to begin as a little child. I went and waited at the feet of Jesus with the old love of my childhood. I saw the rays of light around his head, and bent the knee to the Father's anointed. To me he became all this—my soul's link on to God the unseen. My wish was to place on the brow of him I had dishonoured the bays I had torn from it, to make men love the soul that I had despised. I became child like, glad that I knew the life of man was not measured by the little time of earth, but was to endure from generation to generation, till he knew the source of life and being, till he was knit to God in fullness.

Spiritual communications were to me inspirations, and I drank in with my knowledge much that should have been tried with the cooler reason of my sceptical days. Still, I knew of friends come back from the lost shore, who told through mediums' lips of that other world, bright and fair, or dark and sad, as the lives of men had made it. Glimpses of a higher earth I saw when I knew there was a backbone of spirit. All things become possible in the progress of man; the Lord's Prayer of the kingdom of heaven on earth, the peace free from petty strife, the justice so calm and gentle, the sweet honour of preferring one's neighbour before oneself, the lofty joy of being free from thoughts of the sad condition of Society, the satisfaction of the longings after perfect living. All my life was full of satisfaction when I knew that a force stronger than dynamics was in touch with earthly conditions, that the loves of the angels were going to be showered down on earth again. I wondered at living so long in blind ness, satisfied with my blindness, and the light being *dispersed all around me. I took to literature with avidity. My pen was now to tell the opposite story to what my voice had so oft proclaimed. I had to write out the evidence which came to me, and I was satisfied when one told me my work had been a blessing to his life. My satisfaction when an old companion saw with my eyes was the loftiest joy that earth had given to me. Only a tap, only a peculiar movement which I might have overlooked, let me into the secret of God's mighty providence for leavening the life of the earth children.*

I did not weary of my task. I did not falter at letting out from within the messages I got. No doubts ever crossed me once the avenue was lighted up. I saw a mighty awakening in men's hearts coming. I saw the New Jerusalem coming down, and the lords of heaven breathing the gospel of the new life into the sad hearts of men. All will come yet, though it is slower than I once thought it would be, but it is better that the building be drained and dried before it is open for the occupancy of man. Steadily, surely, the fabric is being erected with durable materials that will stand the blast. Your own life is being lodged in it, so that it shall last, and your bright hopes of early years will be more than realised. A little time, and my life's story will be told through your pen as fully as I can give through mortals. Then you will see that your own interior life makes you my kinsman, hence the reason of my closeness to you.

I was unaware of the pages I filled. There was no conscious volition; all rushed along like a torrent, which I could hardly stop. My own mentality, no doubt, played some part, but to what extent is the question. There are sentences which were foreign to my mode of thought. I ask myself the question at the end, "Am I to take this as real, or the emanation of my own fancy?" and the response given is "Wait." It is but one of many such writings which bear the initials, "R.D.O."

CHAPTER XX

A TRAVELLED SPIRITUALIST

In June 1888 I was brought into contact with two remarkable men who had for long laboured in the fields of human progress. One of those was Elder Frederick Evans, of the Shaker Community, Mount Lebanon, New York; the other, Dr. James M. Peebles, one whom Spiritualists must ever hold in the highest reverence.

Elder Evans had been made known to many through Hepworth Dixon's New America, where the Shakers are fully dealt with, and, let it be said, with a sweet reverence so different from Dixon's treatment of the Spiritualists, whom he seems to have looked at from a considerable distance. The Shakers he had lived with for days, seeing them at their meals and at their prayers, in their private amusements and in their household work, and he said, "The people are like their village soft in speech, demure in bearing, gentle in face—a people seeming to be at peace not only with themselves, but with Nature and with heaven." So deeply moved was he by the attentions of those amongst whom he sojourned, and their mode of living, that he further said, "If any chance were to throw me down, and I were sick in spirit and broken in health, there would be few female faces, after my own wife and kin, that would be pleasanter to see about my bed." Elder Evans personally is made much of in this volume of New America. He talked to Dixon of the Shakers' communion with the dead, and of the sweet and tender messages of love they received from those who had gone from their sight. Dixon, no doubt, had gone to America with his companion, the present Sir Charles Dilke, for the purpose of making a book, and though he writes about many of the other sects too, one can see that he has not gone below the surface. He talks about Andrew Jackson Davis and Spiritualism without knowledge, simply giving voice to the prevailing opinions. He notes the claims of Spiritualism with a sneer, as if such claims were sufficient of themselves to be laughed at. Libellous is the word which I could apply to most of his criticisms of Spiritualism I have met with. It was the leader of this strange body of people, called "Shakers," who had come over on a visit with Dr. Peebles as a councillor and guide. I was at once charmed with the sweet simplicity, the naturalness, and purity of the man. He told me that the Shakers were Spiritualists long before 1848, and that the return of the dead to influence their lives was not simply a matter of faith, but of knowledge. I could not say that I was able to make much out of Shaker theology, though the patient old man took pains night after night to instil into me their basic ideas. I was not specially interested in the second advent, and might at the time have had doubts of the first advent, but I could admire the large fund of common sense, the repudiation of ancient errors, and the strong desire to bring about a state of society in which righteousness and peace might reign.

At odd moments I got the story of Elder Evans' life. Born in Worcestershire, he had gone to America while quite a young man, fired with the Radical spirit, which had developed into Socialism and Materialism. Robert Dale Owen was then at the head of the Atheists of the country. He had still to be awakened from his sleep of death, and have his vision pointed to a realm of finer realities than he had conceived possible. Robert Dale Owen and Francis Wright were Frederick Evans' high priests. The Communism they preached appealed to his nature. These were the days when it was thought that the Community system would solve the problem of ignorance, of want, and of crime. Robert Owen had made his experiment at New Harmony, scattering the fortune he had made in New Lanark, but the world was not ripe for a heterogeneous mass of men and women to live in amity. However powerful circumstances may be, they are not all. Without individual culture there can be no city of peace.

The spiritual vision granted to Robert Owen before the change seemed to him to point to the fact that circumstances before birth play an equal part with environment after birth. The within is after all the potent factor in the life of man, and the external, however elevating, cannot accomplish all. The literary and philosophic minds of Boston had also made their attempt at attaining a paradise otherwise than through the rough battle of life.

> Not they who soar, but they who plod
> Their rugged way unhelped to God,
> Are heroes; not who higher fare,
> And flying through the upper air,
> Miss all the toil that hugs the sod.
> 'Tis they whose backs have felt the rod,
> Whose feet have pressed the way unshod,
> May smile upon defeated care,
> Not they who soar.

Nathaniel Hawthorne, Dana (afterwards of the *New York Sun*), and George Ripley, with their Brook Farm experiment, found the life insipid, and were glad to go back to the life they had left. It has ever been one of the dreams of men to get away from the world, and in some sequestered spot work out an ideal state of things. Humanity, however, is only in the making, and the battle of life can best be fought and its lessons best learned amidst the heat and burden of turbulent life. When we have got to know ourselves better, read our own interior swayings after good and evil, and have brought will forth as something which we can ever sway in the direction of whatever is lovely and good, then the

201

spirit sought for by Communists will be found in our great cities. When we can love ourselves last and not first, the dreams of Fourier, Owen, and, others will be facts in the national life.

Frederick Evans, however, in 1830 was full of the communistic idea, apart from all religion, and had been appointed to look for a site for a settlement. When wandering to Mount Lebanon he made inquiries at the home of the Shakers. Here he was hospitably entertained, and to his surprise nothing was said about religion; in fact, he found them very much in agreement with his own views. As a philosophic materialist, he had been denouncing the past religious history as being false, and as having turned this earth into a hell. This the Shakers denounced in as strong terms as he had done. He found for the first time religious people who were also rationalists, ready to render a reason for the hope that was within them. They prayed for him, and he met with spiritual experiences which convinced his reason that there was a spirit world. Evidence so strong was presented to his outward senses as to completely destroy his materialistic ideas. All his physical, mental, rational, and spiritual senses were satisfied. He knew for all time that intelligences not clothed in flesh were present with him, who reasoned with him as logically as the friends in the body had ever done. Conviction, certainty on the great question, was his, and after three months' absence he returned to New York to report to his confreres the result of his mission.

To his materialistic friends his conversion was incomprehensible, but for himself the old order of thought had passed away for ever. He had an interview with Robert Dale Owen before returning to take up his residence amongst the Shakers. Mr. Owen promised to go to New Lebanon and stay two months, and if matters were as had been reported, he said he would become a Shaker. Robert Dale Owen never seemed to be able to fulfil his promise, but the spiritual facts met him a quarter of a century afterwards, when he became American Minister at the Court of Naples. The blessed knowledge redeemed a choice intellect from materialism. As I have said, I could not follow nor grasp Shaker theology, nor admire the great truths which Elder Evans had found in the Book of Revelation. I was not a mystic, and though I could recognise the great truth of Shakerism that God was our Mother as well as our Father, much else seemed to me of little import. I could love the man, however, with all my heart, though failing to agree with him on all intellectual points.

The Elder's companion, Dr. Peebles, had been for many years a central figure in the movement of Spiritualism. Already he had been twice round the world, proclaiming the news that the spirit world did not belong to the realm of myth and tradition, but was a natural fact. Since the advent of the movement he had never rested. The importance of the news filled his soul so that he could not be still, but must declare the message. There had been many thinkers in the movement, but Dr. Peebles was a man of action as well as a thinker, and behind this action, deep-rooted in his being, was a lofty ideal of religion and a sincere love of truth.

Like many earnest souls, he had bit by bit cast aside the traditional theology. He had begun while a school teacher to preach at revival gatherings, but a season of reflection helped him to see that humanity was not to be saved by magic, but by growth. He began his university studies, and came under the influence of the Universalists, receiving in due course his licence to preach what he thought was a gospel for all time. Rich in thought and eloquent in speech, he soon became a popular clergyman, drawing many earnest people around him. Emerson, Theodore Parker, and Swedenborg had, however, stirred up within him the thought that there was no finality in the creeds. After twelve years of his public ministry, he was brought into contact with the "rappings," and in 1856, when thirty-two years of age, he made up his mind to be free from churches, and preach only what was the outcome of his own experience. He had done with the "said so"of any man or book. Now it must be the "it is so" of fact. Reverence did not become weaker; his early piety was not abated, though he had come to feel that the Bible was neither supernatural, miraculous, exclusive, nor infallible.

The spirits had work for him to do; he trusted all to them, and went forth confident that he was obeying wise monitors, and soon his name was sounded all over America as one of the most eloquent expounders of the gospel of gladness. Spiritual experiences crowded in upon him sufficient to make him hold up his hands with certainty. When he was forty-five years of age, in 1869, he was appointed U.S. Consul to Trebizond, in Asiatic Turkey, and on his way there paid a visit to Glasgow, where he lectured. In London the commotion regarding him was great, as many had become familiar with his name through his writings in *The Banner of Light*, and the publication of his volume, *Seers of the Ages*. He visited John Bright at his home in Rochdale, when the Quaker statesman said to him, "If spirit communion is true, you have got hold of the greatest fact on the face of the earth today," and it was because Dr. Peebles, through every avenue of sense, knew that what he had seen and heard was indeed true, that he went all over the world to spread this truth, confident of the support of his unseen friends. In China, in India, in Australia, amidst the South Sea Islanders, he travelled, accompanied by a noted sensitive, through whom he was kept in touch with the spiritual realms. His pen produced another volume of singular value, *Around the World*, a book clear and elevating, not only giving knowledge of distant parts, but abounding in philosophic problems and spiritual light. This notable worker I met in 1887, and was immediately attracted by his presence and bearing, which proclaimed a man of righteousness, while his speech showed the

scholar and thinker. Of great men he had much to tell. With
Emerson he had conversed for hours in his home at Concord.
Walt Whitman had been introduced to him by Emerson, and
with Whitman for years he had remained in close contact. With
Victor Hugo he had sat in the spirit circle, and witnessed the great
French poet's abiding faith in Spiritualism—faith which is so fully
expressed in these words, "The tomb is not a blind alley; it is a
thoroughfare. It closes on the twilight; it opens with the dawn."
Peebles' *Seers of the Ages* had given me many hours of intense
delight before I came into contact with the author. Much of it is a
prose poem inspired by heavenly messengers. It is a storehouse
of spiritual treasures. Peebles shows that the light which has
glimmered all down the ages is now shining with a measure of
fulness. Not on the past alone does the author dwell, but from
many modern writers he shows how much of the spirit of
Spiritualism is abroad. Men do not use the name, but the truths
which spiritual phenomena confirm are to be found in much of
the literature of the nineteenth century. The pulpit talk of
Beecher abounded with the thought that the dead were still
working with the living, and that at moments our eyes were
opened so that we could look into the other world. Theodore
Parker came much closer when he boldly said Spiritualism had
more evidence for its wonders than any historic form of religion.
Harriet Beecher Stowe pointed out that there was little value in
St. Paul's statement that we were encompassed with a cloud of
witnesses, unless these witnesses could be seen and recognised.
Peebles' volume, though treating exhaustively of the Spiritualism
of the past, and its seers, prophets, and sages, has dug out from
contemporary literature much that is of the highest value, and
much that shows Spiritualism as an old friend who seems strange
and novel only for the moment. It has come in a new dress and
with different associations, against which we have acquired some

prejudice and antipathy, and so we have shut the door in the face of our best beloved relative. The insight and penetration of the scholar is seen all through the volume: what Socrates believed, what to the early Christian Church were the most potent of its realities (the trances, clairvoyance, healing, etc.), are shown to have come in larger volume to the world today. The continuous operation of this power through the ages, now accepted by the reflective minds of many lands, is set forth as only a student of life and history could display it. Whatever a book may give of a writer's personality, personal contact yields much more. With Dr. Peebles in your midst you can open at any page his encyclopaedia of knowledge, and feel the warmth which quickens the inner life. Like all great men he is modest, and unconscious almost of the great work he is doing. For me, and others, he is an instrument capable of kindling latent emotions, and inspiring us to work as he has done for the mightiest revelation with which mortals have ever been favoured. Dr. Peebles for me was the great normal exponent of the gospel, even as Andrew Jackson Davis was the abnormal.

Each in his sphere has given of his best. Peebles has the power to attract the masses, and link their past thoughts to the present outflowings of truth. He has gathered his knowledge from the objective, though quickened and enlarged, no doubt, by the inspirations which have flowed into his receptive and righteous nature. Davis, of course, is the greater marvel. His story is almost unbelievable, and will certainly not be credited by those who believe that the past was greater than the present.

Davis is still for me the most astounding product in human nature, the greatest acquisition to the world's mental and spiritual wealth, and, if I had room for the miraculous, the most miraculous of human beings. Some men shine brilliantly in one corner of thought and astonish their fellows; but Davis, like

Shakespeare, covers the whole gamut of humanity's thoughts and feelings, and will yet live in the world's regard as one of the choicest gifts to mortals. Had he appeared in churchal attire he would have been treated as something divine. His visions and profound revelations regarding nature would have made men say that God directly inspired him, and we should have had a repetition of Godmen and Messiahs. Swedenborg did something to open the doors of the spirit-world, and reveal its people as still having something like rational instincts; but Swedenborg was a scholar, whose imagination might have done something to manufacture the pictures he presented.

Davis knew nothing of books nor of schools, and yet in what he called the "superior condition" he penetrated all realms of being, and would quote from every writer that had sought to throw light on the problems of life. However incredible it may appear, the thoughts of the ancients before Moses was born were made clear to his vision, and he was more familiar with the thoughts of Plato and Aristotle than any specialists of these schools. The scientific man may say impossible, but we have nob to extricate Davis from some ecclesiastical romance, some legend of the saints, for verification; his whole life is open, and the facts of his strange career are verifiable. We can understand how Shakespeare knew so much when we study this "superior condition" of Davis, who was rendered capable of entering the realm of Causes and portraying the facts he had gleaned. He has set down for all time what no writer had ever caught before of the law, order, and naturalness of the spirit-world, while, if physical scientists would but study him, they would have such help as no school of science could give.

Carlyle, in his *Sartor Resartus*, which many will consider a flight of the wildest imagination, writes of Fortunatus as but wishing himself anywhere and, behold, he is there, thus being one who could triumph over space. For him there was no where, only here:

> *Shooting at will from the fire-creation of the*
> *world to its fire-consummation; here*
> *historically present in the first century*
> *conversing face to face with Paul and Seneca,*
> *there prophetically in the thirty-first*
> *conversing also face to face with other Pauls*
> *and Senecas, who as yet stand hidden in the*
> *depth of that late time.*

A study of this abnormal life of Davis, and its products, *Nature's Divine Revelations* and *The Great Harmonia*, will give some corroboration of Carlyle's seemingly wild thought, and help us to realise that "only the timeshadows have perished or are perishable; that the real Being of whatever was and whatever is, and whatever will be, is even now and forever." We do not always see the significance of what is taking place around us. Davis, to this generation, is almost unknown, but when the noise and ferment of the trivial, which now seem so great, shall have gone to the silence, Davis will stand out from the period as one of the great landmarks.

There never was a great truth but in due season it came to be reverenced; never a great man but the time came when the world thanked God for the gift of his example and work. What Darwin and Huxley saw of the outer, this man also saw and set down before their eyes had caught the view; but he saw deeper, wider, saw also the hidden side, the spiritual in all nature. Whatever the religious genius has caught through his ripened intuition, this obscure American has painted in the glowing colours of fact and reality.

Dr. J.M. Peebles and Dr. Andrew Jackson Davis will stand forth as luminous figures in the story of this great movement; one, the brave exponent of the outward, the other, the great seer of the interior forces. I leave these names for the present. The after years brought me into closer touch with the spiritual pilgrim and the inspired magician of spiritual truths.

CHAPTER XXI

THE MISSION OF SPIRITUALISM

He who shall pass judgment on the records of
our life is the same who formed us in frailty.

I pass for a time from those great luminaries, who are not for one age but for all time, to my association with other workers who by their lives have helped to lay a stone in the great building that must one day command the world's admiration and reverence. One of these, named John Hopcroft, came to Glasgow for a season to set forth his phenomenal gifts.

Mr. Hopcroft was a shoemaker in London, a person easily mesmerised by an operator, and had for long been the instrument who enabled Mr. D. Younger, a magnetic physician, to analyse the phases of mesmerism, and to produce a valuable volume on the subject, in which were photographs of Mr. Hopcroft in the several stages of mesmeric control The spirit people were able to use Hopcroft's organism for manifestations of their power. At one of his first appearances in Glasgow, we were somewhat surprised at the public meeting one morning, when he said, "There is no control with me. I cannot go on. Someone is holding back something."

This was an altogether unfamiliar experience, as during all my association with the subject I have never met with a case where the spirit guide failed to carry out his part. We were all a bit upset for a time, when a strange gentleman rose from the back of the hall and said that no doubt he was the cause of the peculiar circumstance which had arisen. He then went on to narrate that he had drunk deep at the wells of spirit communion in America, that business had called him to this country, and that, dropping into our meeting, he had determined to say nothing about his knowledge of the subject. He said the spirit people behind him were not pleased with his cowardice, and had prevented Mr. Hopcroft from being controlled, so that he might be forced to speak out.

This gentleman, Mr. John M. Hockin, had been for twenty years the Nova Scotian representative of the great firm of Arthur & Co., Ltd., and naturally did not care that his position should be tainted with association with Spiritualism during his business call on his firm. I got to know him intimately, and found him one of the most earnest of men—a man who had literally been flooded with spiritual evidences, and who in after years became a regular correspondent of mine, giving details of his ever-varying experiences of spirit action. We had several private sittings with Mr. Hopcroft, at which he was present, and got many tests of the presence of his friends. I had singular experiences myself while in his company, the sweet influence of his personality seeming to open wide the door through which the spirits could act upon myself. At one sitting I felt as if one of the joints of my finger were swollen and, under impression, I asked him to take a ring off his finger. Immediately the sense of discomfort ceased, and I poured out a stream of loving words to him, which, with the ring incident, were full of meaning.

At another sitting in my house, Mr. Hopcroft, while entranced, placed his hands amidst the ruddy coals in the fireplace, and lifting a piece which was perfectly red, he walked through the room, so that its glow was reflected by the pictures on the wall. He wanted to place it on my wife's head. But she, feeling nervous, shrank from the ordeal, and as she pushed away his arm, a piece of the coal fell upon the carpet and singed it. He picked it up and proceeded again round the room till it became black, when he placed it in the fire and toyed once more with the flaming pieces in the grate. I had several opportunities of witnessing this phase of Mr. Hopcroft's mediumship, which was very similar to that recorded by S.C. Hall as having taken place with D.D. Home. Hopcroft was a good clairvoyant, and one of his controls sang very finely in some foreign tongue. Another, whose name I forget, was a peculiar character, harsh and shrewish, who did not always create a pleasant feeling. Poor Hopcroft is now a faint memory to the Spiritualists. Ill-health overtook him shortly after we saw him, and relief came in his pro motion to that other world, the evidence of which he sought to establish.

During the year 1887, i was first brought into personal touch with Mr. Andrew Glendinning, of London, though his was a name I had been familiar with, as an ardent worker in the Cause, ever since I was first brought into contact with the movement. It would scarcely be possible to meet a human being with a more winning presence than Mr. Glendinning, and his virtues are not painted on him, but are the man him self. No one has ever come within his sphere, but has learned to trust him, and as the years have rolled on, increased in admiration for his sterling honesty, his sincerity and affection. The many friends he has gathered during a long life look up to him as a pattern of all the manly virtues.

From his earliest years he has been devoted to every good cause which can tend to the uplifting of his fellows, and there has never been any cessation of his labours. His friendships with men of all sects have been close, and he has been as much reverenced by the orthodox clergyman as by the agnostic writer. The great secret of his power is that he is naturally a religious soul. His feelings are warm and tender. His intellect has ripened with the years, and his hand has ever been ready to help in every practical work.

A word, a look of sympathy,
A penny generously bestowed,
A simple act of courtesy,
A kindly influence shed abroad,
Can from the soul lift many a load.
These angel deeds, grand and sublime,
Like ripples on the restless sea,
Sweep o'er the fretful stream of time,
And reach into Eternity.

His early years were all associated with Glasgow. At the age of twelve he joined the Eastern District Total Abstinence Society, and has remained a total abstainer all his life. While a boy he was in the habit of deliver ing addresses in town and country, working in the slums at night, carrying a hopeful message wherever he could. His name was well known fifty years ago in all that related to temperance work, but this important task did not utilise all his energies. He became secretary of the anti-war agitation at the time of the Oregon difficulty with the United States. Anti-slavery and free labour movements also attracted him, and he came into touch with many notable workers for these causes whose names are but a memory to the present generation.

Amongst these was Frederick Douglass, one of the noblest champions of the coloured race, who had him self been a slave. George Jacob Holyoake relates a story of this man; how, wandering homeless at night, no minister would open his door to him, a slave, though Douglass was himself a preacher, when a passer-by told him to knock at Colonel Robert Ingersoll's gate, and he would find shelter and welcome under the generous heretic's roof, which he did. Holyoake also tells of him that when he was hissed on the platform by slave-owners, he paused, and then said, "Yes, a hiss is what you always hear when the waters of truth drop on the fires of hell."

213

Another noble worker with whom Mr. Glendinning had been associated was William Lloyd Garrison, that brave man who rose up and would not compromise or be silent; who would be heard, and who began the anti-slavery movement, publishing the Liberator in an obscure hole in Boston, his only auxiliary a negro boy, and his supporters a very few insignificant persons of all colours. He shook the nation, and lived to see the fruit of his labours. Mr. Glendinning had also the pleasure of entertaining the learned blacksmith, Elihu Burritt, in his home.

Wherever there was a noble cause or true men to be supported, his wide sympathies were enlisted. He interested himself in the formation of penny savings banks, workmen's libraries, building societies, and the secular education on Sundays of children from the slums, and each and all gave him pleasant occupation. It was a life of service. Creeds did not trouble him much. His religion was ever practical. He worked with all who would work with him in reclamatory work, inside the church or out of it. Not that he was a heretic in those days; on religious questions he was so engrossed with real religion that he had little time to devote to theology. His great article of faith was the absolute goodness of God; all else he did not care to dispute about. Such was the man who in the early days of Spiritualism caught hold of its truth, and has ever since given it his heart's devotion. It swallowed up all the vague half beliefs, and gave him the solid ground of certainty on which he could plant his feet. It was larger than the old faiths, full of .blessing, for in neither the Old Testament nor the New is there a single word which tells the sweet truth that penitence hereafter can make reparation, or that the agony of repentance which men will suffer will wipe out the scars of many years of wickedness.

Spiritualism brought him into personal contact with souls in that other life, who, though badly shipwrecked, had repented and caught some degree of happiness. It is little wonder that a nature born to heal, and soothe, and bless the suffering, would welcome the glad tidings of infinite progression for the most depraved; that in all the family of God there is never a son of perdition.

Mr. Glendinning had been the first president of the Glasgow Association of Spiritualists, and had witnessed all the early stages of the movement in Glasgow. As the story of its origin has never been told, I cannot do better than set down all I have learned from old minute books and annual reports.

Among the events which preceded, and, in great measure, gave rise to the formation of the Association, was the publication, in December 1863, of a pamphlet, entitled, Narrative of Facts Observed. Though intended for private circulation, the contents soon became public, some portions being reproduced in the columns of the daily press. I can well recollect reading a lead ing article in the *Glasgow Herald,* dealing with the pamphlet, in which the whole matter was brought into ridicule, or talked of as wild imposture, unworthy the serious consideration of sensible people. I suppose I echoed the sentiments which were given forth by the press, not dreaming that the subject would one day charm my life, and satisfy my religious aspirations. It was to me, then, the most inconsequential of subjects. The pamphlet would probably have been scarcely noticed, but that it was an open secret that the author was a well known town councillor and a prominent iron master— Councillor Bain, afterwards Sir James Bain, Lord Provost of Glasgow, and for many years Member of Parliament for a borough in Cumberland. It was the position of the writer which caused the excitement, not so much the facts narrated. He had been with Mrs. Marshall in London, and vouched for the genuineness of the phenomena, if not for their spiritual source. To those who already knew the facts, there was nothing peculiar or exceptional in the narrative. Soon in many quarters was heard the inquiry, "What is this Spiritualism? What new thing can this be?" Those who knew of the communion between the two worlds, and who were known to be interested in the subject, had to submit to a considerable amount of abuse and calumny. Men and women whose purity of life had never been questioned were put upon the rack and assailed daily in the press.

But though opposing pamphlets appeared, Spiritual ism did not die; it persisted in keeping alive and demanding a hearing. The few Spiritualists then in Glasgow brought Alderman Barkas, of Newcastle, to give two lectures in the Merchants' Hall, where he bravely advocated the spiritual theory, and answered much that had been said in the press. William Howitt, the well known *littérateur*, had also done something to meet the virulent abuse that was heaped upon Spiritualism by writing letters of trenchant, burning criticism. While so many would have, it that Spiritualism was a mockery, a snare, and a delusion, the Spiritualists in their own homes obtained manifestations and developed mediums. As the number of Spiritualists increased, a desire sprang up for an Association, by aid of which mutual encouragement and advice might be given, as well as means taken for the advancement of the Cause, and so, in January 1866, a notice was circulated amongst known believers, asking them to attend a meeting in Buchanan's Temperance Hotel, Carlton Place, for the purpose of forming an Association. One of the names appended to the circular was that of James Nicholson, a local poet of some note, many of whose pieces I read with pleasure, without knowing anything of the cause of his healthy optimism regarding a future life. The other name was that of Mr. Hay Nisbet, a well-known printer. Both of these men, as already mentioned, I knew in after years, and admired for their courage and devotion. Some thirty persons attended the meeting which had been summoned, and a work was begun which is never likely to cease. Mr. Glendinning, though residing at that time in Port Glasgow, where he had had many spiritual experiences, was appointed president, and amongst those who were associated with him in the work were Mr. William Burns, a well-known Glasgow merchant, still to the fore, the brother of James Burns, the doughty editor of *The Medium* and *Daybreak* (whose great services were scarcely recognised until the change of death came); Gavin B. Clark, afterwards better known as Dr. Clark, and M.P. for Caithness, who was secretary for a season; Mr. Alex. Cross, a good writer and speaker; Mr. Jas. Walker, a man of considerable scientific attainments; and others, who in after years were close friends and fellow-workers in the Cause.

Sir James Bain never publicly associated himself with the movement. Like Nicodemus, he attended sittings by night, and gave now and again a liberal contribution to the funds; but he had suffered so much through the publication of his pamphlet that he feared further publicity. When he stood years afterwards as M.P. for Glasgow, his opponents had not forgotten his Spiritualistic leanings, as cartoons abounded on the walls, showing him getting advice on political matters from the spirits.

The Association at its origin had several clergymen amongst its members, and altogether the meetings bore quite a Christian, sectarian character. It was said that the visitors from the unseen world must have applied to them the Apostolic test, "Every spirit that confesseth that Jesus Christ is come in the flesh is of God, and every spirit that confesseth not that Jesus Christ is come in the flesh is not of God," which showed at least that they had not realised the mission of Spiritual ism. The acknowledgment that the man of Nazareth was a historical personage, and not a myth around which had become associated the legendary and the miraculous, could have little relation to the religious life. That such a question as to whether or not Jesus had lived should have had to be asked in the first century goes to show that the stories in circulation of the marvellous man had not too much relation to fact. Spiritualism calls no man master, neither Jesus nor Paul. It is no personal Christ, but the spirit of wisdom, holiness, and love that creates the well-being of man. It will not call a false word true, though the greatest of the earth speak it; neither will it ignore a true word, though a Pagan give it expression. The Bible to Spiritualists is not a finality; it is no man's master, it is every man's servant. The precious truths it contains they prize, but they recognise that all its heroes and saints only drank a cupful out of the great ocean of truth. Even as Christianity in its early gropings was saturated with Judaism, so the early Spiritualism in Glasgow was but the Christianity of the creeds with the fact of spirit return added, and the great majority of its members kept in close relation with the churches. Soon much of the spirit teachings destroyed belief in a Fall, or the necessity for an Atonement, or any such Judgment Day as theology painted. Spirits came back with their story that progress was a law of life over there, that "man makes his own future, stamps his own character, suffers for his own sins, and must work out his own salvation; that we are our own accusers, judges, and executioners, and that the judgment comes not in any far-off day, but that we daily come forth to judgment." It was quite a long time before the early Spiritualists felt that they were the representatives of a great religious movement, or entered upon any public propaganda. They met and discussed problems and related experiences in a quiet way. But there came amongst them those who had gone through the "unrest of a ceaseless search, and the pain of a never-satisfied desire," who, awakened to new life, and full of hope and courage, determined that the light should not be hid, and so in a few years they began to hold regular Sunday meetings, which have never ceased.

Mr Glendinning has ever been amongst those who recognised Spiritualism in its larger bearings. He has been ceaseless in his search, and has caught the full reward. Helped by a wife to whom he was joined in spirit, he has done much for all the workers, and though not a speaker or writer in the public sense, he has continually sought to cheer the heart of the mourner by giving out the sweet knowledge that has filled his life. My own indebtedness to him has been great, outside his kindly cheer, more of which will be recorded in my after years' experience. He has shown me how high the tide of humanity can rise in noble worth, and how inspiring and lofty is a movement that retains such souls in its ranks. No man or woman who has been privileged to share the friendship of Andrew Glendinning can help feeling that the race of saints has not quite died out from the earth.

CHAPTER XXII

DAVID DUGUID'S VARIED MEDIUMSHIP

It was in the house of Mr. Hay Nisbet that the marvellous gifts of Mr. David Duguid were first brought to light. Phenomena more striking than aught else helped to make the Association a strong power. Mr. Duguid was then a young man, little over thirty. He had attended sittings in Mr. Nisbet's house for a considerable time, and it never crossed his mind that he was likely to become a medium. He had no artistic aptitude, being by trade a working cabinet maker, employed by Wylie and Lochhead. From one of the workers there, a Mr. Whittaker, he first heard the word Spiritualism. A devoted Church member, he followed the subject for long, with doubts as to whether or not he might be working with Satan. The strong common sense of his close friend, Hay Nisbet, however, kept him to the subject. As one day the life of this extraordinary medium will be anxiously inquired for, I think it right at this stage to set down all that is known regarding his early development.

I came into the movement when all those associated with Duguid were still in the body, and for thirty years I have been in almost daily contact with the man himself. He had been at several sittings before he felt any peculiar sensations, but one night he began to feel alarmed when his arms commenced to shake, and when Mr. Nisbet touched him he experienced a cold current running down his spine. Soon this was followed by violent movements of the table. The question was put, "Who is the medium?" It was answered, "Mr. Duguid." The movements became so violent that all rose, and the table followed Mr. Duguid round the room.

Mr. Duguid soon began to see shadowy human forms moving about the room, men and women of different countries, and belonging to different periods of history. This was followed by a further development, the artistic phase, which has been manifested ever since, and which has caused a considerable amount of commotion all over the world.[3] One Saturday evening he had been sitting with Mr. Nisbet and others, when he was impressed to call in the aid of a young lady who was a writing and trance medium. Having sat for some time, and feeling that her hands were cold, the young lady put her right hand on Mr. Duguid's left, and at once his left hand began to move. Thinking he was about to develop into a writing medium, a pencil and paper were laid down, when the pencil was picked up and with the left hand there were drawn some crude designs. At the conclusion of the sitting the spirit who had claimed to operate

through Mr. Duguid's hand gave his name, "Marcus Baker," and promised to come back at the next meeting and, continue. The interest of the sitters was so great that they met again on the Monday evening, when the medium's left hand made more finished productions, one of the drawings being a portrait of the spirit operator. The sitters were asked at their next gathering to provide water colours, and with these the medium's right hand painted an elaborate symbolical picture, the aid of the young lady now being discontinued. The most sceptical member of the circle was a Mr. John MacKay, himself an artist, who was much impressed with the drawings produced by the left hand, and his scepticism was entirely overthrown when the medium began to work with closed eyes, and was so deeply entranced that he did not hear what the other sitters said. By continually experimenting

---

3. For a more complete study of the artistic mediumship of David Duguid, readers are referred to *The Direct Phenomena of Spiritualism*, by E.T. Bennett (London: Wm. Eider & Son, Ltd., 1908).

they found that though the medium did not hear what was said, the spirit did, and replies were made quite unknown to the medium. They learned that the spirit was a Dutch painter who had lived in the seventeenth century; that he was born in 1636 and died in 1681; that "Marcus Baker" was not his real name, which he declined to give, assigning as a reason that he would furnish them with the means of discover ing it for themselves, viz., by reproducing one of his pictures through the medium. This promise was soon fulfilled. There were sketched the outlines of a water fall; a wild scene of rock and crag, with solitary pines growing from their clefts; a hill crowned with an ancient fort towards the right, on the left a hermit's hut, with a rustic wooden bridge leading to it over the foaming waters. The whole time occupied in its production was four hours. When completed the initials "J.R." were observed in the left-hand corner. The medium while in trance had heard someone on the spirit side call the artist "Jacob," but the sitters could not recollect any eminent painter of that name. All were most curious as to whether or not the original of the picture was in existence, and whether it might be found amongst the masterpieces of the old painters, but they knew not how to prosecute their inquiries. Very fortunately Mr. MacKay, the artist sitter, who had been taking a lively interest in the work, one evening brought a brother artist to see the painting and get his opinion as to its merits. This gentleman no sooner saw the picture than he observed, "I have surely seen the original of that somewhere, or at least an engraving of it." He promised to try and recollect where he had seen it, and a few nights thereafter he handed to the circle a book of engravings, entitled, *Cassell's Art Treasure Exhibitor*, in which they saw to their surprise an engraving, entitled, "The Waterfall," by Jacob Ruysdael,[4] acknowledged to be his *chef d'oeuvre.* The information which had been gained as to the real name of the artist was kept from the medium's knowledge. At the next meeting, after the medium had gone under control, the spirit said that they now knew his real name, which was "Jacob Ruysdael." On comparing the engraving with the picture, the resemblance was very close, the only difference being that in the engraving there were some figures on the rustic bridge, which were absent from the work painted by the medium. On being questioned as to this difference, the spirit replied that the figures in his painting were put in by his friend Berghem, which was found to agree with the statements given in the biography of Ruysdael. When the medium came out of trance he was shown the engraving, also a likeness of the painter, when he exclaimed, "That's the very man, and the very dress!" And thus was begun a great work which has made some impress on the age, and will yet do more.

Innumerable tests were received as to the Dutch painter "Ruysdael," and also the notable "Jan Steen." The sitters were all men of intelligence, who laboriously examined the evidence presented, and established beyond a doubt the identity of the spirit artists. Soon there were other developments, to which I have already referred ; the production of paintings, direct, without the medium's hands being used, and the dictation of that marvellous bit of literature, *Hafed, Prince of Persia,* a work which no unlettered man, as David Duguid was, could have written unassisted by spirit help. *Hafed* will be prized for many years as the first-fruits of the spirit's work, and a testimony to the devotion

---

4. Both the original picture and the copy painted through David Duguid are reproduced in Mr. E.T. Bennett's book, previously referred to.

of those brave pioneers, Mr. Glendinning, Mr. Hay Nisbet, and others.

After my first introduction to Mr. Glendinning he was often in Glasgow, and on my visits to London his was the face that ever welcomed me most cordially. Our interests ran together very closely on one special subject, viz., that of Spirit Photography. Mr. David Duguid, to whom I have so often referred, had on one occasion photographed a shadowy form standing beside a visitor from Australia, which form the visitor declared was the portrait of one he had known well in the body. The picture was taken in my drawing-room, and our surprise and delight were very great. I had seen many similar productions during my investigations, but this was the first time that such realities had been brought to my own door. When Mr. Glendinning heard of the event he was most eager to prosecute the matter further. He had witnessed many wonders during his long association with Mr. Duguid, but photographing the so-called dead seemed to him of greater interest than aught else. Our success was indeed marvellous. Sitting one afternoon on the green behind my house, the camera was brought out and a picture taken. When we went in side to develop the plate, my surprise was great to see the form of a child about two years of age sitting on my knee, every part clearly formed; also another face, that of a young woman, looking towards the child. There were few things I had met with which stirred me more than these forms making their appearance on the plate; personal experience of strange facts being of much more value than any testimony given by others. I knew then, and for all time, that the camera could take cognisance of objects which were hid from the physical sight. Our vision has its limitations. The invisible, in relation to the stars, has been brought into the realm of the visible. Thousands of stars, whose light no telescope, however powerful, can show to the human eye, have been revealed by the camera. Almost all Spiritualistic phenomena are found to be related to modern discoveries, if we only widen our observation and take in a larger view of nature, not limiting it to the things of matter, but taking in the realm to which these modern marvels point—a world of intelligence able to act on this material plane.

But for the enthusiasm and skill of Mr. Glendinning little would have been accomplished in the domain of psychic photography. Under the most exacting test conditions—conditions entered upon so carefully that we could speak with authority—we got together a considerable number of choice pictures, which were the product of others rather than those engaged in the experiments. Some of these were realisations of a high ideal of beauty; others were those of faces we had known; while some were of the most puzzling nature.

While these experiments were going on, a friend of mine, occupying a distinguished position in connection with the Court of Session, a lawyer and a scholar, was most anxious to get a picture of a dear boy who had been translated some years before, and whose death had first interested him in Spiritualism. He did not require this form of evidence to convince him that—

> The two worlds—the seen and the unseen,
> The world of matter and the world of spirit—
> Are like the hemispheres upon your maps,
> That touch each other only at a point.
> But these two worlds are not divided thus,
> Save for the purposes, of common speech.
> They form one globe, in which the parted
> seas
> All flow together, and are intermingled,
> While the great continents remain distinct.

My friend had had some years' experience of spiritual realities, and frequently had messages from the boy, whose form was seen and described by a sister who was clairvoyant. So many test pictures had been obtained at this period that we had no doubt of success, but in this we were disappointed for a season. The mother and daughter came to Glasgow, and though the daughter clearly saw the features of the loved one, somehow his form did not come upon the plate. Another attempt was made, and some of the boy's toys were brought into the room, so that the conditions might be helped, but again disappointment met us. Other faces, welcome in themselves, were there, but not the desired one. Though there was a measure of discouragement, the parents did not give up hope, for the reason that all the time they were cheered with messages that their wishes would yet be realised.

A few weeks later Mr. Duguid was in Edinburgh, and, having his camera with him, he left it at the gentleman's house, and made arrangements to call there the next day and make another attempt. When he had gone a letter was written automatically, through the clairvoyant daughter's hand, in a handwriting which they knew well, in which full directions were given them as to the experiment to be tried the next day.

When Mr. Duguid arrived they went to the bedroom where the boy had died, furnished with dry plates which they had themselves bought at a shop in Edinburgh. The six plates, taken out one by one by a member of the family (a daughter), were handed by her to Mr. Duguid. He, in her presence, as it was required, put each plate in the dark slide, which was taken to the bedroom and inserted in the camera. On development, it was found that on four of the plates there was a child's face and form close to the two sitters—the mother and daughter. When the sitting was over, Mr. Duguid proposed to take the four plates to

Glasgow next day and have them printed, but left them overnight, promising to call for them before leaving. The family, however, were eager to see the child's face and could not be induced to wait, so one of the daughters, who had some little experience in amateur photography, took the plates and put them to be printed at one of the windows. To their intense delight, on each of the copies printed there was a clear and well-defined likeness of the boy, so long wanted by them.

In one picture the boy is sitting up in the bed, in the very place where he had died, with a star over his head. The second depicts him in a boy's suit, sitting on his mother's knee. The face is the same in each picture, and each member of the family felt, beyond a doubt, that there had been granted to them in response to their longings, and in harmony with natural law, a portrait of the loved one. Every part of the evidence is such that the most finical critic can find no loophole of escape from accepting the facts as authentic. Mr. Duguid had never been in the house before, nor had he seen any portrait of the boy; the only portrait they had was taken when he was two years old, and it was not like what he was when removed by death, whilst the psychic picture was in full agreement with the child's features shortly before death, as they were impressed on the tablets of memory. Outside the facts of the true like ness, the dry plates used were the family's own, and were not handled by the medium until he placed them in the slide, whilst the development was witnessed all through by a daughter.

It would be difficult to find a more striking or better attested fact, .or one of such paramount importance. Truly, as Carlyle has said, "The uses of some patent dinner calefactor can be bruited about the whole world in the course of the first winter; those of the printing press are not so well seen into for the first three centuries: the passing of the Select Vestries' Bill raises more hopeful expectancy among mankind than did the promulgation of the Christian religion. ... The great, the creative and enduring, is ever a secret to itself; only the small, the barren and transient, is otherwise." The gentleman who attested the facts was a man of keen, critical faculties, with a large experience of sifting what is called criminal evidence; a person of social position and worth, whose word on any other subject would have been accepted without cavil. The public position he so long occupied no doubt prevented him placing his many proofs of spirit action before the world. Robert Chambers only spoke with bated breath on Spiritualism, and to those who knew the facts as he did; and Sir James Bain, in our own city, ran the gauntlet of abuse for many years after publishing his pamphlet. Even modern scientific men who come near the subject in their writings take care not to be too positive in their statements. As the late Rev. H.R. Haweis once said in an article on "Ghosts and their Photographs," which he wrote for the Daily Graphic: "Like the wise man he is, Sir William Crookes, after having tasted the quality of scientific bigotry, and having already suffered somewhat for his ardour in the pursuit of unpopular and novel truth, keeps certain experiences, together with his abnormal photographs, to himself, and will not now even show them." "Be not righteous over much," says the prudent Solomon," neither make thyself other wise; why shouldst thou destroy thyself?"

Though there are many Spiritualists who keep the consolations of Spiritualism to themselves, and pursue the subject, Nicodemus-like, by night, I am not going to ascribe blame to them. Mr. Glendinning, however, was born with a nature which was ever able to stand in the right with two or three, or even alone, if need be. To keep such facts as had come under his notice to himself always seemed to him the betrayal of a great trust. He has ever felt that Spiritualism alone gives that evidence which the world needs: the great truth of a future life having relation to a universal reign of law.

There is an extract from some spiritual writings, the source of which I cannot recall, which presents pretty fully Mr. Glendinning's views of Spiritualism: "Spiritualism is the religion of personal responsibility, of never-dying hope, and of eternal progress. It is the religion which meets every need and every trial of life, holding a clear-burning beacon to light the way. And as men live up to the highest knowledge of truth within their hearts, newer and greater truths shall be given them, and they shall be led by spirit hands. Spirit voices shall whisper in their ears, and their souls shall be attuned to the harmony of heaven. The knowledge of the spirit is the fountain of living water which flows from the great central throne, whence proceed infinite wisdom and infinite love. The spirit and the bride say ' Come,' and let him that heareth say 'Come,' and let him that is athirst 'Come,' and whosoever will, let him take the water of life freely."

Mr. Glendinning never felt that he had done all he could to spread the light, and so he prevailed on Mr. Duguid to visit London, that a man of scientific attainments might be able, without sentiment, to vouch for the reality of these phenomenal occurrences. Mr. Traill Taylor, the editor of the British Journal of Photography, and an authority on light and optics, readily agreed with Mr. Glendinning to carry through several experiments. The meetings were held in Mr. Glendinning's home, and I was privileged to be amongst those who witnessed them. Mr. Taylor has placed on record his modes of procedure. They were that he for the nonce would assume the sitters to be tricksters, and to guard against all possibility of fraud he used his own camera and his own unopened dry plates, purchased by him from dealers of repute. Under no circumstances did he allow a plate to go out of his hand until after development, and to ensure still further exactitude he used a binocular stereoscopic camera, and dictated all the conditions of operation. Under these circumstances, Mr. Duguid being simply an observer, he got what he calls psychic figures beside the several sitters. Some of the figures are in focus, others are not, but again there was corroboration of Mr. Glendinning's and my own experiments in Glasgow, that forms unseen by the naked eye were able to make their impress on the sensitive plate.

Undoubtedly, amongst those pictures got by Mr. Taylor were some which the average person would at once have called spurious and fraudulent; but he was manly enough, in a lecture he delivered before the London and Provincial Photographic Association, to stand forth in defence of the genuineness of all, fraudulent as some might look.

A peculiar circumstance arose one afternoon during the operations. We had with us a Church of England clergyman and another professional gentleman, who had craved admission to witness what was taking place; but, singular to state, each effort made ended in failure. There were no forms on the plate other than the physical sitters. I followed Mr. Taylor again and again into the developing room, ever expecting that the previous successes would be repeated, but in vain. No doubt these gentlemen felt that it was their superior vision which prevented any imposition being played upon them, but the cause must be attributed to some other source. The auras of certain individuals contain elements which prevent the manifestation of psychic phenomena. Even of Jesus of Nazareth the statement is made that he could do no mighty works in certain places on account of unbelief; but here the failure can scarcely have been occasioned by unbelief, else Spiritualism could have made but little progress. The majority of converts have set out on their investigations with a deep-rooted feeling that such things as were related could not take place, but the facts beat them, dissipating their unbelief. It may be that an inordinate prejudice against the subject may set in operation certain vibrations against which the unseen operators cannot work; but honest doubt or critical observation have rarely any deterrent effect. As yet we are but "children groping for the light" as to causes and effects, but observation helps us to discover the prime conditions needed for satisfactory results.

Mr. Traill Taylor met with a similar reception to that meted out to Sir William Crookes when he published his Researches. His scientific confreres expected that he would curse the subject; but, unfortunately for his reputation, he gave it his blessing, and similarly, though everyone would have agreed that Mr. Taylor was the ablest person to enter on such an inquiry, when he made his report he met with the usual amount of ridicule. No one could point out more subtle precautions which he might have taken. Yet many said that undoubtedly he must have been tricked in some inexplicable way. Mr. Glendinning did great service to the Cause by publishing Mr. Taylor's address, with other matter relating to the subject contributed by himself and others, under the title of The Veil Lifted, with illustrations of many of the plates. This little volume has circulated in many quarters, and has on the whole been fairly criticised by the Secular press. The leading newspapers, such as the Glasgow Herald, and the Scotsman, of Edinburgh, did not doubt for a moment the honesty and sagacity of those engaged in the experiments. Mr. W.T. Stead, in the Review of Reviews, said the reputations of Mr. Taylor and Mr. Glendinning were "above reproach." This he could say with all confidence, as Mr. Glendinning had been for long one of his esteemed and cherished friends.

CHAPTER XXIII

WONDERFUL MATERIALISATIONS

To Mr. Glendinning I am indebted for a careful study of the phenomena of Materialisation, which prove that spirits in these days can and do clothe themselves in matter, so that we can see with our eyes and feel with our hands those who have literally come back from the grave. The ancient records of such occurrences have for long been met with a half belief, or a positive denial. And, after all, statements about a man who had a miraculous birth and a miraculous resurrection can scarcely be of much service to an age that must see some kind of law ruling everywhere. I had witnessed many materialisations, had read and re-read the carefully tabulated experiments of Sir William Crookes, but again and again in the home of Mr. Glendinning I had the privilege of looking at the phenomena so closely as to settle to my entire satisfaction the reality of such appearances.

My friend had for years literally dwelt in the presence of these risen dead, and his loving spirit and open mind had been warmed and cheered thereby. The medium through whom these phenomena were brought into view was a Mrs. Titford, a young married woman, whose family had all some portion of mediumistic gifts. Her father, Mr. Davis, had for a long time been a Secularist, feeling, like so many, that on the question of a future life no evidence had ever been forthcoming. A man of intellect and insight, he found nowhere a theory of the universe and of man's destiny which was at all satisfactory.

Charles Bradlaugh and G.W. Foote were to Mr. Davis (Mrs. Titford's father) the best exponents of what could be learned of nature and her methods. At the Hall of Science a debate had been arranged between Dr. George Sexton, who had himself been at one time the champion of Secularism, and G.W. Foote, of The Freethinker. Mr. Davis, accompanied by a fellow-work man, a Mr. Eglinton, attended this debate, and listened to the pro and con statements which were made by the debaters. At the close they stood for a long time talk ing together on the subject to which they had been listening. Dr. Sexton had given out some strange and seemingly weird stories of spirit intervention. That a man with some pretensions to scholarship should see in this Spiritualism facts worthy of the attention of man kind was sufficient to make these two Secularists pause and wonder.

"What do you think of it ?" the one said to the other.

"Let us try at home, and see for ourselves what, if anything, will be revealed." And thus they parted with open minds.

Both families began their quest to find an entrance into the society of the dead, and each in due season received the reward which all earnest, honest endeavour meets with. Out of Mr. Eglinton's family there came one of the most useful mediums, William Eglinton, whose phenomena for many years created much excitement. Books were written about the marvels which occurred in his presence, and so great a man as Mr. Gladstone was startled by what have been called Eglinton's slatewriting experiments.

Mr Davis was equally fortunate with the members of his family, two of whom were present when I first sat at Mr. Glendinning's. We gathered in the spacious drawing-room, across the middle of which was spread a curtain, and behind this was placed an organ. We sat in the front portion of the room around a table. At one end was Mr. Davis, at the other his daughter, Mrs. Titford, on each side of whom were her sister and an artist friend of my own, who had come with me from Glasgow. Mr. and Mrs. Glendinning, with myself, made up the other sitters. We had not been seated long when raps were heard, and these raps intimated the positions the sitters were to take up. We heard a voice speaking quite clearly, but saw no one. The voice was addressed as "Harry," and I soon knew that he was a young boy, one of Mr. Davis's children. The gas was lowered by unseen instructors, and immediately "Harry's" presence was felt by all the sitters. For each he had a word and a touch, while to his father he was most affectionate. Not a doubt was in the mind of this father but that here was his boy, once regarded as lost. To myself he came close, and he put his soft face to mine and kissed me. At my back was the piano, which he played in a very amateurish way, chatting away all the time in the bright happy tones that a boy in the physical world would use. Soon he was at the other end of the room, where the organ was, and we heard him pulling out the stops and bringing forth music.

Other members of Mr. Davis's family came and touched us; solid beings, with all the characteristics of earth. A form, with a light, came and stood beside me and Mr. Davis, who at once said, "Is that you, darling?" "Yes," the voice responded, and the form stooped down and kissed him. It was the wife of his bosom come back to soften the break, and give him the certainty of her presence.

I thought to myself at the time: "The thing which I behold is actually taking place at this moment; it is not a dream, but a veritable reality, which all through life I shall be able to bring out from memory to refresh and sustain me."

Mr Davis, speaking as he would have done had his wife still been an earth inhabitant, said to her, "I am better than I have been," and asked her if she would magnetise his chest. I felt the form opening his vest (I had still the grip of his hand; Mrs. Glendinning held the other) and rubbing him vigorously. Each spoke of the troubles and worries that had been, and of the joy there would be when all of earth was over and the re-union took place. I prayed while these things were occurring that I might be left with the clear memory to set down all that was taking place. A heavy musical box was several times lifted up in the air, played over our heads, and wound up again and again by the unseen operators. We had on the table some sheets of paper which had been treated with luminous paint, and these were lifted up by the visitors so that we might see their faces. I looked at "Harry" carefully, and saw a young face, about ten years of age, with curly hair. This is a record of but one of many such gatherings that I was privileged to attend.

At other times I heard the organ played with wonderful effect, showing that a skilled musician was at work, in contrast with the childish efforts of "Harry." I might chronicle pages of similar phenomena occurring in the presence of this medium: a simple, loving-hearted woman. At times she would retire behind the curtain, and then the several forms would walk out in our midst and come quite close to us. Members of Mr. Glendinning's family would make their appearance, and cause tears of gladness to run down the old man's cheek. His faithful, loving heart had received for years all the consolation which the spirit circle alone can give—a perennial outpouring which bathes the soul with warm sunlight.

I was once present at a small gathering in the home of Mr. Davis, at Mildmay Park. We numbered six—Mr Davis and his two daughters, Mr. Glendinning, Mr. David Duguid and myself. It was a small room, containing a couch, table, a few chairs, and a small organ. Several portraits were around the walls, which I looked at before the sitting began. There was no curtain or screen in the room, and we had placed the piano stool and chair against the door, making certain that no one could come in. Several luminous slates were placed upon the table, so that we might see the forms when they built up in our midst. I sat with the medium's hand in mine, the hands of all the other sitters being joined. When the gas had been put out, I at once felt hands touching my legs and patting my back, but saw no one. I then felt a form pressing between me and Mr. Davis; I was conscious of a being crushing against my shoulder, and bending down to the table it took up one of the luminous slates. I then saw quite clearly the face and form. It was again the wife, who kissed Mr. Davis as before. "Let me look into your face," I said, when she turned round, holding the light over her head. I looked at the face intently for several seconds; there were the full cheeks, and I recognised the likeness to the portrait I had seen before our sitting began. I was calm and composed in every sense, thinking to myself: "What would the out side world say about this great reality? "She bent over me and kissed my forehead. There was no room or place for doubt; this person had come amongst us, a spirit, and from the psychic emanations of those assembled, had built up a structure like the one she had possessed on earth, which, like the appearance of Jesus in the upper room, we could see and feel. It was a death blow to what was engraved on tombstones about resting in the grave with the" sure and certain hope of a joyful resurrection." "Harry" again came, and talked to his father about events which had occurred in the home at other times, showing that he was often present, though unseen.

Shortly after a tall form made her appearance behind Mr. Davis and myself, and I heard the word "Uncle." "Is that you, Annie?" Mr. Davis asked. She had now the luminous slate in her hand. "Come here," he said. She went close up to him, while I looked eagerly at the form and features while she was speaking.

"Will you come close to me?" I asked, and then she bent over, and, looking into the face, I saw the sparkling dark eyes and the altogether pleasant face of a young woman. The face was only a few inches from mine, so I could have recognised it anywhere—

a spirit clothed with matter. She then went to the organ, and, pulling out the stops, played "The Lost Chord" with fine execution.

I asked what her age had been when she left the earth, and said that I judged her, from appearance, to have been twenty-five or twenty-six years of age, when I was told by Mr. Davis that she had died at twenty-five, and that while on earth she had been acknowledged as a fine musician. "Harry," who always seemed to be about, asked us to sing, after which he played over some bars of a nursery rhyme which Mr. Glendinning had taught him. The difference in execution between "Harry" and "Annie" was very marked. The one was a childish effort, the other that of a finished musician.

Truly it was a Pentecostal time. We were like the apostles of old, "all of one accord," and therefore no retarding influence kept the spirits back. The truth of Tennyson's lines was realised:

In vain shalt thou, or any, call
The spirits from their golden day,
Except, like them, thou too canst say,
My spirit is at peace with all.

The reverse side of the picture was never felt at these gatherings:

But when the heart is full of din,
And doubt beside the portal waits,
They can but listen at the gates,
And hear the household jar within.

There now stood beside Mr. Glendinning a tall, thin form holding the luminous card over his head like a college cap, so as to throw light on the features. "This is our John," Mr. Glendinning said. No doubts were there, and the lost son leaned over and caressed the worthy father, bringing forth joyous tears.

Other departed members of this family came, each with his message of love and cheer. "John," the son, said to his father that he was going back to help his mother, who was in poor health at home. As the time went on the power seemed to increase rather than diminish. "Harry" seemed to be more solid than ever, moving about and chatting, and letting us feel the fine drapery with which he was clothed. While he was at my left side, talking, I felt a tiny hand on my forehead, a touch with which I had been familiar for years, and which had in the past ofttimes strengthened me for the battle of life. "What do you see, Harry?" I asked. "A child's hand on your forehead," he replied. While he was speaking I felt an arm placed round my neck, though I saw nothing, all of which was of deep import to me. I think this was the climax of all the sittings I had ever attended. No doubt the power contributed by Mr. Duguid helped to strengthen the manifestations, but the sweet harmony that prevailed amongst us did more than aught else. When we had let hands go and lit up the gas there were the stool and chair against the door just as when we sat down. I have had many similar meetings, at which Mrs. Titford was present, where friends of my own have come back in this way and made their presence clear, not in Mr. Glendinning's or Mr. Davis's house only, but in my own abode in Glasgow. One striking circumstance I will mention before I have done with these manifestations. Once, when the conditions were not very good, some of the few sitters being in indifferent health, and a difficulty felt in obtain ing the necessary darkness, a form stood beside the medium, which we all saw in the dim light without the aid of luminous cards. I instinctively knew who it was, a close relation of my own, who went out of the physical life while I was living in the darkness, and whose removal at the time raised within me much of question ing as to the "whence and whither," if any.

I said, "I know it is you, Maggie," naming her in full, but I was at once corrected. I had used her maiden name, with which I was most familiar, when she gave her married name, which was far from being a common one. All I have been saying regarding these form manifestations is only on a par with what Sir Wm. Crookes has vouched for in his Researches into the Phenomena of Spiritualism. These are actual occurrences, and I have sought to set them down with the accuracy with which they were recorded in my diary immediately after the sittings.

It is because Spiritualists have had such experiences as these that their faith in the future life is strong. Haeckel may say that people cling to the doctrine of immortality owing to conservative tradition, and the stamping of untenable dogma on the mind in early years, but those who have the confident assurance of the after life cast aside tradition and dogma. It was the Spiritual facts they met with which beat them, and helped them to vanquish and abolish the fear of death. A new and brilliant star has arisen over the world, but the appearance of a newly created star is notable at first only to star-gazers and weather prophets, who point out its reality in the galaxy of the heavens. And so this star of hope and promise is shining on men, who one day will wonder that they did not sooner observe its movements over their heads. The duty of man should be to show hospitality to new thought, to look at the untried with open mind. Newspapers and tongues may defame what is true and noble, but the KNOWERS of a real truth should stand erect, feeling that heaven has sent them its angels to give a new and brighter colouring to human life.

CHAPTER XXIV

WORKERS AND ORGANISATIONS

In the summer of 1889 many people were stirred when Annie Besant, so long the champion of cultured Atheism, gave out that she had swung back to a recognition of the spiritual in man. She called herself a Theosophist, but Theosophy to many was but one of the sides of Spiritualism. Without spiritual evidences there could have been no cult of Theosophists. The newspapers were flooded with matter relating to the conversion, all of which tended to open the minds of many to the important truth that there is more in life than is visible. The old spirit, which once upon a time pronounced the man or woman who did not accept the orthodox faith as being guilty of all forms of immorality, had been dying down. The noble and pure lives of such brave souls as George Jacob Holyoake and Annie Besant destroyed much of the old spirit of malignity, so that when Mrs. Besant stood forth in her new dress there were few who did not give her credit for heroism and honesty. Gerald Massey had, in the days when she was militant against all spiritual belief, felt proud of her courage, and said that while she might murmur that there was no soul, the great of the past came back to earth with power. He called her one of God's faithful few, though she knew it not. She had gained a unique position in the world's esteem. The world saw that all through her life she had been seeking to follow truth with an earnest spirit, and that she was brave enough, when she met with facts which contradicted her old beliefs, to speak out with boldness. The infidel is not he or she who opposes the popular faith, but he who speaks words with the tongue which he does not believe in his heart—who speaks with a half-shadow of a belief what is plausible, contented with saying a nothing that will look like a something. The man in a pulpit, who screens his unbelief amidst scriptural phrases, and holds back that which he does know, is the real infidel. Mrs. Besant has been an inspiration to many, and the fine quality of her life will form a bright page in human history. Since that turning-point in 1889 she has been ceaseless in her advocacy of the spiritual in man, and of a spiritual universe, towards which we are all hastening.

Several books appeared at this time, which did not fall from the spiritualist press, but which dealt with spiritual truths, such as had been revealed to those who had been in close touch with spiritual phenomena. Mrs. Oliphant, the well-known writer, issued a series of volumes from the reputable publishing house of Wm. Blackwood, the basic facts of which could only have been gained through mediumship. These were *The Little Pilgrim*, *The Little Pilgrim in the Unseen*, and *Old Lady Mary*, which were read by thousands, and must have made a deep impression on many readers. They were not given forth as facts, nor did they present the brightest side of Spiritualism. Still, all who read them must have felt they were more than dreams of the imagination. Mrs. Oliphant, when she wrote the life of Edward Irving, was forced to look upon the occult side of his life, with its "gifts of tongues"and inspirings from an unseen source, and, no doubt, the influence derived from that connection followed her in after years. Since then she has written *Laurence Oliphant's Life*, which abounded with the spiritual, much of which I have already dealt with in the story of the Owens. So many are prone to dwell upon the surface, and will not enter into the palace of truth and new life; they speak of the outer as if this were all, while deep down are treasures which would supply the wants of humanity. When Dr. Johnson was asked, "Have we not evidence enough of the soul's immortality?" orthodox in creed as he was, he exclaimed, "I wish for more. "Today the thinking man or woman who has cast aside Bible infallibility needs this evidence more than Dr. Johnson did, but how few are so earnest as he was in seeking to find it. On such a question each one needs to believe with the whole united soul: a belief that can be checked by every faculty. The old Spiritualism belongs to myth and tradition; the new Spiritualism demands the facts of a common experience.

One who has been largely instrumental in bringing such facts before the view of the world I first met at this period of my spiritual journey: one who had been tuned by the heavenly messengers and who sang out the truths of that other real life— this was Miss MacCreadie. Her spiritual sight had been open from childhood, and she had long felt she was strangely constituted ere chance or direction brought her into the spirit circle. What numbers of hearts she has been the instrument of gladdening! Mothers have told me how she has given them back their dead, and healed the old wound. Slowly and steadily she won her way into the loving hearts of many who esteem her for her sincerity and devotion to the truth. Tests in abundance, which satisfy the hungering hearts, she has given forth for many years, and when the inquirer asks, "Where shall the authentic be personally met with ?" satisfaction is almost invariably found through her. For years past in London she has occupied a high position as a clairvoyante, and hundreds of times from the public platform has she given descriptions of the departed, and messages conveying knowledge which only the dead could give, so clearly as to startle many inquirers and bring them nearer to a knowledge of the truth. Scotland gave her birth and education, and the land abounds with many seers such as Miss MacCreadie, who, however, are afraid to speak of their experiences. Old friends, through her lips, have made their presence perfectly clear to me, as vividly real as any other event in life. People whom she has described as standing beside me have afterwards made their appearance by my side on the photographic plate. I have watched her progress as a public worker, and have ever admired her kindliness of spirit, her real trust in the spirit people be hind her, and her devotion to the cause of Spiritualism in its public propaganda. She is a woman who has been a source of blessing to hundreds.

In the home circle, where only harmony reigns, evidence of spirit presence is readily obtained, and many mediums who in private give the moat satisfactory results, when placed upon a public platform, where all qualities of aura are presented, fail to present clear pictures which can be recognised. With Miss MacCreadie, however, it is otherwise. Strangers have often dropped into public meetings, perhaps to scoff, and have been arrested by hearing a description given of some lost one, or by getting some message which could only have come from beyond the veil. Though Miss MacCreadie has many calls on her in a private capacity, she has ever recognised the need for a public presentation of facts, and her spirit gifts have done great service to the Cause in this direction.

We scarcely ever see or know what changes of thought are taking place in our midst. What is going to mould the next generation steals upon us almost silently. The ideas which were held by our fathers have, imperceptibly to us, been modified. There is still the same name, Christianity, used glibly and without much meaning in it, and the same Church standards, but our views of these have altered. We have got hold of brighter conceptions, more rational and just. What has been thrown away is no loss, but a gain. The quickened souls of humanity could not now believe in a hell of brimstone, or a devil who was continually the victor over man and God. The old hell fire has been damped down, and the wild blasphemy against the Most High that He was the jailer rather than the Father of mankind rooted out, never to arise again. The brighter thoughts which have slowly found their way into all churches regarding the Bible, the atonement, the person of Jesus, are part of the evolutionary process that has been going on, and has been fanned and kept ablaze by the spirits' influence. The truths enunciated by Carlyle or Emerson might have "Thus saith the Lord" written over them with more truth than much that is in the Bible. No modern prophet has ever had such degrading ideas of God as were entertained by some of the writers who have been called infallible. That the teachings of Spiritualism are in harmony with the most exalted thoughts of modern seers shows clearly to many minds that the spirit world works through many avenues, fertilising the soil and making it ready for new grain. The great fact established by Spiritualism, that dead men come back to earth, settles so many questions about which the world had doubts. It destroys the idea of waiting in the grave for a physical resurrection. It abolishes the theatrical conception of a universal Judgment Day, when, through years of communion, you witness the moral and spiritual growth of those who were once degraded. When the breathing in of sentiments and ideas from another plane of being is seen to be a fact, and inspiration becomes rational, it helps you to comprehend how Bibles were written. In the light of modern mediumship Jesus is seen to be a man, capable of imbibing and revealing truth, through whom the denizens of that other world manifested as they do now.

Spiritualism is the one key to all the religions of the world, the emancipator of man from priestly tyranny, and the uplifter of his being to the realm of real religion. What an idle dream it is that it can ever be submerged! Men might as well war against the growth of vegetation or fight against the elements, as seek to battle with this strong force that now comes with full life to take its place in the homes and hearts of humanity. It has the omnipotence of

God upon its side, and the loving power of His servants, who, with seeing eyes and loving hearts, will work for human redemption. Men may cry "infidel" and "devil worship," but those of pure minds and feelings, who have felt the joys that the knowledge has brought them, who have the certainty through every faculty that they hold a mighty truth, are not discouraged. It is the largest and best message of God to man, part of the evolution which the ripened faculties of mortals have seen in other realms. It ever marches onward, gaining adherents each day. Some only see it dimly at first, but soon it will dawn upon all that it is in our midst for a mighty purpose, the outline of which we only see faintly at present. There is never any retreat on the part of those who have seen its great realities, though there are too many who are afraid to speak out boldly that which they do know, and who still outwardly walk as if they were satisfied with the religious think ing around them. They are waiting until Spiritualism becomes a recognised truth, and then we shall hear of their great devotion. It was men and women of a different stamp to this who called together a conference of spiritual workers at Manchester in July 1890. There had been conventions in the earlier years of the movement, the first taking place at Darlington in 1865, and another at Newcastle in 1866, followed by one held in London in 1867; but these were minor affairs in comparison with the gatherings which took place in Manchester at the instigation of Dr. and Mrs. Britten, John Lamont, J.J. Morse, and E.W. Wallis. It was inspiring to come into close touch with so many whose souls had felt the immense value of the truth of spirit communion. To be in a world where all is vague regarding that other life, where nothing is known about messages of love and sympathy coming from the beyond, where all is shut out, or so nebulous and weak as to be valueless, and then to cross from this into the sphere of knowledge, lifts one into an atmosphere of content and peace, which no pulpit theology can give.

> *Ah! we are not alone. The countless dead are near us.*
> *Their warm, strong hands we feel.*
> *For fifty living souls, ten thousand dead souls hear us,*
> *And answer with their love our passionate appeal.*

To come into touch with such men as John Lamont, so self-contained, so sympathetic and brave, and yet so mild, simple-hearted and humane, was to receive evidence of how much nobility was enshrined in our human nature. His presence transmitted a light which shone in his own heart; the reality and meaning of the new revealment had caught hold of all his faculties, and he had given himself fully to make it known to others. Its advocacy had cost him something in the worldly sense. A strong Presbyterian in Liverpool, closely connected with church work, when he set forth the new light that had entered into his life he lost severely in pocket. He was a most picturesque figure, not dramatic, yet moved with vehemence and soft feeling alternately, to which his Highland accent gave additional effect. He was a great figure in many ways, worthy to be ranked amongst the world's heroes. He had got free from church creeds and articles of faith, for he knew for certain that he was spiritually related to the unseen world. This was his religion; not a mere profession or assertion, but the outcome of knowledge. Dr. and Mrs. Britten, ever full of the subject, threw themselves into the work at the conference with their whole hearts, while Mr. J.J. Morse and Mr. and Mrs. Wallis were everywhere, to see that all went on successfully. The secretary was Mr. James B. Tetlow, earnest and sincere, nimble and orderly, who had spent days and nights in focussing all the arrangements. Much enthusiasm was kindled as the result of the gathering, the full result of which will never be known publicly. Valuable suggestions were offered, brilliant settings forth of the truth given by many speakers, and an amount of fervour shown which did good to all. At one of the meetings during the week there was present a young woman connected with the Salvation Army, and wearing their uniform. She had been seeing spirits for some time, and had had so many strange experiences that her convictions had been changed, and she came amongst us to get more know ledge. When I heard her story of the Army work, I understood how this movement had existed for so long in spite of its association with an antiquated theology. It had been an expression of real piety; men and women, out of the divine sympathy of their nature, going down to the depths to seek out and save the ungrown, and this woman dwelt on the heroism and sacrifice of those who, without thinking much of creeds, gave themselves to succour the fallen. In after years this Army worker became an apostle of the new truth she had imbibed. Known as Miss Cotterill, she became a lecturer and clairvoyante, and has done much good work for the Cause.

It was not an easy path for her to take, as she was subjected to much contumely, her old associates of the Salvation Army following her about at times, and calling her a child of the devil. Many pleasant memories were left with me as the result of the Manchester conference. I felt strengthened and encouraged, and more eager than ever to listen to those who beckon us onward.

> The hearts whose loss our faithless souls deplore
> Were never quite so close, nor half so sweet.
> The lonelier we are here,
> The less we have to fear,
> For on the other side more dear ones stand.

At this period I was brought into correspondence with one of the most notable of men, whose name will one day be sounded forth in many quarters as one who was an instrument to throw much light on the mystery of life and being—W. Stainton Moses, then editor of *Light*, and a medium through whom was given a volume of spiritual treasures called *Spirit Teachings*. It is a book which, if read, will break down much of the scepticism which exists regarding the possibility of light streaming from the other world. A clergyman of the Church of England, he was full of the bewildering delusions and confusions of what makes up traditional Christianity. Some day it will be surprising that sane men with open eyes could ever have believed the set of doctrines which once ruled in this world of ours. This man fought tenaciously for the truth of these doctrines when the spirit teachers first came into rapport with him. He would not be moved from his position that they were all the world needed, and though he admitted the teachings of Spiritualism were lofty and pure, still they were not Christian. He was forced to acknowledge that those personalities who used his own hand to set down their message of love and wisdom were intelligent, but he criticised and warred for long against their thought, until ultimately his prejudices were broken down, and he saw that after all Christianity might be one of the "little systems that have their day and cease to be." Truth is ever being transformed. As the Rev. H.R. Haweis has so well said in his *Dead Pulpit*:

> *Less and less of what belongs to the past shall*
> *be of any avail for the future, only a residuum*
> *can be used, and even that, like old building*
> *material, seldom in its original form.*

Mahomet called his spiritual experiences "Revelation," and credited the Angel Gabriel as being the revealer; but though Mahomet's word has become the spiritual food of millions, it lacks the evidential authority which a close study of the life of Stainton Moses gives. Prophets of olden time came also to Stainton Moses, but this was never set forth as an authority for accepting the message. It is the message itself which becomes of value, not the name of the inspirer; and these messages, when read with an open mind, will help to shape the thought of the future years, and bring home to the world the confident feel ing that none of the saints of old drank dry the inspiration of heaven, but that all the time it flows in on receptive minds.

So much of value from the spirit spheres had never before been chronicled. Pregnant truths given at the spirit circle leave their impress only on the hearers, but these records of what was given to Stainton Moses will be reprinted again and again, for there are embedded therein truths which will make our old idolatries fall, and build up a religion of use and beauty in harmony with the ever-widening thoughts of men. They help us to get free from tradition and bring us close to natural fact.

Charles Buller once said in a letter to his old tutor, Carlyle: "I have not yet found that faith which I can believe, and none among the creeds of the world that I could wish to be true. I could picture to myself a bright creed truly, but to think it could be real because it was pretty would be childish indeed." Minds such as Buller's have already found in the philosophy of Spiritualism, and in such books as Stainton Moses's *Spirit Teachings,* all that was needed for the heart's hunger; a gospel in harmony with reason and with nature, in unison with what noble souls in all ages would wish to be true, and strengthened by such facts as appeal to every faculty of our human nature. As speculations, many parts of the spiritual gospel have filtered into the hearts of men, but these impulses have been as much the spirits' work as the fuller blossoming with which the world is becoming familiar. We can see the spring from which so many have had draughts of comfort, and can understand the brave thoughts which find expression in the writings of a Carlyle, an Emerson, or a Theodore Parker, for these also were but servants of the spirits proclaiming the fuller day of light and knowledge.

The year 1892 was marked by the publication of a very remarkable book of spiritual experiences written by Florence Marryat, which for a season caused considerable noise. The fact that she was a well-known novelist led some persons to think that her somewhat strong statements regarding the spirits' contact with mortals must also be part of the fiction which she had formerly dealt with. She was, however, a strong and confirmed Spiritualist, somewhat of a medium herself, or at least one of those susceptible beings who give such conditions as enable the spirit people to come close to them. Her book, *There is no Death*, undoubtedly set very many persons thinking, and drew a consider able number into our ranks, where they have remained. She very naturally asked why she should be disbelieved. Readers accepted readily the statements of other travellers of repute, and had any one of them affirmed that in their wanderings they had encountered a goldfield of undoubted excellence; thousands of fortuneseekers would have left their native land and rushed to secure the glittering treasure. She claimed the same ground for obtaining belief. She also had a well known name and a public reputation, a tolerable brain and sharp eyes, and was firm in her assertion that what she had witnessed, others, with the same perseverance, might witness for themselves. Spiritual phenomena, however, do not find the welcome we are inclined to give to new discoveries relating to mundane affairs. Dr. Robert Chambers, in writing to Alfred Russel Wallace, regretted that Huxley would not give a moment's patience to the consideration of such a subject — a subject, he says, "so infinitely transcending all those of physical science in the potential results." Chambers found the fullest satisfaction while in the body, and once at a séance where Sir William Crookes was in charge rapped out the message, "It is a glorious truth. It was the solace of my earth life, and the triumph over the change called death." Many strong attestations as to the reality of the facts are scattered through books of the past thirty years, but somehow we have the faculty of ignoring these and only seeing what is of much less value. There is nothing in Florence Marryat's book to which the Spiritualist of experience cannot subscribe. I have sat with several of the mediums she names, and with some have met with even more striking phenomena. My personal contact with Miss Marryat enables me to say that she was just such a person as would naturally give forth the best conditions to bring about a satisfactory séance. The Glasgow Association, taking advantage of the popularity of the book, brought her to Glasgow, where, in the Waterloo Rooms, she thrilled many hearts with her recital. I had the privilege of having her as my guest for several days, and learned much from her regarding her father, Captain Marryat, the famous novelist of our boyhood's days. He also had been much attached to the occult side of life, and had met with spiritual experiences, but in his day there was wanting the key which had opened so wide the door of spiritual realities to his daughter.

There is undoubtedly in many quarters an intellectual repugnance to the subject of Spiritualism. Why, it would be most difficult to say. Many of my friends will listen to me on other topics; but on this, to me, the subject of subjects, they keep silent, and care not to discuss it; though it is not a question for discussion, but rather for experiment and observation. Nathaniel Hawthorne, while in Italy, was surrounded by Spiritualists—Mrs. Browning, Flowers, the sculptor, and many others—but his wife, when at séances and inclined to give the question a fair hearing, had to restrain herself, because, as she said, her husband had such a repugnance to the whole thing. His own words are a revelation of his state of mind, and these words pretty well portray the position of many: "What most astonishes me is the indifference with which I listen to these marvels. They throw old ghost stories quite in the shade; they bring the whole world of spirits down amongst us visibly and audibly; they are absolutely proved to be sober facts by evidence that would satisfy us of any other alleged realities; and yet I cannot force my mind to interest itself in them. They are facts to my understanding, which it might have been anticipated would have been the last to acknowledge them, but they seem not to be facts to my intuitions and deep perceptions."

Here, surely, is the revelation of a dual nature, but it is at all events of more service to other minds than the contemptuous denial of the facts which some great men have recklessly set forth. They are at least recognised as realities, and some, reading those Italian Note Books of Hawthorne's, may from his words be pointed to a realm of activities greater than Browning cared to explore. The year 1892 saw the translation of many eminent men, some of them eminent to the world, others only great to those who had been brought into touch with spiritual facts. One of these, Tennyson, the great poet, was much of a Spiritualist, and even delighted to con verse on the subject. Stainton Moses he sent for when in his neighbourhood, to talk over his wonderful mediumistic experiences. Alfred Eussel Wallace, in his *My Life*, tells us how William Allingham, the poet, was asked by Tennyson to bring the great naturalist with him on a visit. Dr. Wallace says: "The poet lit his pipe and we sat round the fire, and soon got on the subject of Spiritualism, which was evidently what he had wished to talk to me about." Wallace gave him the names of one or two trustworthy mediums, but whether Tennyson ever had sittings with them he did not hear. A great soul to me, James Murray Templeton, also passed over at this time: one of the sweetest truth-loving men I have ever met, with but one desire—to stand on the side of truth and right. Only virtue and the uplifting of his fellows had any charm for him. He saw in

Spiritualism something of a new Redeemer and he followed it devotedly. Here in Glasgow, I introduced him to Rosamond Dale Owen, who became his wife after the decease of her first husband, Laurence Oliphant. James Murray Templeton passed away at Haifa, Syria, where they were resident at the time. It is rare to meet with those great souls who sacrifice wealth as he did for the sake of a beautiful ideal. A golden memory of human worth he is to me, and though only known in his inward parts to a few, the world is all the better that he has lived. Ofttimes have I been stirred with the thought, "Am I living uprightly as he did, and not skimming over life's duties?" Stainton Moses passed over shortly afterwards, a man whose name will gather fame all through the coming ages, and the full purport of whose life's work will not be clearly seen for a season.

A man of sterling honesty and devotion to human weal, his memory has been truculently treated by some who had not the vision to recognise the true grandeur and nobility of this phenomenal man, who, along with D.D. Home, will ever stand as a worthy apostle of the great Spiritual Reformation.

CHAPTER XXV

SPIRITUALIST PERIODICALS

Almost from my first association with the movement I had been giving expression to my feelings in the spiritualist journals. To the pages of *The Medium* and *Daybreak*, conducted by James Burns, I contributed many articles dealing with phases of the movement, and later on, when *The Two Worlds* was set agoing, under the editorship at first of Mrs. Britten, and afterwards of Mr. E.W. Wallis, I was a pretty frequent contributor. Mr. Wallis was a considerable help to me, with his kindly encouragement and advice. Many of the addresses which I prepared for delivery before the Glasgow Association found a larger constituency in the pages of *The Two Worlds*. Four lectures on "The Rise and Progress of Modern Spiritualism" were printed from week to week, and afterwards issued in a small volume. This résumé of the Spiritualism of the age brought down to date has already found a large sale, and may form a skeleton upon which a larger history may be built. Nothing delighted me more than the receipt of a letter from Andrew Jackson Davis regarding my little book. Carlyle was never more thrilled by letters from Goethe than I was by the kindly words of commendation of the greatest seer of this age. He said of it: "It is a clear, manly, true presentation, and the world will be better for it." In a postscript he added some words regarding his own life's work, which I have treasured. It read as follows: "Since the noble Galen's first visit in 1843 to this hour my life's motive may be stated thus: To make it a paramount duty to develop to the utmost all natural faculties, whether of mind or body; not as instruments of self-gratification, nor even self-advancement, but in order to render them more efficient tools in the service of humanity." Since that day I have had many letters from the great spiritual teacher. No honour could have been conferred which I should have valued more than this coming close to one of nature's nobles, the most highly-illuminated man of any age.

> *In him are gleams of such heroic splendour,*
> *As light this cold dark world up like a star*
> *Arrayed in glory for the eyes of heaven;*
> *And a great heart that beat according music*
> *With theirs of old—God-likest kings of men!*

The Rev. John Page Hopps, in the columns of *The Coming Day*, also had an appreciative notice, saying: "It was the very story that wanted telling; it is all very simple and unadorned, but that is an advantage." During the year 1893 the name of another prominent public man was heard of as giving acceptance to the facts of Spiritualism. This was Mr. W.T. Stead, acknowledged to be a person of great journalistic power. The courage which had characterised him in his warfare against the sin of Babylon was still to the front, and it seemed sufficient for him to know a thing was true to speak out boldly all in its behalf. There is never a welcome for the man who comes forth to declare the higher truths of life. Mr. Stead's declaration that he knew spirit people only brought him the rough treatment that had been tendered to Sir William Crookes when he entered on the same field of exploration. Mr. Stead was known to all as a man of action, and no sooner had he witnessed the phenomena than he began to weave his experiences in the form of fiction in a Christmas number of *The Review of Reviews*. Soon that popular periodical had much in its pages relating to Spiritualism. The subject had caught hold of him as it has done so many, and would not let him go. His own experiences in automatic writing were most conclusive to himself. A friend whom he had known in the earth life, whom he calls "Julia," made her communications to him through his hand, and showed her individuality so clearly that he could not doubt. All manner of the most conclusive tests met him on the way, and these he let the public know of without any hesitation. Some men would have published such experiences privately, in fear that such beliefs might damage their worldly prospects. Not so W.T. Stead. The truth at all cost, as it is seen by him, has been the dominant feature of his life. Knowing how real were spiritual facts, and conscious of the world's need of the knowledge of them, he ventured in 1893 on the publication of a spiritual quarterly, which was named *Borderland*, on the suggestion of that time-honoured worker, Mr. J.J. Morse.

Before the first number appeared he invited counsel from all the great men of his day, bishops, parsons, psychical researchers, scientists, politicians, and men of letters.

It was amusing to read some of the epistles which his request drew forth, and a few of these, one day, will be recalled and placed in line with the Italian philosophers' treatment of Galileo. Christianity, which today so much needs facts to strengthen it, casts off the one power which alone can relate the marvels on which it has lived to present-day occurrences of a similar type. The Church is dead, insensible, and blind; it ignores the living forces, or, worse still, denounces them. It does not see the dry rot which is eating into the whole fabric, nor will it until the whole building collapses. Spiritual evidences—the future life evidenced by facts that can be seen and felt—should have been welcomed with open arms, and hosannas to the Highest sung in gratitude for the precious gift. Not so, however; reviling and contempt have been its reception. The benefactor is not seen, or, if seen, is despised and rejected. The Archbishop of Canterbury (Tait) had no helpful words to give. He who drew such an immense salary for preaching about an invisible world, and was an avowed believer in the possibility of communications reaching mankind from the great beyond, could only write such twaddle as "It might be dangerous to touch the subject!"

It was the old story. Every wonder performed by a Jew was of God; every other marvel must be of the devil. Bishop Temple, of The Essays and Reviews, once considered a heretic who had destroyed the faith of many, could only say that there was the extreme probability that investigators would be self-deluded, and tempted to delude others. All this shows how much the broad Church needs Spiritualism to give it a satisfactory resting-place. Spiritualism alone answers the craving for an assurance that there is a life beyond the grave, and that our loved ones survive.

A person is guilty of treason against the highest human instincts who fears the result of any investigation, be it philosophical, scientific, or historical. Roman Catholic Bishops and Fathers were satisfied with the revelations they already had, and could only regard with suspicion and aversion any other revelations than those which bore their "trade mark." The Psychical Researchers, whose mission should have been to prove or disprove the evidence that had been collected by Crookes, Wallace, De Morgan, and so many others, but who had only become chatterers and manufacturers of theories about which they quarrel amongst themselves, had little light to give. Balfour, Sidgwick, and Myers (until just before his death) were neither seers nor discoverers, and, with all their speech, they threw little light on man's survival of physical death. They ignored and neglected the gathering of the harvest, contenting themselves with looking at withered straws that served their purpose.

Some of the men of science revealed the common knowledge that a person may be great in one sphere and a Dogberry in another. The most notable exhibition of folly was that made by Lord Kelvin, whom the world looks upon as one of its greatest men. Carlyle regretted that the wise Tacitus saw nothing more in the Christian religion than a sink of abomination. What will the future Carlyles say of Lord Kelvin's great pronouncement on a subject which in a few years will be recognised by all? "I have nothing to do with *Borderland*," he says; "I believe that nearly everything in hypnotism and clairvoyance is imposture, and the rest bad observation."

Luckily the progress of the race is not much retarded by such blind and ignorant outbursts. It wants reasons for such condemnation. Thousands of men and women who may not be so famous as Lord Kelvin have found the truth which he ignorantly passed by. It was an unscientific, hasty statement, which will expose him to the ridicule of the scientists, even of the present day, who have had something to do with *Borderland*, and have found there the choicest blessing and the richest discovery of all the ages.

Wallace and Lodge, of course, had met with spiritual facts, and therefore their welcome to the new journal was cordial. Hay Lankester, who thinks that he exposed Dr. Slade, has not lost the old narrow spirit. His hatred of the whole matter is intense. Unashamed of his past, he still talks of fraud and insanity as being causes and results of psychic phenomena, ignoring all the light that has dawned. As Thomson J. Hudson has so pointedly said in his Law of Psychic Phenomena, "The man who denies the phenomena of Spiritualism is not entitled to be called a sceptic; he is simply ignorant; and it would be a hopeless task to attempt to enlighten him." Such curiosities as Ray Lankester and Frank Podmore we should have in our museums along with the extinct mastodons. They reflect not the spirit of this age, which seeks to give attention to every seeming trivial fact. They belong to an age of men that existed in some profusion, perhaps, before the introduction of the printing press. To call such men "scientific" we must alter the meaning of the word.

Borderland existed for some few years, and was the repository of many spiritual records. From its pages the future historian of the movement will be able to cull many spiritual facts. Unfortunately, Mr. Stead had associated with him in his work a lady called Miss X., who, unlike himself, had not much sympathy with Spiritualism. No doubt she was a medium of some power, but she was dominated largely by Professor Sidgwick, and was more representative of psychical research than Spiritualism. More than once her own experiences as a crystal gazer pointed to the spirit world seeking to bring home the facts of personal identity, but stubbornly she resisted all such evidence, spirit control being the point she would not admit. Even through her own powers "Sir Richard Burton" called her a Sidgwick-ridden seer. Spiritualism did not walk in silver slippers, and this lady did not care to be associated with a movement whose workers belonged largely to the common people. Had many rulers of the Pharisees been at the head of the movement it would have found her one of its most useful supporters. *Borderland* was brought to a conclusion in 1897; it was called a suspension of its operations only, but Mr. Stead has not since seen fit to resume its publication, though all the time he has given evidence of his devotion to Spiritualism, which crops up continually in all he writes.

I paid many visits to London and Manchester in 1893. When at the former place I had some long interviews with Mrs. Emma Hardinge Britten, who had by this time retired from the control of *The Two Worlds*, and had begun a monthly magazine called *The Unseen Universe*. How pleasant it was to sit and converse with one who had such an interesting history! In all lands and by the most prominent people she was held in esteem. I recollect how she told me the story of "Sir John Franklin" coming to her, and of how she knew for a certainty of his death when the first search parties were sent out to follow his trail in the Arctic regions; how "Sir John" stood for his portrait to a poor unknown lad called Weila Anderson, who limned the features, but did not know what to do with the picture when finished. The spirit, however, told him to send it to Mrs. Britten, who at the time was resident in New York. Mrs. Britten was quite a stranger to Anderson, who resided in the Far West.

"My joy was full," said Mrs. Britten, pointing to the Spiritualistic periodicals picture on the wall, "when I received the portrait of my long familiar control in this strange way." Some Spiritualists fail to appreciate to the full the many tests of identity which reach them: they are like Oliver Twist, ever asking for more; and though they know spirit return is perfectly true, with outsiders they fail to speak of its reality in a positive tone. Mrs. Britten was of another stamp. She lived on the communion, and could not contain herself regarding its power and beauty. She gave added strength to one's own conviction, and made gratitude spring up in the heart at being the recipient of so much choice blessing. In 1893 I was also, for the first time, brought into contact with Mr. and Mrs. Everitt, who had been for many years in the front of the movement, giving them selves for it without fee or hope of any earthly reward. I have spoken eulogistically about the work of so many mediums, that now, when I come to name this pair of devoted souls, words are almost lacking. How few there are, after all, who, blessed with great gifts, give them forth ungrudgingly as Mr. and Mrs. Everitt did! For forty years they either opened their own home or went out in many directions with the single thought of blessing others. Mrs. Everitt's powers as a medium for spirit raps and direct writings are so marked that no one can be in her presence without feeling that such potent facts are capable of redeeming the world from its materialism. In her presence, through the spirit raps, you are conscious of unseen visitors, who listen to what you say and respond each with his distinct characteristics. Clear and intelligent are the messages telegraphed by their code. It has been my privilege—a privilege which I shall ever esteem—to have been present at many successful meetings in their own home at Hendon, at other places in London, and in my house in Glasgow. The first time I was in their presence was at a hotel in London where I was staying. We were at the tea table, and when the visitors had gone out who were strangers to the subject, the flowers in profusion on the table at once began to wave, as much as saying, "Now we are ready for a talk." Soon we heard the raps, loud and clear in response to our questions, in all parts of the room—on the flower glasses on the table, or on the chairs where we sat. When a waiter came in for a minute, the flowers would cease to move and the raps stop, and when he had gone out again, the familiar friends would again make us conscious of their presence. Many thousands of persons have become familiar with these rappings, through the unselfish spirit which ever characterised these workers. Their highest joy has been to extend this knowledge wherever possible. All has been contributed without money charges, so that the scoffer cannot here offer the usual objection.

The phenomenon of direct writing has ofttimes been manifested through Mrs. Everitt's mediumship: one of the great spiritual facts not readily believed in by the outside world. I have handled, without any feeling of doubt, such writings, many of which relate to the early history of the Christian religion. I have seen one message with 794 words, which was written in five seconds; another of 786 words, which took seven seconds; another of 745 words, which took seven seconds. Sir William Crookes, who has sat several times with Mrs. Everitt, was the first to notice that there was no indentation on the back of the writings, each being as smooth as if lithographed. Several portions of the writing were in Latin, which they had to get translated, as neither Mr. nor Mrs. Everitt could claim scholarly gifts. Writings have also come to them in closed boxes.[5] I have had such evidence, getting some personal messages from their spiritual guides while partaking of their hospitality in their home at Hendon, near London.

A remarkable case of this direct writing took place while they were paying me a visit at Gourock, in the autumn of 1896. One Sunday we had been sitting in the dining-room, talking about old friends and fellow workers who had gone onwards, our speech being punctuated by the showers of raps all the time. While thus engaged, Mrs. James Bowman, the widow of that old, enthusiastic Spiritualist, who did so much to further the Cause in the early days of the movement, dropped in to pay a friendly visit. The greetings to her from the spirit side being so marked, and the sweetest of feeling prevailing amongst us all, we felt that a satisfactory séance might be held. We went upstairs to the drawing-room, prepared to wait for any manifestations that might occur. We sat down without either pencil or paper. Mrs. Everitt said she had an impulse to write something, and each began to search his pocket for pencil and paper. A young friend tore off the blank half from a letter he had, and handed the sheet over to Mrs. Everitt, with his pencil. She then began to write, automatically, a message purporting to be from "James Bowman" to his wife, which was most characteristic of the man and appropriate to the circumstances.

By this time it was getting dark, and we lit the gas. The paper was being handed round when my son and other members of the family came into the room. My son at once said, "This is very like Mr. Bowman's writing," a fact which I had noticed at once.

5. See also *The Direct Phenomena of Spiritualism*, by E.T. Bennett, already referred to.

He went to the piano and began singing "Rest in the Lord," while the paper went round from one to another. My brother-in-law turned the sheet over, looking at the other side, which was perfectly clean. I had looked carefully while the message was being written and had received the pencil back from Mrs. Everitt when she had done writing, and I returned it to the young man to whom it belonged. The sheet was handed back to Mrs. Everitt after all had carefully examined it. She kept it in her hand until my son had finished singing, when she said to Mrs. Bowman, "Perhaps you would like to keep the message ?" She was about to hand it over to Mrs. Bowman, when she said, "Why, here is something on the other side!" and we were all much startled to see that there had been written in the light, and without the aid of a pencil, for it had been previously returned to the owner, a response to what my son had said a few minutes before, about its being like Mr. Bowman's writing; the words were, "Yes, it is your husband's writing," and signed "J.B." Undoubtedly this part had come upon the paper by "direct" spirit writing. It bore a close resemblance to the writing of Mr. Bowman, and I would have accepted it as his hand writing had it been sent me while he was in the body. Nothing more satisfactory and conclusive as to spirit action could be presented. It was an example of the spirits' power to act on mortals when favourable conditions were given. We were all of one accord, of one mind; each of us was free from doubt, and so we were ministered to. Such phenomena do net come to all, nor when they are most greedily desired. There are persons, even amongst believers in spiritual realities, who are so constituted that they paralyse all phenomena.

There are again those who suspect fraud, and their state of mind acts as a blight on the work of the spirits. The spiritual medium of Galilee could perform no wonderful works in certain parts on account of unbelief. The spiritual mediums of today do not put so much stress on unbelief as on the element of suspicion and distrust which disturbs the spiritual atmosphere. The great majority of those who have accepted these truths were unbelievers, but they entered on their examination with open minds, prepared to receive truth from any source, and facts which appealed to all their faculties broke down their unbelief. All honour to the many noble and true servants of the spirit world, like the Everitts and others, who have laboured unceasingly for the coming day, when all the world will know of the closeness of the spiritual realm; when doubts will be no more heard in the land; when each will look up with trustful heart, because he knows more than of old regarding the goodness of God, and recognises in death the kindly hand that leads him into brighter chambers of His kingdom.

CHAPTER XXVI

FURTHER PUBLIC TESTIMONY

There are very few persons who really think and feel that death is a good thing for mortals. The strongest religious sense that most people have developed through life is a dread of death. Even those who have cast off the old theological idea that death came into the world as the result of Adam's sin scarcely recognise at all that the processes of nature in relation to death are wise. Let us boast of our freethinking as we may, the old beliefs with which we were fed in youth affect us all through mortal life.

What a world this would be if nobody died! How old fashioned and conservative and bigoted it would become! What progress would be possible? We speak of the wondrous adaptability of nature in every other realm, but somehow think that there has been a blunder here. We must recast all our thought, and spiritual phenomena alone will help us to do this, before we can recognise that death must be a blessing to man, else it would not be here.

If it is a good thing to be born into the flesh and wear it for a season, it is a good thing to be born out of the flesh and live elsewhere under better conditions.

A long experience of spirit communion has made the fact clear to me that once the link with the body has been broken, nearly all who have passed on are glad to be free, and would not, under any circumstances, seek to live the earthly life again. The few exceptions are in those cases where the transplanting has been sudden, or where there was much need of the bodily presence, but even in such cases the sense of being wronged lasts but for a short season. The Infinite goodness is recognised soon, and the love and wisdom of ministering spirits open the eyes and bring a sense of trust and satisfaction.

Religion, when life is lived under the influence of a spirit world in close contact with this, will take on an entirely new colour. It will become actual, vibratory to the holiest emotion and performing the noblest deeds. That truest manhood will be aroused, which seeks to do good for its own sake, and not from the selfish fear of hell or the bribe of heaven. The bridge which Spiritualists have discovered between the two realms of existence is the one means by which we can get to know of that other world and its people; it is the only revelation man has ever had or is ever likely to have. All bibles and all religions which ever were, are but the products of spirit messages. In saying this it is not necessary to vouch for the truth of all we find in so-called sacred writings. That which is incredible we leave discredited. We test all things by the laws of nature—there is never a miracle: ever a law. What ever excellence one generation gains is maintained for all following generations.

Strong as Christianity seems today, it is not stronger than the complex mythology which Greece and Rome had two thousand years ago—yet that has gone! The gods and goddesses have only left their footsteps in the marble, or their breath in the literature. Nobody prays now to Pan, no sacrifice is offered to Pallas, though in the first century the wisest of Romans perfunctorily bent the knee to such gods. All forms of religion are fleeting, and some day Christianity, with its Virgin birth and resurrection of the physical body, will be discarded, because it parted company with Nature and cut itself adrift from the ground of phenomenal fact. We can be none the poorer for losing that which was never a real possession, but only the shadow which deluded us with its seeming substance. To find the trice we must first let go the false.

In Goethe's words, "Until we let the half-gods go, the whole gods cannot come."

The early Spiritualists, like S.C. Hall, William Howitt, Dr. Elliotson, and others, were of opinion that Christianity would have its strongest support from Spiritualism. They believed that because spirits in the séance room built up bodies for themselves which could be seen and grasped, the feeding of five thousand with the loaves and fishes must also be true!

Materialisation is a scientific fact which men like Sir Wm. Crookes and the modern school of Italian scientists have proved, but Bible miracles need to be evidenced by some authority beyond the bald statement of those who only heard that such things had taken place. Spiritualism means a new light of revelation in the world. Its freethinking is no longer on the side of negation, but on the side of eternal facts. It is going to out the ground from under many beliefs which Christianity has fostered. It is going to conquer, as Gerald Massey has said, because "it is not afraid of any new facts that may be dug out of the earth or drawn down from the heavens." It has a place for evolution, which the Christian system was entirely without, and it will have a place for every glimpse of light which may come to mortals from every source. For a season no doubt its purport and power will be slowly assimilated by those who know of its phenomenal facts, but are not strong enough to let the old fables die at once. Its great prophets, like Davis, Tuttle, and Massey, have been terribly iconoclastic, because full of courage and assurance. They have worked for a future day, which must come when we learn to think freely and reverently. As yet we can only set down the great fact that the cable is laid between the two worlds, and that messages of truth and intelligence come from those who, at the other end of the line, tell their own story in human language.

I have referred to the work done by W.T. Stead by the publication of *Borderland.* By giving to the world the matter which came through his own hand, Letters from Julia, he made known much that is rational regarding the after-death state. He has been fearless in the promulgation of spiritual facts since the hour when the veil was lifted from him. It was my privilege to have a visit from him in April 1894, on his return from a long tour which he had made in America, where he had witnessed some marvellous phenomena. Those who know Mr. Stead would scarcely regard him as an ideal experimenter in the domain of occult facts. His energetic and impulsive temperament, his hasty modes of reaching at many things, do not usually give such conditions as are requisite for the spirit circle, but, strange to say, he has there been flooded with evidences. He has the capacity to receive truth and the power of telling it, which are admirable, while his courage is undoubted. He has been able all through life to stand alone, as it were, when he once became convinced of the truth or righteousness of any matter. That he has a genius for justice can scarcely be gain said, and he has paid the penalty for standing forth on behalf of the weak and oppressed, when no one else cared to lend a helping hand. I heard from his own lips how again and again he got writings on closed slates under the most conclusive circumstances. He had asked his spirit friend, "Julia," to write to him through other mediums, and she managed to give him a clear message in her well-known handwriting. This strong piece of testimony in favour of continued existence, like so many other spiritual facts of today, is passed by, while matters of trivial moment are flashed from continent to continent. At one sitting the medium asked for gold, whereupon a bracelet was put upon the outside of the slate, and in some mysterious manner the spirit chemists were able to extract some of the particles from the bracelet, so that the message came on the slate written in letters of gold. I was astonished to hear from Mr. Stead that he had no knowledge of Andrew Jackson Davis, the most profound product of the spiritual movement, the man whom Theodore Parker called the greatest marvel in literature, and whose name will one day be sounded in all continents as that of the most transcendent man of his age, the mighty magician whose inspirations have thrown the clearest light on Nature's divine processes.

In 1894 I was privileged to visit Mr. E. Dawson Rogers, at his home in London, and listened to his ex tended experiences of spiritual phenomena. He told me how he had looked at the spirit forms walking out in the clear light and afterwards going back to the body of the medium. Mr. Rogers had been a close student of the subject for many years, and its facts had been woven into the fabric of his being. The subject of a spiritual conference had been for some time talked of by Mr. Rogers, instigated by Stainton Moses, his predecessor in the editorship of Light. Instructions in the direct voice with regard to it had been given through the mediumship of Mrs. Everitt. While I was present this honoured instrument paid a visit to Mr. Rogers, and it was my good fortune to listen to the clear, bold voice of "John Watt," her oldtime control, advising how the work of the conference should be carried through. There were a great crowd of spirit friends there, who spoke at intervals, each in tones quite distinct from the others. One especially, an old personal friend of Mr. Rogers, "the Rev. Mr. Bailey," revealed how, after all, the old friendships are not sundered by death, as so many think, but are enduring, and helpful to those still in the body. I had expected to hear "Stainton Moses" speak, but "John Watt" told us the conditions did not permit of his manifesting. While the voices were speaking the raps sounded from nearly every corner of the room.

Mr Rogers told me of a wonderful clairvoyante he had known in Norwich, when engaged on his journalistic work there, who described to him Dr. Peebles in his robes, addressing some Arabs, while a spirit stood behind the doctor whispering words in his ear. At this period Dr. Peebles had not been in this country, nor was he known to Mr. Rogers personally. When he did arrive in England some months later and was introduced to the clairvoyante, she at once said she had seen him before. Dr. Peebles knew the spirit well which she had described as whispering in his ear, and at the time named he had been wearing his official robes at his Consulate in Asiatic Turkey.

The conference which had been arranged by the spirit people was carried through in May 1895, at the Portman Rooms in London. I was asked to contribute a paper, and did so, on "Public Exhibitions of Spiritual Phenomena." All the notable men and women connected with the movement were present. Mrs. Emma Hardinge Britten, Mr. J.J. Morse, Rev. John Page Hopps, Traill Taylor (editor of *The British Journal of Photography*), Mr. E.W. Wallis, John Lamont (of Liverpool), Dr. Abraham Wallace (who had but newly come into touch with the facts), and others either contributed papers or entered into the discussion. One notable person whom I then saw for the first time, and about whom I shall have much to say, was Mr. George Spriggs, who was over on a visit from Australia. Amongst those who read valuable papers were Thomas Shorter, the veteran writer, who had stood in the front of the movement for many years, editing the *Spiritual Magazine*, and issuing tracts innumerable. It was a link with the past to look upon the old sightless warrior eloquently pouring out his philosophic thoughts. Traill Taylor's address was also amongst the most searching and positive that could have been penned. I was the guest of my old friend, Rev. John Page Hopps, during the proceedings, and each night participated in the rich flow of thought that fell from his lips. In the old days in Glasgow, when he was the minister of St.

Vincent Street Unitarian Church, I used to listen to his sermons and wonder what could be the source of his deep piety and spiritual insight. In those days I dwelt in the darkness, feeling that no light had ever come from beyond the tomb. Mr. Hopps left Glasgow before I had come into touch with the subject, or at least before I heard he was interested in Spiritualism. To me he had been much of a teacher, helping to quicken my intellect, even if I could not accept to the full his positive affirmations of spiritual realities. He it was who first stirred me to read Carlyle as the outcome of one of his lectures. Few men who toil earnestly as he has done see what the seed they sow will bring forth. They are contented to do all the good they can, leaving the rest to the Great Power that overrules all for good.

I had from Mr. Hopps at this time a wonderful bit of spirit ministry. He had been laid up at Leicester through arduous work, and was scarcely expected to recover. One day he was a little better, and desired 'his wife to try to get some automatic writing; but she, after taking a pencil in her hand, said it was of no use, there was only a scribble. Mr. Hopps looked at the scribble, as it was called, and found there the signature of George Dawson, of Birmingham, whose assistant he had been on beginning his ministry. As Mr. Hopps put it, his old friend had just called and presented his card, to congratulate him on his convalescence. How few outside our subject know of the multitude of evidences such as this which are being continually given to make the earthly life full of cheer by this added companionship!

The conference at Portman Rooms was brought to a conclusion with a conversazione, where were gathered some hundreds of true and tried workers or sympathisers with the Cause. Amongst, others I met with Maurice Davis, D.D., the author of *Orthodox and Heterodox London,* who had written much on the subject of Spiritualism; Mrs. Guppy, the wonderful

271

medium, whose phenomena, as narrated by Dr. Alfred Russel Wallace, have caused no end of discussion—hers was a valuable life, which helped to establish the future life as a fact, but she had her reward in contumely and abuse from those whose prejudices prevented them from looking at the actual facts; Jesse Shepard, the musical medium, whose great gifts have been frequently reported in the spiritualist journals; Miss Chandos Leigh Hunt, a niece of the poet, now Mrs. Joseph Wallace, whom I had met with years before in Glasgow; Mrs. Bessie Russell Davis, whose work has been particularised by Florence Marryat in the volume *There Is No Death*; Mr. and Mrs. Wallis, and many other persistent and faithful servants of the spirit world.

Amongst the company was one who could scarcely be called a Spiritualist, seeing that he edited the *Agnostic Journal*, William Stewart Ross, a brilliant poet and prose writer, who would have made a front position in literature but for his advocacy of Agnosticism. His was indeed a burning pen. All he wrote bespoke the man of courage. I had known him in the old days when he was a student at Glasgow University preparing for the ministry of the Church of Scotland, and eking out a living by writing works of fiction for the *Weekly Mail* and *Penny Post*. Even then he had published a volume of poetry, *The Harp of the Valley*; like some few others, when he did not find any Christian evidences, he was brave enough to say so. I had not met him for many years, and when we once again came to speech we talked of the old days, of Robert Buchanan, Charles Gibbon, William Black, R.L. Gentles, and other Glasgow *littérateurs* whom we had both known before he had faced London life and created a name. "Saladin" (Mr Ross) made a strange confession to me. Agnostic as he was, he told me that when reading my little work on the *Rise and Progress of Spiritualism* some occult influence said to him, "This is written by an old friend."

His was a poetic nature, and when he gave full play to his intuitions there oft times streamed forth a flood of spiritual thought. He was at one time a not infrequent visitor at Spiritualist conferences and *conversaziones*, and was for long a close friend of that highly esteemed veteran Spiritualist, Andrew Glendinning. He passed, on November 30th, 1906, to the search for Truth on a higher plane, where agnosticism has no place, and where his ardent spirit cannot but progress in true Knowledge.

CHAPTER XXVII

MR. GEORGE SPRIGGS

As I have already said, the Conference gave me an opportunity of meeting for the first time Mr. George Spriggs, a spiritual worker whose life for many years had revealed the kingly virtues of humanity, and whose mediumship had brought in its train a rich blessing to many. Spiritualism has had within its ranks scores of individuals whose life stories have revealed guidance as wonderful as any that is set down in what we call sacred writ, but many of these wait for an audience and an interpreter. Our eyes are holden so that we see not that which stares us in the face, else we would sing songs of gratitude for the revelations of Davis and Tuttle and the rich wisdom which has fallen from the lips of a Morse and a Wallis.

These have been amongst the most important benefactions given to this generation. All have worked as faithful servants of the spirit world, studying how the greatest human blessedness might be obtained. The world is greedy for pleasure and strives for money, reputation, and office beyond aught else, but the spiritual servants whom I have named have thrown into the treasury of the world their priceless gifts, heedless whether or not they would be valued in this life.

Herbert Spencer once made the remark to Huxley, "One cannot hope for much more than to make one's mark and die." But Huxley replied from a nobler altitude, "Never mmd about the mark, it is sufficient if one can give a push." A man must needs have courage whose eyes are opened to spiritual realities and who feels that the rare powers which are his were given for use and not to be hidden away Most of us hate to be in a minority, and so the price has been heavy which the bulk of spiritual mediums have had to pay in standing forth and making proclamation of that which the world would hold in scorn.

The story of George Spriggs' mediumship is amongst the most wonderful on record. Were it printed as a romance it would call forth plaudits for its marvellous invention, but it is a story of fact, and fact only, and no one who knows the integrity of the man has ever had cause to doubt his honesty and purity. Close on thirty-five years ago, when quite a young man with a deeply religious bias, he had his attention called to Spiritualism in Cardiff. A circle had been held for some time at the house of a pure-minded man, Mr. Rees Lewis, and to this circle the unassuming young seeker was admitted. The sitters were earnest, high-souled, devotional people, whose lives had been thrilled by the, to them, new fact of spirit return. They had had tidings of their own loved ones through the simple agency of messages rapped out on a table. None of them could have conceived the possibility that the latest introduction to their gathering would establish their faith on firmer lines. Amongst those people in Cardiff there was no thought of money or fame, or anything beyond the joy of holding communion among their unseen friends. It was a sacred service, where all sought to condition themselves in mind and body so that the spirit people might come all the closer. As in the story of the Apostles, they were all of one accord at each gathering, and the circle was seldom changed. Each new arrival was admitted only when he showed an earnest desire for light and knowledge.

Mr. Spriggs soon manifested that he possessed the gift of automatic writing and messages from the unseen were given clearly and with many evidences of identity. Then his spiritual eyes began to open, and he described in distinct outline the forms of those who had passed beyond the physical life. Greater things were promised, and these were soon fulfilled in the shape of materialisations. All valuable things in any realm are matters of slow growth. Time and effort have to be expended before the day of fruition comes round. It was a tiny luminous cloud which first met the sitter's vision, moving about the room and proving that spirit chemists were at work. It soon would grow in power and size, until some face would be made clear. The sweet blending in spirit of the devoted sitters gradually brought about more effective manifestations of the spirits' power. Full forms, covered with dazzling white drapery, would come out amidst the circle and repeat their messages. The Cardiff circle gave for all time evidence of what may be accomplished when patience is exercised and only the spirit of love prevails. Pure hearts and sound minds, where love of self is last, are the only things which can draw the people of that other world down to our midst and let us know that continuity of life is real.

Sometimes at these gatherings as many as twelve different forms would come out and walk round the room, Sir Spriggs himself being visible at the same time. At some moments these forms would melt away in front of where the medium was sitting, and then in sight of the people would assume their form again. I know that the unknowing ones, who never touched this joyous realm, will only say that such things cannot be, and that those who say they occur are only fit for the madhouse. But Sir William Crookes, with the critical scientific spirit, has vouched for similar occurrences, and numbers of such statements have been affirmed again and again by those who are wise in thought and sound in judgment. The Cardiff séances of course gave even better results than Crookes or any other professedly scientific workers over obtained. When the testing spirit is uppermost, then, indeed, much of the spirit energy is dissipated. These people in Cardiff did not trouble about what are called scientific tests. They had the evidence of their eyes, their ears, and their hands. The faces of those they had known, the voices they knew of old, were sufficient for them.

One of the sitters was Mr. A.J. Smart, a clear- headed man of some literary gifts, and he carefully tabulated much that occurred. The records of these events will no doubt one day be searched out, when the facts are more common than they are today, even as the Italian scientists who have been devoting themselves to the subject of materialisation bring forth Crookes' statements and compare them with their own observations. It was at the Cardiff gatherings that the spirits left the room where they had built up their bodies and walked a long distance from the medium. Well-authenticated records of this wonderful manifestation were made and published.

In the majority of circles, where the sitters have not been harmonised by long meeting together, the form has to go back again and again near the medium to obtain power to manifest. Again, where there are not the best conditions, when a promiscuous gathering is brought together, strong light is usually a deterrent At Cardiff, however, the light at times streamed in, permeating every comer of the room, and falling on the form of the spirit so that the veins and even the flesh tint could be seen. The very acme of materialism, the ignorant may say, but it is less so than the doctrines of Christianity which are based on a physical resurrection, which could never demonstrate for us a spiritual continuity. These efforts of spirit beings to clothe themselves in matter that may be seen and felt, are but temporary, and are only carried on that we may realise that there is a more subtle chemistry at work than we have yet realised.

Spiritualism demonstrates for the first time that if the right conditions ate furnished we can converse with our dead. The prophets and oracles of old who spoke their messages, or the spiritual visitants who appeared, were thought to do so by miracle and and not by law.

The spirit friends who come today reveal that they have lost nothing of life or love, and are here because they wish to brighten our lives and dissipate forever the gloomy fears which have been so long inculcated. Step by step these appearances at Cardiff grew in intensity. They would come out of the sitting-room into the hall and there show themselves in good light. They would ascend a short flight of stairs, open the doors of the rooms, and enter them. In the full blaze of daylight they would bring articles out of a room, when from the known position of the articles it was evident that they must have passed in front of the open window. While this was going on the direct voice of the unseen spirit would be heard by all. Two of the sitters went down to the front garden on one occasion, and there they saw at the window the form of the spirit named "Peter," who waved the curtain and dropped the speaking tube which he had been using into the garden. The stair was afterwards descended by the form, and he showed himself through the folding glass door which opened directly into the garden, afterwards opening the door and standing before the observers in all the glory of his white raiment.

Then he would be seen returning to the circle room for power, and coming back again, walking through the open door and down the three or four steps outside till he stood on the lowest one, showing his features plainly. There were many similar exhibitions of the spirit's power even more remarkable than any of these. That it was no case of the "transfiguration" of the medium was fully evidenced when the form would return to the circle and dematerialise in front of the curtain, apparently sinking through the floor. While the form remained in an upright position, the head and shoulders gradually sank until within a foot of the floor, finally dissolving there. Never before had the materialisation of the full form been obtained so perfectly as at Cardiff. Sir William Crookes walked and talked with the spirit form in the room where the experiments were carried on by him, but at Cardiff some of the spirit forms would take the arm of Mr. Rees Lewis and walk down the stair, a distance of fifty feet The world did not hear of these remarkable occurrences, beyond those who read the spiritualist journals, hut those who were privileged to be present accepted the facts as real and nursed the great joy in their own hearts. This work went on for several years, and Mr. Spriggs has revealed other faculties of mediumship, the most notable of which is medical clairvoyance This power is most marked. The sitter becomes an open book, and the whole interior of the body is laid bare to spirit sight, so that the most subtle diseases can be diagnosed and remedies suggested.

The spirit friends of Mr. Spriggs, on whom he leaned with a perfect trust, advised in due course that he should visit Australia, where, it was promised him, he would meet with troops of friends. I have been struck ofttimes in my life with this confidence in the unseen which sustains spiritual mediums. Weak men and women, who of their own normal selves could not utter a word, have gone forth into many lands to utter the message, knowing that the help promised would be given them. And so Mr. Spriggs, whose faith was real, entered upon the voyage in 1880, accompanied by his friend, Mr. A.J. Smart. A cordial welcome was given him by those Spiritualists who had read about Cardiff, while the man's modest, genial, and unassuming character soon endeared him to everyone.

At the sittings which took place in Melbourne the same remarkable phenomena took place as had been witnessed at Cardiff Men of the highest integrity, clear-headed and clear-sighted, of undoubted character, had no hesitation in vouching for the reality of these wonders. Mr. Terry, then editor of *The*

Harbinger of Light, has stated that he has been present at over fifty séances, where he recognised distinctly friends whom he had known in the body. At times the medium and two separate forms would be seen together. There are no facts in the universe which have been more satisfactorily evidenced than that of the mediumship of Mr. George Spriggs. When he left his old friend, Mr. Kees Lewis, at Cardiff, Mr. Lewis promised to show himself to Mr. Spriggs when the death change took place. Mr. Spriggs asked him, when the time came, if it were possible, to appear to him in the daylight, and not in the dark. He had not heard from Mr. Lewis for some eighteen months, when one afternoon in blight sunshine, while walking on the verandah, Mr. Spriggs felt his coat pulled, and, turning round, he saw and recognised Mr. Lewis. This happened in Melbourne seven days after Mr. Lewis is had parsed away at Cardiff. Clairvoyance of a very marked character has been manifested by Mr. Spriggs during all these thirty years of his wonderful life. There are on record many instances of this faculty, such as we might only expect to read in some wild romance. Yet the facts are real facts, and have been vouched for by men of social position and known integrity.

Perhaps the most notable instance is that associated with the name of Hugh Junor Browne, a prominent merchant in Melbourne, who has placed all the particulars on record in his own published works. The story is well authenticated, and all the carping criticism in the world cannot destroy or weaken its essential points. Mr. Browne had a son aged eighteen years, who, along with another young man, became the possessors of a yacht called the *Iolanthe.* On a Saturday afternoon two of Mr. Browne's sons, much against their mother's wish, started with this other young man on a trial trip in their yacht A promise was made that they would be certain to be back on Monday morning for business. As they failed to return as promised, the mother became very anxious, fearing some calamity must have happened. Mr. Junor Browne, who was a Spiritualist and knew of the reality of Mr. Spriggs' gifts, having known him since his arrival in Australia, made a call upon the medium on the Tuesday' morning. Mr. Spriggs knew nothing of the absence of the lads, nor was anything told him by Mr. Browne when he called. He was simply asked to give a sitting, being told that Mrs. Browne did not feel well. When Mr. Spriggs went into the trance state he at once said, "There seems to be sorrow and trouble connected with the sea. If you will give me something belonging to *them*," not stating who the "*them*" referred to, "I will endeavour to trace them." The lads' pocket-books, which had been left in their bedrooms, were placed in Mr. Spriggs' hands. He then began to trace them from the time they had left home, describing minutely the course of the yacht until it had foundered on Monday morning through the jib-halyard fouling in a squall. He further proceeded to say that the yacht had gone down in deep water, and that it could not be washed ashore. When Mr. Spriggs came out of the trance state, he was told of the sons' absence, whereupon he promised that he would sit the next day and see if further particulars could be obtained. When the sitting took place the next day, Mr. Spriggs was controlled by the younger of the two lads, who corroborated in every particular what had been said regarding the foundering of the yacht.

The anxiety of the parents was so great that they had a further sitting the following day, when the other son spoke, giving fuller particulars of the tragic mishap.

Both of the lads gave their parents the assurance that there was no bodily pain in the drowning, but that when they found themselves in the water they had much remorse at the thought of having disregarded their mother's warning. The young man named Murray, who had accompanied them, also spoke. This young man held a mate's certificate, and so Mr. Browne had made no demur to the lads a voyaging.

The fact that all of the lads had been familiar with the subject of Spiritualism while in the body was a great consolation to them when they realised that they were spirits, free from earth's limitations. They each said that their misery would have been much greater had they not known of the power of spirits to return and let those left behind know that they still lived and loved. They were so glad that the spiritual gates were open, and that they could come back to unburden their minds and ask forgiveness. Mr. Browne now made every endeavour to get the information he had got from spiritual sources corroborated, but no earthly information came of either the lads or the yacht until two weeks afterwards, when the body of the youngest, minus an arm, was washed ashore about ten miles from Melbourne. At the funeral service the father himself spoke over the remains. Many wondered at his nerve, but be said that but for the glorious knowledge of Spiritualism his eyes would have been bathed in tears.

A few days after the funeral a friend of Mr. Browne's in Adelaide, some 600 miles from Melbourne, who was the possession of some spiritual gifts, wrote to him that the elder son had paid him a visit, and said that a large fish had bitten part of the right arm off his body, and had taken his waistcoat also. Two days after the receipt of this communication a large shark was caught at Frankston, 27 miles from Melbourne. A young friend of one of the sons, who was present at the capture, suggested to the policeman present that the shark should he opened, to see if there might he anything inside belonging to the young men who had been drowned. On opening the shark, the son's right arm, almost up to the elbow joint, was found, also part of the vest, in the pocket of which was found an old gold watch, which the mother had lent him, his own silver one being out of order. There were also his pipe and keys and 12s. in silver. The watch was found to have stopped at nine o'clock, the exact tune, as had been stated three weeks before by Mr. Spriggs, when the accident to the boat had occurred. At Mr. Spriggs' séances in Melbourne the lads made their materialised appearance once or twice a week, and the father and others recognised them distinctly, and were cheered by the messages they gave.

As I have said, no romancer could have penned from the wildest imagination a more wonderful story. It was the sensation of Melbourne and many other parts for a long time, and the details were criticised in every conceivable way, but there was nothing to break down the volume of testimony. There was no loophole of escape from the important fact, which is being repeated in so many quarters, that denizens of the other world can come back to earth and solace the mourner, while establishing the larger fact that the future life is but on unfoldment of the life here, a natural evolutionary process. We applaud great men who demonstrate to us the wonders of material things, while we ridicule those true men and women who seek to make clear to the world the greater wonders of the spiritual kingdom. But those who know of these spiritual revealments can afford to wait, they have the assurance that all truths must conquer at the last, and that, though they may be retarded for a season, they will bear fruit eventually and feed forever the hungry souls of men. The march of Spiritualism has been steady and persistent. In spite of being decried and hounded down as a vile superstition, it rears its head higher than ever before, and many are now drinking from its fountains who once upon a time said its waters were poisonous. Mr. Spriggs, amidst all aspersions, has maintained a character for spotless purity. His unselfishness and sweet nature have drawn around him troops of friends who know to the full his genuine manliness, his sincerity and devotion. The striking facts which followed his course made him for years an important personage in Melbourne. Hundreds waited upon him to have obscure diseases diagnosed who cared not to acknowledge the spirit people who were behind him.

It is a truth, which is only being grudgingly admitted, that in the trance state some clairvoyants are enabled to perceive the state of each organ of the body, and in cases of diseases to designate with accuracy which organs are principally affected. Hence there is no need for the patient to describe symptoms, or to be examined physically, or questioned as to his ailments What is hidden from the eye of sense is made plain to the eye of the soul. This blessed power has been long before the world, but charily have its claims been admitted. No one who has stood many times in the presence of the clairvoyant physician but has felt that this faculty is one of God's choicest gifts to man.

Mr Spriggs, during the many years of his residence in Australia, carried on a priceless work. No one came into his presence but was startled by the remarkable dearness of his spiritual vision. In many cases where the old-school physicians could do no good, cures were effected by the spirits. Even those who could not visit Mr. Spriggs personally, when they sent some clue to their personality, such as a lock of hair, got the same intimate diagnosis as if they had been present. Many prominent men in Victoria gave their testimony that the faculty Mr. Spriggs claimed to possess was a real faculty, which looked through the physical body and described the nature and cause of any want of harmony that existed in the system. Mr. Spriggs made several visits to England before finally taking up his residence in London. I felt at once, when I met him, the impress of a generous, happy, cheery, healthful nature, a man who shed his sweet influence on all who came near him. After his many years of close work, he could not be still. If there are souls needing help, his powers are ever at their service, his highest joy is in blessing the needy.

Largely through his vigorous temperament the Psycho-Therapeutic Society has been formed in London, where for years he has, without price, diagnosed the diseases which are treated by the Society. *The Health Record*, which is published monthly, tells how much good work is being done silently to heal and soothe and bless. Many eminent physicians, who are beginning to see the folly of much drugging, have joined themselves to forward the good work. No doubt one day Mr. Spriggs' unselfish and untiring efforts to make human life brighter will be recognised, meantime he labours on, seeking no applause. "Absolute purity of heart and life is the richest human possession, and perfect obedience to the highest attractions of the soul is the only means of attainment," says the great seer of *Nature's Divine Revelations*, Andrew Jackson Davis. Mr. Spriggs, in his life, fulfils this high standard to the full. The public work of Spiritualism has held him closely all the time, both in Australia and London. He is a Spiritualist because ha recognises that from the unseen all his strength has come, that he is but the servant of those wise and loving souls in the beyond.

The Spiritualist Services held at Cavendish Rooms, London, have the benefit of his presence and voice, while on the Council of the London Spiritualist Alliance he has been one of the strong towers. His has, indeed, been a noble life in a field where fame is not considered of much value. Like a star he has shone through the folds of thick darkness, and manifested to the full a love of Truth, Justice, and Wisdom.

CHAPTER XXVIII

MORE SPIRIT PHOTOGRAPHY

A VERY distinguished writer on psychical subjects, Dr. Maxwell, of Bordeaux, in speaking of mediums, says we ought to consider them as precious beings, forerunners of the future type of our race. How few, however, take this view of those through whose instrumentality we have been able to catch glimpses of the future life, its people and their conditions! No medium has yet appeared who has escaped the snarls and suspicions which abound. The noblest men and women with gifts not of their own seeking have all had to submit to calumny and abuse. There have been none considered righteous, no, not one.

The life story of D.D. Home will one day be brought forth as evidence how a people could not only fail to recognise a great benefactor, but even take him for the opposite of what he was. What splendid gifts have been lost to the world because of the fact that those who saw and heard strange things could not bear the oppression of the world, and so kept to themselves or the few what was of tremendous importance! That men and women possess these spiritual gifts is hardly admitted yet in many circles, in spite of all that is recorded in the New Testament about trance, clairvoyance, foreseeing, etc.

If in the past there was evidence that at rare intervals mortals were endowed with powers strange and peculiar relating to the spiritual, why not now? The race has progressed on many lines. For the isolated cases of mediumship in the past, we have now the hundreds. Humanity has not yet reached its apex, but is steadily progressing to a fuller manifestation of the gifts of the spirit. We have in the past been ignorant, tactless, and incautious in these matters, but the better day is dawning when the discovery of spiritual powers will he welcomed amongst us as tending to elucidate the mysteries of life and being, here and hereafter.

These thoughts have been suggested by the coming upon the scene, in 1895, of a new worker whose psychic gifts caused no end of controversy. Spirit photography, it was thought, would be the most valuable evidence which could he presented, and yet, when Mr. Boursnell was first heard of, there was little in the way of welcome accorded him, but much in the way of suspicion. Mr. Stead, in *Borderland* for October 1893, gave a lengthy article dealing most carefully with the phenomena he had met with, but holding back the worker's name. All that was set down in that article bore within it pretty fair evidence that here again was one with those abnormal gifts that threw light on the realm of spirit. Spirit photography was not a new thing, even at a much earlier day there had stood forth those who really got authentic likenesses of the so-called dead. W.H. Mumler, in Boston and New York, succeeded in getting many pictures which were recognised as portraits of friends once in the body. One of the most remarkable cases was that of Mrs. Lincoln, wife of the murdered president, who went to the photographer a perfect stranger, thickly veiled. There came on the plate an unmistakable likeness of her husband and of one of her children, and yet not a copy of any portrait in existence. Though Mumler got so many pictures about which no one could cavil, he had to bear some martyrdom, as he was dragged into the law courts and assailed as an impostor. The evidence offered on his behalf, however, was so strong that his character was vindicated and he triumphed.

In this country for some years a Mr. John Beattie, of Clifton, along with a friend, Dr. Thompson, made many experiments for their own satisfaction, and they were rewarded for their patience by getting undoubted evidence. Stainton Moses gave considerable attention to the subject, bringing his clear and searching intellect to bear upon it in a series of papers which swept the entire field and conclusively established the great fact that portraits of the dead had been obtained again and again. The medium, Hudson, who gave so much satisfaction to Stainton Moses, had to tread the thorny path of suspicion like his fellows, though the evidence of his honesty would be sufficient to establish any truth in other branches of knowledge.

I have already referred to the work of David Duguid in this realm. He also brought home to many that photographing the invisible was a natural fact. All through a simple, brave life he kept a reputation for honesty, for faithful service to the spirit world, and for true friendship to humanity. David Duguid's many sacrifices for so many years will yet find recognition. Boursnell was welcomed as a valuable instrument by a few Spiritualists, but attacked fiercely by others.

I first met him towards the end of 1895, when the controversy regarding him was at its height. Mr. Traill Taylor, the first of photographic experts, was certain of the genuineness of Boursnell's gifts, and no one was more capable of weighing up all points than he—the editor of the British Journal of Photography, and an undoubted authority on light and optics. I have no doubt Mr. Taylor would have stood to the front in defence of Boursnell as he did on behalf of David Duguid, but that, taking a trip to Florida, USA., shortly after Mr. W.T. Stead had shown him the pictures which he had obtained, ha was cut off by a fever and so prevented from continuing his valuable work in England. What he did see of Boursnell's photographs convinced him that no photographer with days at his disposal and confederates to assist, could have produced such pictures as Mr. Stead obtained with him under the conditions set down.

The laws which regulate spirit phenomena are, as yet, largely hidden from us. We know, however, full well that the spirit of calm receptivity, neither credulity nor incredulity, the spirit of the truth-seeker who feels that we have not quite exhausted all nature's secrets, gives forth an atmosphere through which the spirits can work. William White, the author of *The Life of Swedenborg*, an ardent Spiritualist, who had witnessed many marvels in his day, used to declare, "The question is not what can spirits do, but rather what is it they cannot do, provided they have proper conditions." I know such speech as this will be considered the veriest raving of ignorance and superstition, but it has been evidenced in the case of all notable investigators. Crookes got his most telling evidence when he cast away the spirit of the sceptic and gladly received what came. Eusapia Paladino sat with the "very clever" people at Cambridge, the so-called scientific men, and was declared a trickster, while the same Eusapia, under more harmonious, yet even stricter, conditions, has convinced the ablest scientific men of France and Italy that her powers are genuine. Mr. Boursnell had run the gauntlet of some very unfavourable criticism in the correspondence columns of the spiritualist journals when I called upon him one Sunday morning in December 1895. I went accompanied by my friend, Mr. Andrew Glendinning, taking several marked plates with us. On our arrival, however, we found the photographer so much upset by the aspersions which had been made on his character, that he declined to give us a sitting. We spent several hours in his company, and I was soon convinced that here was a simple-minded man on whom these special gifts had been bestowed.

He had gone to some circles where he had shown the power of clairvoyance, and the subject had engrossed him day and night. When at his regular business, forms which he did not want had come upon the plates, and by and by, when he told these things to his friends at the circle, several came and got test pictures of friends who had gone out of the physical life. I was obliged to return with my package of plates unopened; but, on leaving, he said to me that he did not like to disappoint, and that if I cared to come out the following day he would make a trial. On the following Monday morning I was out at his studio as early as nine o'clock, when I handed him my marked plates and placed myself before the camera. On five of the plates figures were seen standing close to me, though none of them were pictures of anyone I had known in the earth life, while some were very like those I had seen on other plates taken by Mr. Boursnell. This aspect of the matter did not for me bear any impress of fraud. I knew that in materialisations there are cabinet spirits who regularly manifest, while the friends of sitters only come forward at intervals. I think what "Julia" wrote through Mr. Stead's hand conveys some measure of truth regarding these photographs: "They are all pictures of real people, not thought forms; the real spirit to which they may belong may, or may not, be present; they may leave their picture without their spirit. The picture or bodily mould which appears is only a shape created by thought or the mind for the sake of showing the identity." And I would further add that these "moulds," once made, can be used again and again by the spirit. We know that some of the most carefully attested pictures which have been given, where the form and features revealed are those we have known in life, cannot be the appearance of the spirit today. The spirit has memory of what he was like, and the photo may be the recollection of some portrait of himself. By power of will he creates this portrait and impresses the sensitive plate. Of course there are many pictures procured where we need no theories, but can accept the fact that the spirit is present, and has, out of the aura of the medium and sitter, been able to cover the spiritual body with the material that can make an impress on the plate.

On one of my pictures a beautiful female figure appeared, who held up a wreath in front of me. As a work of art the form is striking, the face full of character, bearing an expression akin to what we speak of as the heavenly. I was much struck with this piece of work from the fact that the previous Thursday evening, while in Glasgow, Miss MacCreadie, sitting at the tea table, described such a person as being close to me and holding out the wreath. When I got back to Glasgow the following Sunday with proofs of my pictures, and was speaking from the platform of the Association on the subject of spirit photography, Miss MacCreadie entered the hall. I asked her to come upon the platform. When she did so she was controlled by her guide, "Sunshine," and after describing some spirits whom she saw in the audience, I asked her, pointing to the bundle of photographs which were before me, "Have you ever seen any of the spirits which are on these cards?" She could not see, from where she stood, anything but a packet. "Yes," she said, "I see amongst these the form of the lady whom I described as standing by you with a wreath." Of course, to those who knew nothing of entrancement, or who would not recognise the personality of "Sunshine" apart from that of Miss MacCreadie, all this is of little value as evidence. To me it counts for something, but I have other and perhaps more striking testimony to bear regarding the reality of Mr. Hoursnell's gifts.

Amongst my earliest friends in the spiritual movement were Mr. and Mrs. John Dewar. When I first went to the meetings, I was astonished at the extreme scepticism of Mr. Dewar. No matter how clear was the evidence, he was always prepared with some theory which left the spirits out. A man clear in intellect, well read, yet determined to yield to nothing readily, for long he gave me the impression that spiritual phenomena were not likely to make a convert of him. I was wrong, however.

Mr. Dewar was brought into somewhat close companionship with Mr. David Anderson, the conclusive nature of whose valuable mediumship soon dissipated all doubt, and Mr. Dewar, like so many others, had to bend to the weight of facts. He was for years literally overwhelmed with the choicest proofs of spirit identity it would be possible to receive. The death angel in due course knocked at Mr. Dewar's door, taking away a favourite daughter named Jeanie. I knew the girl well, as also the other members of the family, for all of them were in the habit of attending the Lyceum which I conducted for some years in the Trongate Hall, and I can mentally recall each of them well. After Jeanie's departure, many consoling messages were received from her; she was never looked upon as lost, but as being present with them, taking the old interest in their welfare. In the course of a few more years, Mrs. Dewar was also called hence, to the deep regret of all who knew her. Her eldest son, John, at this time resident in London, who had been brought up all his life with a knowledge of spirit presence, thought that if he went to Mr. Boursnell he might be able to get a photograph of his mother as a spirit. There came on the plate, however, not the face of the expected one, but that of his sister, Jeanie, whose remains we had borne to the grave some ten years before. There could be no mistaking the likeness. You did not need to read anything in. Here were the veritable features of one whom we all knew well. The photographer had no knowledge that such a person had existed.

Mr Dewar had no expectation of getting his sister's picture, yet here it was, complete in every way, surrounded with the drapery which such spirit pictures usually bear. All the "faking" in the world could not have produced this authentic likeness, which gladdened all our hearts. I took the photograph round and showed it to many old friends, all of whom, without hesitation, said, "Joanie Dewar, beyond a doubt." Relatives of the family who were not at all sympathetic towards the subject of Spiritualism were forced to admit that, by whatever means the picture had been procured, it was a correct likeness. Mr. Stead, hearing of the circumstance, asked me to make a report of it, which I did in the pages of *Borderland*, where was printed the spirit photograph along with one of the girl taken while in the body. I place considerable emphasis on this picture, because I feel there is no link lacking in the chain of evidence.

I have seen scores of portraits, obtained by some of the clearest-headed men and women in the movement, who have been strong in their pronouncements that these were veritable likenesses of their deceased friends. Whatever statements may be brought forward about "faking" such pictures, there is a strong body of testimony that Mr. Boursnell has been the instrument for producing innumerable test pictures No medium has undergone more severe criticism than Mr. Boursnell, but, as Miss E. Katharine Bates has said in her admirable volume, *Seen and Unseen*: "If Mr. Boursnell, or any other photographer, can produce (*as he has done*) my old nurse, who died twenty-three years ago, and was never photographed in her life, then we must find some other suggestion than that of 'common or garden faking' as a solution of the mystery. There she sits, the features quite unmistakable, and no one knew the dear old woman as well as I did."

I have sat again and again with Mr. Boursnell in the intervening years, and never found any circumstance to arise which clouded my first impressions as to his honour and honesty. I have had pictures of those I knew while in the body, and I have seen undoubted portraits of other friends of mine obtained when others were sitting. These pictures were not copies of any other photographs, but betokened the presence of spirit visitants. In spite of any suspicions that may arise in individual cases, there is the great and startling fact that hundreds of visitors from all parts, entire strangers to the medium, have got authentic portraits of those whose faces they longed to see.

CHAPTER XXIX

SPIRITUALISM: A REVELATION

With all the spread of knowledge and the great discoveries which have so changed the face of Nature, there has been no access of knowledge, apart from the revelations made by Modern Spiritualism, regarding the future life. This, the most important question which concerns us, has been left in the old vague atmosphere. The millions depart year by year into what by many is considered the great darkness, for the feeling remains that there is no avenue open through which news can be transmitted. What has been named revelation reveals nothing which the rational mind can assimilate. It has only created innumerable sects which war with each other, and consider this warfare a part of their religion. The heaven, hell, and purgatory of today are perhaps if anything less rational than the conceptions held in Egypt six or seven thousand years ago. No one claims that ancient races had a revelation from heaven. They looked at the phenomena of Nature and interpreted them according to their own knowledge and experience. These gave them, however, conceptions which pointed to a future life, and many of the symbols seen on Egyptian tombs vividly portray a life after death.

The Old Testament, with its story of a chosen race, does not trouble much about any after-life. It is filled with matters that relate to the earth only. Spirituality of thought and development of the higher faculties are scarcely found in the books of Moses. There is no hint that souls gone out of life are still interested in the progress of the race. Evidently they followed the Egyptian belief that all the dead were living in the under world, Amenti, or Hades, and that the only humans in heaven were Enoch, who was translated there miraculously; Moses, who was thought to have reached there in a similar fashion; and Elijah, who went up by a whirlwind. One can find evidence of this belief in the story that those who were seen to stand by Jesus on the Mount were two men who had reached heaven in irregular fashion. The other spiritual visitants who came to mortals, it was thought, did not belong to the race of humans, but were angels, a species of being about whom nothing is known. The one instance outside of these non-human messengers is the story of Samuel appearing in response to Saul's request to the Woman of Endor; but Samuel was called up from this same under-world, and not brought down from a heaven. The philosophy and poetry of Greece and Rome did not improve upon the ideas which prevailed as to the life after death.

It is claimed for the New Testament that it gives greater light as to heaven and hell than anything which went before, but can anyone honestly say he is satisfied with the meagre light scattered through its pages? Is there to be found any foothold on which we can walk or rest? We still talk about resting in the grave, and waiting for a great day of judgment. In the Egyptian Book of the Dead we find the very phrases which are used in the New Testament in connection with this day of judgment, so that we are forced to come to the conclusion arrived at by Max Muller that "everything new is old, and everything old is new, and there has been no entirely new religion since the beginning of the world. The history of religion, like the history of language, shows us throughout a succession of new combinations of the same radical elements." Look where we may, it is hard to find evidence of any revelation to man other than that which is in our midst today. We do not belong to the dotage and decay of the world. Our reverence for the past is just in proportion to our ignorance of it. We have to get rid of the false idea that God was once everywhere in the world and in the soul, but has now ceased from taking the old interest in mortals.

The real Scriptures which are finding acceptance, and which harmonise with all we do know, tell us that we have not come from any state of perfection, but are, as Gerald Massey says, "As animals emerging from the animal, wearing the skins of animals, uttering the cries of animals whilst developing our own; and thus the race has travelled along the course of human evolution with the germ of immortal possibilities in it, darkly struggling for the light, and a growing sense of the road being up hill, therefore difficult and not to be made easy like the downward way to nothingness and everlasting death."

The most ancient races were well acquainted with some of the abnormal phenomena which are now pressing themselves to the front in this age, and which for a long season have been ignored. The old stumps of devil worship and of imputed righteousness have to be pulled up before the ground can be cleared for new seed. Churches may oppose for a season, but there is not force enough in the human race to annihilate a single truth. Science cannot efface nor uproot a single reality in Nature, and the evidences of spirit return are a part of Nature's reality. Gerald Massey, in his last great work, to which he unselfishly devoted the later years of his life, says truly, "The 'science of religion' with the ghost left out is altogether meaningless. The ghost offers the one unique objective proof of spiritual existence."

It is spiritual beings who are preaching to this generation clearer ideas than the world has held before as to the true resurrection. They are freeing men's minds from the cruel fables of ignorance and bringing reason forth as God's choicest gift.

The middle of the eighteenth century marked a new era regarding an authentic spirit world. Emanuel Swedenborg, who had been labouring for years at the problems of material science, when fifty-four years of age gave forth that man had spiritual possibilities within him: the faculties for seeing into the spiritual realms, and conversing with the so-called dead. As Emerson has said, "He sees with the internal sight the things that are in another life more clearly than he sees the things which are here in the world." Those who are familiar with modern mediumship recognise that Swedenborg was simply an instrument through whom spiritual beings could transmit gleams of thought, not a perfect or infallible messenger of truth, but one who saw real scenes and people, and coloured all with the dogmatic theology which he had imbibed. We can separate the facts of his life from the inferences which he drew from his visions. The influence of his writings on religious thought has been very much greater than has been admitted. Men of all schools have imbibed something from him, while a sect of his followers has sought to place him in a position he did not claim—one of those miraculous and special teachers sent from God. His faculties were natural faculties, held in some degree by every soul of man, but in his case unfolded much beyond that which is common with man. We have to march through much that is unintelligible to get at his facts, but statements are to be found in his writings which are now, with more highly developed instruments, corroborated as being true regarding the spiritual world. Before his day reports of clairvoyance or second sight were fugitive, belonged to tradition, and those who possessed the gifts of the spirit did not care to submit their evidence to a world which was prejudiced against these matters, as belonging to the kingdom of evil.

But Swedenborg, with his scientific reputation, and being possessed of courage, hesitated not to talk about his experiences, and invited investigation of his claims. He was tested by many in high places as to his holding converse with the dead, and he gave forth messages which were considered as settling the question. His clairvoyance on mundane matters was certainly remarkable, and clearly evidenced the possession of a real faculty. Just as the powers of D.D. Home overturned the scepticism of many in our own day and produced a large number of believers like Brougham, Mrs. Browning, Crookes, Wallace, etc., so did Swedenborg's powers amongst his contemporaries.

It was the evidences obtained through Swedenborg which drew forth from Immanuel Kant that remarkable prophecy, the truth of which is coming nearer each day: "The time will come when it will be proved that the human soul is already, during its life on earth, in a close and indissoluble connection with a world of spirits."

It was my privilege during a visit to America, in 1897, to come into personal touch with a greater seer than Swedenborg, one whom the Swedish seer watched over and assisted to unfold from the spirit side of life. I have already dwelt on Andrew Jackson Davis as one of the most profound and comprehensive teachers who have blessed the world for centuries. A man without scholastic advantages, he entered a realm of real knowledge, and handed to us truths not hitherto conceived. The truths he scattered are so clear and rational that we have in him a prophecy of a coming day when mortals will not prate about the inspiration of the past, but be conscious of it in the living present. Nature's Divine Revelation, with its encyclopaedic unfoldment of massive truths, will yet charm a generation when the spiritual faculties are more recognised than they are today. Each year his philosophy will find more admirers, and the word revelation has no meaning if it be not recognised in the life and works of Davis. William Lloyd Garrison, the brave apostle, said of him, "Who exhibits to the world in his own person a more beautiful life than Andrew Jackson Davis? Who can deny the extraordinary phenomena attending his mental development? Who that really knows him, doubts bis sincerity, his honesty of purpose, his extraordinary enlightenment?" Modesty of a beautiful type has ever characterised his noble life. He has resolutely asked the world to lose sight of his own personality and take his statements to the bar of reason, conscious that "error is mortal and cannot live, while truth is immortal and cannot die." Humanity will yet go to this store house and be fed with new life. To look in the face of this remarkable man was the realisation of one of my fondest dreams. Even as Carlyle had a golden day when some missive reached him in the wilds of Craigenputtoch from Goethe, so I ever experience a thrill of delight when I receive a letter from the illuminated Davis.

America to me had much charm, embracing Boston with its rich literary associations, and being the country of those men I reverence, Emerson, Theodore Parker, and the great group of seeing souls who gave to the world such transcendent views of a nobler religion. I felt that all of them were but preachers, in another tongue, of the gospel of Spiritualism. I met with many who had given up their lives to devotion and sacrifice, so that the world might be lifted out of its lethargy, and a higher religious thought abound. I met with much brotherly kindness and help from Harrison D. Barrett, then editor of the Banner of Light, who, meet ing with the spiritual evidences, gave up the pulpit to speak out unshackled the brighter story that witnesses and helpers are working continually with us. To see in the Banner of Light lecture room, amongst the portraits of the men and women who had given their gifts to the Cause, one of Gerald Massey, the bravest apostle the movement has had, was a source of joy. Since I began these records this heroic soul has finished his work on earth, and been translated to the land of the reality of which he had no doubt. Even as in Germany the works written for the hour were sold in thousands, while the bookseller despaired of the unsold sheets of Immanuel Kant, so it may be that the truths Massey brought to light in his Book of the Beginnings, Natural Genesis, and Egypt, the Light of the World, may have to wait for an audience. We so rarely recognise the great man, and therefore cannot thank God for him when he comes. Spiritual facts were at the root of all that Massey penned during the last thirty-five years of his life. He cared not for the reward of the present hour, only that such truth as he had caught should be given forth to work its mission. Whatever subject he touched had real light thrown on its path. His work on Shakespeare's sonnets called forth the admiration of eminent Shakespearians like Charles Cowden Clarke, Salvini, the great Italian actor, and others who revered the name and fame of one who was not for an age, but for all time. Lord Coleridge, writing on the subject of Massey in 1907, calls his Shakespearian work his magnum opus, a wonderful marshalling of facts, and perhaps the most learned work on Shakespeare ever written. Spiritualists, with their key of interpretation, can perhaps see how the Bard of Avon poured his inspiration on the singer of Democracy. The heroic has not died out from amongst us, and it was heroism of a noble type for Massey to bring to light the true foundation stones of the Hebrew legend and Christian dogmas, to make war against the false truths, "letting the half-gods go in order that the whole gods might come."

I had regrets while in America that I did not come into personal touch with Hudson Tuttle, the seer and farmer, whose writings Darwin and Buchner had quoted, not knowing that the author only claimed to be an amanuensis of the spirit people. Tuttle himself had never known that Darwin made reference to his works until his attention was drawn to it by an address I de livered in London, which was printed as a pamphlet.

The literature of Spiritualism has not received as yet the marked attention of the world. Books like Florence Marryat's There Is No Death were sold by the thousand, and no doubt for a season stirred up thought and consideration as to whether the strange events recorded were actual or not. The fact that the authoress was a writer of fiction may have militated against its taking a permanent hold. Mrs. Crowe's Night Side of Nature at an earlier date stirred many minds, but here also the fact that Mrs. Crowe was a novelist caused it to be soon forgotten. There have been many writers familiar with the phenomena, men like Rev. H.R. Haweis, who have continually brought forth the subject as one capable of making religion real. Scarcely a volume of Mr. Haweis's, The Broad Church, Current Coin, The Dead Pulpit, etc., but has numerous paragraphs wherein he shows how important to his mind were the modern evidences of a future life. The unripe and unready pass these over as speculations on the writer's part.

Many of the volumes associated with what has been called the New Thought are impregnated with the spiritual teachings. We have somehow the faculty of regarding what belongs to the next life as but poetical speculation when we come across some stirring sentence in a book, but it will invariably be found that the writers of these books are Spiritualists.

Miss Lilian Whiting, who has written a charming study of Elizabeth Barrett Browning, The World Beautiful, and other volumes of a lofty type, is a declared Spiritualist. It is the consciousness of being close to the spirit-world, and having held speech with its inhabitants, that helps her to pen such words as these in The World Beautiful: "We at once realise that death is not the end of life, but merely one phase of experience in life, and its nature is to uplift and purify the friend left on this side, and to offer its absolute testimony to the persistence of the communion between the two—the one still an inhabitant of the visible world, the other of the unseen world. He who has gone into the life beyond is as real a personality as ever. Indeed, he is even more alive than before, having entered into the 'life more abundant.'"

I had the privilege of meeting with Miss Whiting in Rome during the spring of 1907, and conversing with her on the wealth and beauty of the spiritual gospel.

It is not, however, those who write books only who have built up the great movement which is talked about in every corner of the land. The powerful addresses delivered in the trance state for nearly forty years by Mr. J.J. Morse have helped many to realise a natural spirit world. It has been my privilege to stand by his side all these years during his visits to Glasgow, and to be charmed and assisted by the inspired utterances, the veritable thoughts of souls who once dwelt on earth. What perplexing questions has he not thrown light on, what real cheer has been sent forth! And yet all this wealth of intellect and spiritual knowledge has only been heard by a comparative few. Seeds have, however, been dropped which take root, and the noble and faithful service he has rendered cannot be lost. One who, like myself, has been fortunate to have Mr. Morse as a guest for many years has gathered rich treasures of thought, which are stored in the archives of memory. The public movement in Glasgow has been built up largely through the wisdom of his controls, "Tien" and "Strolling Player," who, to me, are not only spiritual beings, but close personal friends.

The work which has been done by Spiritualism through such labours as Mr. Morse has given, is such as has been pointedly set forth by the genial Oliver Wendell Holmes in his Autocrat of the Breakfast Table, in that striking paragraph which the bulk of readers will pass over: "While some are crying out against Spiritualism as a delusion of the devil, and some are laughing at it as a hysteric folly, it is quietly undermining the traditional ideas of the future state to a larger extent than most good people seem to be aware of. You cannot have people of cultivation, of pure character, sensible enough in common things—largehearted women, shrewd business men, men of science—professing to be in communication with the spiritual world and keeping up constant intercourse with it, without its gradual reacting on the whole conception of that other life."

There can be little doubt that the brighter and better ideas which are preached in the churches today —the disappearance of the devil, the silence regarding eternal punishment, the doctrine of eternal hope—are largely the result of the spiritual facts which are in our midst. Many of the clergy know all about Crookes and Wallace, and the fact that many scientific men of eminence are giving attention to the matter. Spiritualism faces them continually; members of their congregations talk to them of what they have seen at séances, and so, unconsciously, the harsh, unjust dogmas which formerly ruled have been modified. There are hundreds of clergymen who know that the facts are real, the evidence unsurmountable. Many are so situated that they dare not say all they think, but others have confessed to me how much of joy the new light has given them, how it has held up their hands and strengthened their hearts in the face of death, and made them discard forever the old doctrines. Almost every town and village has set up a temple where the good news of the immortal life is proclaimed, and where, it may be, the forms of their loved ones are described. New and bright ideas are coming into life each day, and if the Church, called Christian, had to disappear it would give place to something better, something not related to myth and tradition, but to what we really know.

Three hundred years ago men said it was wicked to study the world: that to know God you must read the Scriptures, the Hebrew of the old and the Greek of the new. Who could have fancied, once, that the deities of Greece and Rome would be displaced, and the gods become only the playthings of poets? All the gods called heathen have been turned out of the heathen heaven, and the playful fancy of a Heine pictures them in exile. Nobody prays now to Pan or Jupiter or Zeus; no sacrifice is offered to Pallas; not a worshipper of these old deities remains in all the world. Rome has still its temples of Jupiter, Mars, and Minerva, whom humanity has banished. The stone has outlasted the deities. The God of Abraham, Isaac, and Jacob, the God of David and Israel, will also disappear in due season. We shall get rid of the fancy sketches which make up the ecclesiastical Jesus. We shall cease to mumble over words which flamed out of the religious consciousness of saints—words now dead to thinking minds. But better institutions, better forms of religion will appear, and better men will tread the ground. They will gather up every good thing we have brought to light, to be kept forever. A living and progressive people has need to alter its ecclesiastical institutions as it improves its other machinery, industrial or political. It is the ecclesiastical institutions which have been the greatest obstacles in the way of progress. They have for years retarded and perverted the intellectual, moral, affectional, and religious development of mankind.

CHAPTER XXX

THE STRUGGLE OF SIXTY YEARS

Spiritualism sixty years ago was but some strange noises heard in a farmer's home—noises which had a voice for those who would hear. Now it is the spiritual food of millions, who find in it a something which the churches cannot give. For long it had no great man in its ranks, not a philosopher, not a scholar, but it had new fire on its hearth, and soon it warmed the souls of mortals. With more of evidence for its wonders than the miracles of the Christian religion, it yet destroyed the belief in miracles.

If there have been extravagances and follies amongst some of its followers, this is not to be wondered at. Some will always swing to extremes when suddenly taken from their old moorings. In Scotland for long the progress seemed but slow. At moments you would have thought that the censor of the press would have blotted out all reference to Spiritualism, but it had a true word, and those who heard it were eloquent with its new force. Men were quickened by its power, and could not keep still, but told out their story, repeating the forcible evidence that came to them. Some saw it but dimly for a time; others, who seemed to be waiting for the consolation, gave it ready welcome. But a handful of people met in an upper room less than thirty-five years ago, afraid almost to declare that there were such facts as that spirit people could make their presence known. Now there are meeting-places in every district of Glasgow, with congregations which add to their numbers daily. In Edinburgh, in Dundee, and many other places the public hear the new gospel gladly, while the Glasgow Association gathers audiences of several hundreds together each Sunday. The spiritual teachers tell out a message which does not insult the common-sense of mankind.

It is only right that I should put on record the great work done by Mr. E.W. and Mrs. M.H. Wallis, who, like Mr. Morse, have for many years spoken out the spirits' message. New workers continually come to the front. Mr. John Lobb, of the City of London Common Council, has done yeoman service both by his books and voice, and his great regret is that he should have passed through life for so long unconscious of the precious gift which all the time was at his doorstep. The Glasgow platform has been filled by men of social position and deep insight, who have not hesitated to let the world know where they stood on this question—men like Dr. Abraham Wallace, Rear-Admiral Usborne Moore, and Gambier Bolton, F.S.A. The public workers whom the spirits have more specially called to their service, who through their phenomenal gifts have evidenced the message, have stirred up many. For years Miss Rowan Vincent, a cultured woman, by her intelligent speech and forcible clairvoyance, built up the faith of many. Dundee also produced a striking seer in the person of Mrs. Inglis, an untutored but brave woman, whose descriptions of spirit people, so marked and clear, gave food to many a hungering heart. In South Africa a great movement is on foot, and a call is being made for missionary mediums. Many of those in that part of the world received the knowledge while resident in Scotland. Already several workers have traversed that land with singular success; first Mrs. Green, then Miss Florence Morse, daughter of Mr. J.J. Morse, an admirable speaker and clairvoyante, then Mrs. Place-Veary, and latterly Mrs. Inglis, of Dundee, all of whom by their real spiritual gifts have brought hundreds into the fold.

Spiritualism continually shows forth how much a single man or a single woman can do when sustained by the power of the spirit people. The great strength of the movement, however, is not in its public aspect. In thousands of homes the spirit circle is a veritable altar, from which hearts are fed, and a new joy given to life. A sanctuary is provided for the weary, who gather a strength on which they can walk for many times forty days in the wilderness of life. Many noble souls fed from "the other side" go through life scattering the seeds of joy. Much that they do is not seen, but they are planting a religion which will produce blossoms in the lives of a multitude. The names of many labourers who have done perhaps the noblest part of the work may never be publicly heard, but they will march into the next life and receive the cheer and love of numbers who have witnessed their true worth.

Spiritualism will yet join hands with all true science, and enlarge the boundaries of knowledge, in harmony with the facts of nature. It cannot well join hands with a church which has ever been anti-natural and at war with scientific facts. Spiritualism was once thought to be coming to buttress the churches' faith, but the faith which Spiritualism will establish will have facts for its basis and not fables. Spiritualism alone gives a basis for assured belief in immortality. It demonstrates the existence and persistence of man in another life. It can have no contact with the idea that man fell from paradise and was damned forever before the first child was born, or that the world was ever lost, or that it is to be saved, and man restored, by a vicarious atonement, on the plea that once there was a miraculous physical resurrection from the dead. All these doctrines so long preached and believed in are non-natural, non-spiritual, unscientific, and false, and the facts of Spiritualism uproot them.

The school which has claimed to be scientific, the Society for Psychical Research, has not given much evidence that it was qualified or had the desire to get at the kernel of the matter. If there has been any progress it has been of the most creeping kind. A good many nothings have been strung together, which gave neither light nor leading. Some of the men of real scientific bent, like the early investigators, Professor De Morgan and Alfred Russel Wallace, gloried in the great and beautiful illumination without putting forth cold and incredulous reservations to save their credit for wisdom. The new school seems incapable of coming to any conclusion. If something is said which for the moment is direct as well as forcible, in another sentence you get something else which breaks it to pieces. And yet the force of the facts has brought conviction to some of those who laboured for long without sight. This has not come about through the hyper-sceptical spirit which has ruled for long, but rather through casting it off. Some, no doubt, are of opinion that the work of this Society has drawn many into the ranks of the Spiritualists; but I, for one, believe that where one has been drawn into the ranks hundreds have been caused to stand aloof through the uncertain opinions which were held by its members, and the incapacity shown by them of arriving at any definite conclusion.

I gave a lecture in London, in February 1908, on my view of the work of the Society for Psychical Research, which is printed as an appendix to this volume, and in spite of the fact that about the same time Sir Oliver Lodge came into the open with the statement that he believed he had held genuine converse with old friends, and that at last the boundary wall between the two spheres was "wearing thin in places," I have seen no reason to modify the criticism which I then expressed. As a writer in *Light* so well said: "Every alternative to the Spiritualists' theory has been tried, and that only is left. Its acceptance was therefore inevitable."

The Spiritualists who have fought the fight cannot slavishly applaud the last comers who waited outside the gates which were open all the time. It is something, however, that a truth so long despised gets recognition at last from those who hitherto have opposed its march. The volume of testimony grows all the time. The bands of workers on this side increase, and greater power under the brighter conditions comes from those on the other side of life. I find my work coming to an end. For over twenty years I occupied the presidency of the Glasgow Society, and have witnessed the movement grow from a tiny babe to vigorous youth. My interest in the success of the work can never be lessened, but with advancing years I am glad to leave the public work in the hands of those who, with youth on their side and fervour for the truth, will be able to go further than I had the time or power to go. Each day of my earthly pilgrimage I can truly say that I give God thanks for Spiritualism and all it has brought.

> *Though he may cause pain and weeping,*
> *Those whom Death holds in his keeping*
> > *Still live on.*
> *Death is Nature's love transcending.*
> *Life, unsought, unearned, unending,*
> > *Still flows on.*
>
> *Come, for all that is immortal*
> *Passed through Nature's love-lit portal*
> > *Without pain,*
> *And, by that same door returning,*
> *He will come, for love still yearning,*
> > *Back again.*[6]

---

6. From *Poems* by Harold Carpenter.

APPENDIX

SPIRITUALISM AND THE SOCIETY FOR PSYCHICAL RESEARCH

A Review and a Criticism

An Address delivered by Mr. James Robertson to the Members and Associates of the London Spiritualist Alliance, on Thursday evening, February 6th, 1908, in the Salon of the Royal Society of British Artists, Suffolk Street, Pall Mall, Mr. H. Withall, Vice-President, in the chair.

Mr. Robertson said that he was glad that Mr. Withall, in his introductory remarks, had drawn attention to the fact that he would present his own views. He did not desire to commit the Alliance to any opinions which he might express; they were his own, and he fully accepted the responsibility for them. He thought that he would be able to make his meaning clear, and he would present an aspect of the truth as it appeared to him. Continuing, Mr. Robertson said:

It is over thirty years since Spiritualism came to me like a burst of sweet music, and ever since it has claimed the best part of my thought and life. During that time, I have heard and read a good many of the misinterpretations and misrepresentations with which it has been met, but neither the theosophic boom nor the laboured work of the Psychical Research Society has changed one idea which I caught up when I fortunately became a student of the writings of Andrew Jackson Davis, and was privileged to come within the personal sphere of those wise people who have so long used Mr. J.J. Morse and Mr. E.W. Wallis as their mouthpieces. I have never for one moment lost the faith that the Spiritualism of the Spiritualists would ultimately prevail, and I think that the current of public thought during these later years points very much in this direction.

I know that to the outsider it is a stupendous proposition to make, that the dead have found an avenue through which they can impress their identity on the living, and I do not wonder that such a claim should be met with incredulity; but I do say that there has been given to the world during the last sixty years such a wealth of evidence in favour of the existence of man after death as to bring the Spiritualist's position within the domain of demonstrated fact. I would not think of claiming that all the details of spirit manifestations which have been printed in Spiritualist literature are accurate; but what is really important is the great fact that intelligence, not belonging to those in the body, comes out clearly from many sources, and the same remains true, if some of the details set down are erroneous.

From the inception of the movement there gathered round this central truth numbers of sober-minded, intelligent men and women, who found the satisfaction and rest which such a glorious belief was calculated to give. Their experiences were not of the subjective type, but were the result of the exercise of all those faculties which enabled them to weigh up facts in the material sphere. There was borne in upon them that here was a great reality which rolled away a cloud of difficulties, and threw a new light on history, sacred and secular, which had been long obscured. They asked for no patronage, were patient, and listened without a murmur when powerful assailants threw ridicule on their beliefs, feeling that they could always receive a fresh measure of strength from the spirit circle. They could afford to be indifferent to the assertions of their scientific opponents, who had either been ill-guided or unfortunate in their search for light. The simple truth of Spiritualism, that those we have loved and who love us can mingle in our sorrows and our joys, is a perfect armour against any assault.

The opening of the gates between the two worlds represents, of course, a great deal more than our personal consolation. There is a rich philosophy which has been merely hinted at in the religions of the past, and this will unite and bring into line every aspect of Nature. But the first point to be brought home is the one which most nearly concerns our personal affections—that life and love have not been destroyed by death. The Spiritualist has never needed to move from his original position. All these years he has listened to the babbling of adverse voices, considered the theories advanced, only to find that his daily experiences contradict many of them. But Spiritualists cannot convince those whose minds are closed against even the possibility of Nature having such facts as spirit spheres and spirit beings to reveal. Incidents of spirit intervention may be dissected and explained (?) by the critic to his own satisfaction, but his incomprehensible theories never in the least weaken or destroy the incontestable facts which have become a part of the Spiritualist's being. Professions of unbelief or non-belief are valueless. Only those who are free to stand level-footed, face to face with the facts, will ever see; the others grope blindly. The faculty of vision, the gift of hearing, and the capacity to weigh up and take the measure of any occurrence should be the property of the average man or woman as much as the savant. We are apt to get tired of hearing so much about learning alone having the capacity to see truth. The natural man who has never come into touch with a university, who knows nothing of classical scholarship, may see a fact and estimate its worth quite as readily as the most profound scholar. Many things are not calculable by algebra, nor deducible by logic. The mightiest magician that ever waved the enchanter's wand, Shakespeare, was twitted by his contemporaries because he lacked scholarship, and the first biographer of Robert Burns, Dr. Currie, always introduces him with a certain patronising, apologetic air; as if the polite public might think it strange and half unwarrantable that he, a man of science, a scholar and gentleman, should condescend to do such honour to a rustic! There is no ready-made, patent, scientific method by which the scholar has the advantage over his fellows in reaching truth. "He that walks familiarly with humble men," says Theodore Parker, "often stumbles over masses of unsunnied gold, where men, proud in emptiness, looked only for common dust."

It may, perhaps, seem somewhat presumptuous that I should take it upon myself to criticise a body of men making claims to be scientists, philosophers and deep thinkers, who are credited with possessing the culture and erudition which a university training is supposed to give. My warrant is that I have had over thirty years' close experience in the subject which they have sought to examine.

What has the Society for Psychical Research brought to light during its quarter of a century's working? Is there anything made more clear regarding what are called spirit phenomena? What special faculty of vision were its leaders possessed of which gave them an advantage in the way of research over those who called themselves Spiritualists, and who had vouched for the reality of certain phenomena taking place? They set out on their mission because they considered that Spiritualists were visionaries and their facts were too sensational for the general palate. Inefficiency was to give place to a cultured efficiency, which would yield endless diagrams, elevations and sections, that would explain and regulate the phenomena. Theirs was a golden opportunity to let the world have some thing authoritative as to whether these abnormal experiences which had been denied or denounced were fact or fiction: but have we got anything from them which settles anything? Would it be rude to suggest that, with all their high-sounding titles, they were incompetent, and that they failed to show that they were gifted with even ordinary powers of observation? As Mrs. Poyser in *Adam Bede* says: "There's folk 'ud hold a sieve under the pump and expect to carry away the water." I have read somewhere of "moon-rakers": "people who do not see a fact as plain as the luminous orb in the heavens, but will go dredging after the image of it, reflected in their own village pond."

This Research body got credit for possessing some superior furnace, in which they would smelt the Spiritualists' ore, and show the world its poor quality, but their crucible had been wrongly constructed, and therefore it has only produced Blag. They never grasped the revelation that was being given. Time and money have been consumed, and the total outcome has been to raise a cloud of dust, about which there has been much chattering. I know there are a few people in the Spiritualists' ranks who praise the work of the Society for Psychical Research, and flatter its printed Proceedings, calling the fog produced illuminating. They seem to consider that Spiritualism is helped when they meet with the sly pinch of disparagement under the pretended fondling of praise—the honey with a sting in it. The average Spiritualist, however, who has waded through the complex mass, finds little of real value; hardly anything which he did not know before, and very much that is so twisted and entangled as to be utterly incomprehensible.

I know some persons will ask what did we know about the subliminal, the sub-conscious, or unconscious self, before the days of Psychical Research? and I would ask what do we know *now?* Have any of these newly coined and imposing words helped anyone to reach firmer ground? Has it been a great gain to the world to be told that what was heard by Spiritualists was not the silvery voices of angels, but rather a bundle of peculiar forces which had a genius for confusing and confounding? Mr. Myers harped on the subliminal self as explaining nearly all there was in so-called spirit action, and after all his labours, a new leader of the body, Mr. Gerald Balfour, president, comes out with the statement, "I never yet succeeded in forming a clear idea of what Mr. Myers means by the subliminal self." Mr. Balfour does not stand alone, I think. It was an imposing term, no doubt, but it did not lay bare or dissect the spiritual facts with which I, for one, have long been familiar. Then we had the blessed word "telepathy," the second dogma of the Researcher's creed, which was quoted in every direction as the true solvent of all there was in Spiritualism. Whenever some demonstration of a marked character was given that evidently made spirit return conclusive, out came this all-sufficing word to dispute or explain away the action of spirits. But another leader, an American one, dislikes telepathy as an explanation of psychical phenomena. He cannot believe the wild assertions that telepathy can be made to wander all over the earth and read minds, and then neatly palm off the knowledge thus acquired upon the Researchers. After the word had become orthodox Professor Hyslop came out with the statement that Psychical Researchers had used the term illegitimately. Surely here is a presentation of incapacity somewhere. It looks like a case of blind men who feel the raised letters which they touch, but have not first learned to read.

Spirit phenomena had been satisfactorily attested by men of light and leading before the days of these confused ideas. It would be difficult to find anywhere more competent minds than those who vouched for the reality of the spirits' presence amongst mortals. The earlier researchers adopted methods which were simple, clear, and exhaustive. What was actual they reported, leaving speculation alone. They were men and women who would not swerve a hair's breadth from the sternest loyalty to truth. One of them, recognised as having the keenest insight and the most sublime courage, went so far as to say that spirit return was as satisfactorily proved as any other scientific fact.

The work of research had been entered upon years before by a committee of the London Dialectical Society, who reached certain conclusions without wandering in the wilderness of fog. Spirit action on the mortal life is more than hinted at in their report, but they had no doubt about the reality of certain phenomena. What Cromwell Varley narrated, the wonderful incidents spoken of by the present Earl of Crawford, by H.D. Jencken, by Thomas Shorter, by E.L. Blanchard, and many others, was just the kind of evidence which would have established the truth of anything in a court of justice. For a period of fifteen years before theDialectical Society's report was made, there was perpetual commotion regarding the Spiritualists' claims. The controversy between D.D. Home and his friends and Sir David Brewster was more than a nine days' talk. The fact that Lord Brougham, who had been present with Brewster at Home's séances, never uttered a sentence while the war of words lasted, was pretty fair evidence that Brougham knew that a strange realm had been brought into view. When this was followed, a few years afterwards, by his remarkable statement that, even In the cloudless skies of scepticism he saw "a rain cloud, no bigger than a man's hand," and that this rain cloud was Modern Spiritualism, we have surely the proclamation of the coming deluge of evidences of the presence of spirit people. This statement by Lord Brougham ran pretty much in line with one made by the great German philosopher, Immanuel Kant, a century before, when the author of *The Critique of Pure Reason* met with the spiritual gifts of Swedenborg. He said: "The day will come when it will be proved that the human soul is already, during its life on earth, in a close and indissoluble connection with a world of spirits, *that their world influences ours and impresses it profoundly.*"

They were strong men and women in every sense, who acknowledged the open door between the two worlds in the fifties and sixties.

Robert Chambers was something more than a *littérateur*: his penetrative intellect had formulated Evolution as a possible theory before Darwin arrived with his array of facts. Chambers gathered sunshine into his life by observation of the phenomena through Home and others, and acknowledged that Spiritualism was a potent influence in dissipating the materialism which abounded.

There were other literary personages whose eyes and ears opened to the recognition that an important discovery had been made—the Halls and Howitts, Mrs. Barrett Browning, and many others—neither dreamers of dreams nor manufacturers of bad myths.

Not one name associated with Psychical Research, nor all combined, can be compared in capacity with those early Spiritualists. What a strong tower was the great man who went out of the physical life the other day almost unrecognised, I mean Gerald Massey, the most courageous and helpful exponent of Spiritualism! Massey was more than a poet, he was a discoverer and excavator in realms obscure; a man of tremendous range of thought, with powers of vision, and a capacity to tread ground where there was almost no foothold. He brought the character of Shakespeare out of the darkness, and showed to all the world a man pure in thought and deeds. The man who unravelled that story in Shakespeare's Sonnets, and who in later life turned his thought to the secrets of ancient Egypt, was a great explorer. His sacrifice of self in labouring in a realm where there was no hope of remuneration, so that future generations might know the truth, is a splendid exhibition of human nobleness. But it is his clear-ringing, positive strains regarding the spirit world that should call forth our admiration and gratitude. Future generations will rank Gerald Massey as the clearest-sighted Spiritualist of our day.

Sir William Crookes had also contributed something which looked like evidence before the Research days. He may be halting, and not inclined to speak out all he knows as to what the phenomena may point to, but it is clear that there is no doubt in his mind about the actual existence of such phenomena, and no carping criticism can shake his testimony. There it stands—the movement of objects without contact— the unseen intelligence which gives a rational message, the direct writings, the appearance of phantom forms and faces, leading up to the fully-formed materialisations of those who claimed to have once dwelt on earth. No one can read Crookes without feeling that here we have an exhibition of the true scientific, cautious spirit, a man not carried away by sentiment, but one who accurately measured all the ground. The issue of his *Researches in the Phenomena of Spiritualism* will always mark an era of vision and faithfulness.

What Crookes had met with was introduced to a larger public through the bravery of Thackeray in printing in the *Cornhill Magazine* that record of spiritual phenomena entitled "Stranger than Fiction." From many quarters, in those early days, there came forth strong and forcible statements as to the existence of spirit people at work. The *Cornhill* article was followed by a volume from the eminently respectable house of Longmans, entitled From *Matter to Spirit*, in which we had the same objective phenomena vouched for—the very phenomena which the Researchers could never see. The preface to this volume was one of the most masterly bits of literary work, and it was soon an open secret that its author was Professor De Morgan, the mathematician, of London University. It is a scholarly and forcible presentation of the whole matter; nothing is vague; it creates the impression that striking and positive as were his statements, there was more behind which he might say. Mrs. De Morgan, the writer of the book, a remarkably clear-headed, conscientious woman, had recognised that the phenomena could only point to the unseen spirit people as the workers, who, by seeking to touch our sense perceptions, make us realise their continued interest in our welfare. This early setting forth of spiritualistic phenomena was most conclusive, systematising the facts in such a way as to demand attention. It was, how ever, the learned and philosophic preface which elevated the subject at a bound, and showed it to be one of pre-eminent importance. Careful and thoughtful as the writer is, you feel that instead of the spiritual hypothesis being weakened, every other hypothesis appears to be eliminated.

Professor De Morgan seems to have anticipated some of the learned twaddle that was to arise in after years, and pretty thoroughly answers many objections which the Research, thought-transference school have manufactured. His own theories had been destroyed by the strength of the facts which he had met. Here is a striking and clear statement which he makes: "I have seen and heard, in a manner which should make unbelief impossible, things called spiritual, which were not capable of being explained by imposture, coincidence, or mistake," and, modestly, he adds, "The physical explanations which I have seen are easy, but miserably insufficient; the spiritual hypothesis is sufficient, but ponderously difficult." Is it not remarkable that so many of those early investigators could see without difficulty what the later school, with all their learning, failed to realise?

Professor De Morgan, with his uncommon common-sense, could boldly say: "The deluded spirit rappers are on the right track, they have the spirit and the method of the grand time when those paths were cut through the uncleared forest in which it is now the daily routine to walk." Evidently the Psychical Researchers had not got either the wit or the method required for such investigation as they entered upon. They could not distinguish between a conjuring trick and a spiritual phenomenon, and all the time seemed to prefer the shadow to the substance (Young Davey before Eglinton), the phantom to the fact (Maskelyne before Eusapia), cloudland before solid earth. Miss Katharine Bates, in her charming book, *Seen and Unseen*, tells of a Burmese lady whom she met on her travels, who was indignant with the Theosophista because they had muddled everything up, taking little bits and piecing them together all wrong, many of the pieces wrong side upward, and she wound up by calling them "stupid muddlers." I think the *Journals and Proceedings* of the Society for Psychical Research could cap even the Theosophists at misreading the spiritual revelation. There was already in existence, as I have sought to show, a body of striking evidence gathered together—evidence much more weighty than what we have for historic Christianity. It was scientific, it was rational, and it was religious. It converted Robert Owen and his clever son, Robert Dale Owen, while they were dwelling widely apart from one another; and those valuable volumes written by the latter, *Footfalls on the Boundary of Another World* and the *Debateable Land*, are priceless to persons of intellect who have been dwelling in the wilderness of doubt and denial.

Dr. Elliotson, Thackeray's close friend, to whom he dedicated his *Pendennis*, must also be considered one of the strong men who expressed his gratitude for the rich blessing of spiritual intercourse. At first an opponent of the most virulent type, he soon came to look fairly with an open and free mind, and with tears he expressed deep regret for his former opposition.

There can be no doubt that Spiritualism brought cheer into the hearts of thousands, enabling them to breathe a freer air and live a larger life. We cannot calmly consider this remarkable transformation, amongst all conditions of men, without feeling that it could have been no delusion which effected such positive and beneficent results, for we have a volume of testimony that thirty or forty years ago Spiritual ism was accepted by numbers of the shrewdest men and women in the country.

In the year 1882 certain gentlemen of note, who had been coquetting with the subject for some time, came into association with a few prominent Spiritualists and set forth the view that it was a scandal that there should be any dispute about the reality of spirit phenomena. They urged that the question needed to be determined, and that a society should be inaugurated with this object in view. The Spiritualists, who were certain that no amount of investigation could destroy or weaken their position, were most cordial in their co-operation. They had the idea that the principal object of the new body was to examine the Spiritualists' affirmations, but there was never any effort made to deal seriously with Spiritualism; what attempts were made were of such a blundering pattern that Spiritualists were satisfied that no convictions would be arrived at, and most of them, to their credit, withdrew.

The question of a future life is beyond aught else the great question: a truth compared with which it is of small moment whether anything else be true. Spiritualists had been insisting that the phenomena they had witnessed alone offered the means of establishing it as a fact. This new society commenced its inquiry by appointing committees to consider thought-reading, mesmerism, Reichenbach's experiments, and added apparitions, haunted houses, and physical phenomena as something to retain the interest of Spiritualists. I know that a good deal of printers' ink has been consumed in treating about thought-reading, etc., but the research into the physical phenomena of Spiritualism has been absolutely barren of result. The Researchers evidently had never heard that there was a Mrs. Everitt, in whose presence raps and voices could be heard, or that there was such a person as Lottie Fowler, with her gifts of clairvoyance and clairaudience, or that a J.J. Morse entered into the trance condition and revealed abnormal intellectual powers. They never heard or saw anything which was of the least value. They did not know that Spiritualism had given birth to the most profound scientific setting forth of Nature's revelations through unlettered men like A.J. Davis and Hudson Tuttle. We have never heard that any one of the persons named was ever asked to submit to cross-examination. They never wanted to establish anything, but were quite satisfied to trot out their hypotheses in one corner and have them demolished in another.

When natural phenomena have to be investigated, it is essential that the observer be passive and look closely at what occurs in a truth-seeking frame of mind, accompanied by keen perception and common-sense. Unbiassed persons would have inquired, "Under what conditions did the phenomena which Crookes vouched for take place?" and it might be fairly assumed that these sages would have recognised that, given the same conditions, the phenomena would be repeated; but it seems never to have dawned upon them that the character of the manifestations was moulded by the mental and moral status of the mediums and the sitters. Crookes caught something of the method required to get evidential results, and his words cannot be too deeply pondered. When his modes are brought into play there will be less heard of fraud, and no need for the distressful "tests" which rarely bring conviction. The phenomena will then rise beyond all the tests that can be applied. Speaking of D.D. Home, Crookes says: "I used to say, let us sit round the fire and have a quiet chat, and see if our friends are here and will do anything for us; we won't have any tests or precautions. On these occasions, when only my own family were present, some of the most convincing phenomena took place." Crookes, no doubt, had seen that the power with which he had come into contact exhibited, at times, the most complete indifference to scientific theories, and would not be confined within the borders of any speculations, but made itself understood when the free-minded and openhearted listened. Has the Psychical Research Society ever presented this aspect of kindliness and sympathy towards those who claimed to have medial gifts? On the contrary, as I read, they have, as a rule, treated them either as rogues or as automatons. It is not to be wondered at, therefore, that these alleged "experts" have given us nothing but confused ideas. It could have been seen from the first that it was not a demonstration of Spiritualism that was intended. Apparently there was never any desire to reach a conclusion as to the great central fact that the dead return; they were ever repudiating preconceptions and bias, and yet they never accepted anything which was not in harmony with some preconceived notion.

The Society for Psychical Research was an awe-inspiring body—on paper. Notables in abundance were to be found in its list of Members and Associates; no one could lose caste through being connected with such a body of respect ables, while to be a Spiritualist was but another name for ignoramus and fanatic. Very many of the names, however, were only names. It was Sidgwick, Myers, Hodgson, Podmore, and one or two others who composed the Society, and I would like to look at them individually for a short time, and see if they ever revealed any special talents which would make them superior to the average man in the street as investigators of occult phenomena. I will begin with Professor Sidgwick, the first president, whose name is one we have heard mentioned with bated breath. "Such a profound man!" everybody said. Why, I know not exactly. I have heard him described by those who were brought into close touch with him as a philosopher and a saint of the ancient type, but I am not aware of his being gifted with any special faculty for seeing the trend of modern events. No doubt he was a scholar and philosopher, whose great position dominated the younger men, who looked up to him as an oracle, pretty much as did those who gathered round Coleridge in his declining years and devoured his speech, conceivable and inconceivable, as heavenly wisdom, while much of it was really what Carlyle called "bottled moon shine." Sidgwick never seemed to have any settled ideas as to a future life. The Christian's hope of immortality was a thing for which there was no rational basis, he said; but, like Matthew Arnold, he felt that the absence of such a hope would be an evil. "Why he ever troubled himself about the phenomena of Spiritualism is an enigma, seeing that he never wanted to get at the root of anything; his own words being," It gives life an additional interest having problems still to solve." He might truthfully have classed himself as a waverer or an Agnostic, who never could reach any settled convictions. He sat with mediums year after year, but he evidently neither hoped nor desired to get satisfactory results. He might have gone on for a century and have found himself in the same position, because, while he recognised that certain conditions were essential in other realms, he considered that spiritual phenomena were different, and so dictated his own conditions. He admitted that he seemed to paralyse phenomena, yet he never caught the idea that certain vibrations of the ether were needed for their successful production, and that vibrations from the sitters might be as disastrous as is the crossing of the telephone wires when one wishes to hold a conversation. But for the commotion inspired by his position, and the authority of his name, Sidgwick's colleagues would speedily have recognised his unfitness to explore such a subject as mediumship. As early as 1864 he wrote: "I *fancy* I have heard the raps." This gives us a revelation of his character: he was never quite convinced about the reality of anything. He was cautious, however, that even his "*fancies*" should not be betrayed, for he adds to his letter, "but keep it dark about the raps till I blaze forth." Of course there never was any blaze, only blinding smoke! All his life he was a doubter, and I suppose the spirit people did not trouble whether he was converted or not, as he would have unearthed some theory to shatter their proofs and leave himself as unconvinced as before. He was "the old man of the sea," who rode upon the shoulders of his fellows. He failed to see that the laws of physics were not always applicable to spiritual operations.

Crookes' experiments would have been as barren of results as Sidgwick's, but that he was gifted with a little more common-sense. He saw at a glance that material science could not arrange a successful spirit circle. "Katie King," the spirit, called Crookes' children around her, and amused them by recounting her adventures in India; but no "Katie King," or any other spiritual being, could have come within the sphere of the man who only got the length of *fancying* he had heard the raps. I hope we shall hear no more about Professor Sidgwick being an *authority*. In my opinion ha was unworthy of even the slightest attention. He simply wasted years in travelling round a circle, without observing that it was a circle. We cannot call him a. philosopher, only a trifler.

Another influence in this body of scholars was Mr. F.W.H. Myers, a man of quite another stamp from that of Sidgwick; but with rare genius, with the sweetest traits of character, he was continually dominated by his surroundings and afraid to give out all he knew or thought. At times his hands were filled with husks, from which the corn had long ago been shelled out. At other moments there was the appearance of living bread in his grasp. His was truly a. dual nature. Did he meet a spiritualist, he was strong in the faith and only wished there were greater marvels to believe. Let him again get into the Sidgwick-Podmore atmosphere, and his previous faith would vanish. He would once more hug to his bosom his favourite bantlings, telepathy and the subliminal self, and would talk learnedly about multiplex personalities, forgetting, for the time being, all the facts that he had met with. It was his association with the Society for Psychical Research that kept alive the sceptical vein. Naturally a spiritually minded man, he would have been fully satisfied with the clear evidence of spirit return which was all around, but that his nature was timorous, and though never dominated by Podmore, he lent himself too readily to adverse theorists.

He was a poet and essayist, but could not claim to be a scientist, although that would not have been greatly in his favour, for, as David Christie Murray pointed out, "Your man of science is often the last man in the world to be entrusted with an idea, because he often starts from a pre conception which he has to maintain at all hazards." Myers' essays are truly spiritual, and convey the idea that he had something more than intuitions to guide him. He opposes Kenan for his non-acceptance of spiritual marvels, and has almost a feeling of pity for George Eliot in thinking that immortality was unbelievable, and yet when he speaks from the Research atmosphere there is never any certainty. The balanced mind was continually lacking, so that even with his great gifts he would blow hot and cold alternately. Many years before the days of Psychical Research he witnessed materialisations through Miss Wood and Miss Fairlamb in Professor Sidgwick's rooms at Cambridge, but he kept the facts locked up in his bosom. It is only through the publication of Dr. Alfred Russel Wallace's autobiography that we get at the particulars of these investigations. Myers had no doubt that the manifestations which then occurred were genuine, and a hungering world should have had the facts placed at its service. His corroboration, at the time, would have assisted Crookes and Wallace in their controversies with Tyndall and Dr. Carpenter; but he remained silent, contented with keeping the records buried in his notebooks, until in after years, when the better Myers was uppermost, he read them to Dr. Wallace and expressed himself as quite convinced of their genuineness. Myers was ever afraid of the full force of the truth, and would tone down the more pregnant facts with some of his far-fetched theories. Dr. Wallace, seeking to place Myers' attitude in the softest and most apologetic light, says that the introduction of such well-attested phenomena would have been out of place at the early period of the Society's working; but the fact that he gave no signs of possessing such knowledge during a quarter of a century needs some more cogent explanation; even the great book published at the conclusion of his active life does not contain a word on the subject. I hold, with Sir Arthur Helps, that "the withholding of large truths from the world may be a betrayal of the greatest trust."

I have heard it said that Myers believed in Stainton Moses beyond aught else, but conclusive evidence for this is sadly lacking. He got so close to all Stainton Moses' work that he might have reached some definite and clear conclusion, but there is a considerable amount of trifling all the time, and no statement we can grasp that this great seer established the fact that intelligence and knowledge survived bodily death. Stainton Moses was a robust thinker, who was keenly critical of all that happened through bis own mediumship, one who faced and fought his doubts, only yielding when the evidence was overwhelming. Yet Myers' criticism of him was that he was without the critical or legal faculty! In 1894 the London Spiritualist Alliance asked Mr. Myers to read one of Stainton Moses' posthumous papers on "Spirit Identity," certainly one of the most evidential presentations of the subject that could have been offered. This remarkable statement of facts should have brought conviction to Myers, and perhaps it did, but the old spirit showed itself at the close. There were only some platitudes offered about being cautious in our affirmations, and exercising constantly the doubting spirit, as one who should say, "Live ever on doubt, and thy soul shall be satisfied!"

What brought Myers rest and satisfaction towards the close of his earthly career were the simple truths of Spiritualism, not the psychical theories and hair-splittings which had taken up so much of his time. The people from that other world had been waiting at the door: he simply drew up the blinds, and there came to him knowledge which might have been his years before. His theories, in the light of the spirits' presence, were of little service. He opened his eyes, there they stood; he opened his ears, and those of the long ago were heard giving the message of courage and good cheer. It required neither literature, science, nor philosophy to get conviction, only the removal of the obstacles of his own creation. The spirit people came in and supped with him, and brought him at last to the realisation of the larger hope that had gleamed upon him so fitfully for so many years.

Another leading light I have to notice is Mr. Frank Podmore, one of those strange freaks who crop up in human history, like the sages who will have it that the earth is a flat plane and not a globe. He stands alone, conscious of his marvellous vision, and as he hears of others yielding to the spiritual hypothesis, he becomes more and more convinced that there is but one sane man left and that his name is Podmore. There is no wisdom or insight anywhere but what is exhibited in his own marvellous personality. Nature formed but one such man, and then the mould got broken. According to him even his great hero, Sidgwick, was not altogether an ideal investigator. Nothing is of the least value but what receives his own approval. Professor Hyslop's report is so much colossal simplicity, and Podmore can only hold up his hands in amazement at such an exhibition. As for Dr. Hodgson, he had been so completely hypnotised by Mrs. Piper that he lost his power of observation, or he would have protested against Hyslop's methods.

Podmore stands forth proof against a mountain of facts, and can show to his own satisfaction that the mountain is only a bit of conjuring and mal-observation. Not the smallest piece of spiritual phenomena is allowed to pass through his sieve. However eminent and honest his *confrères* may be matters not—they are dupes, everyone of them. There never were raps heard under conditions where it was not possible for someone present to make them. Crookes might assert that he heard them, but he lacked hearing. Wallace was credulous, Myers without capacity, Hodgson hypnotised. In one man alone dwelt the insight to see that pure trickery was the sole origin of what had been called spiritual phenomena. The Chinese in ancient times drew a map of the world, and outside their own dominions they marked "inhabited by barbarians." Mr. Podmore has consistently and practically said: "I am the centre of intelligence and knowledge; outside me are only blindness and desert." Has there ever been such an exhibition of cool egotism and audacity as this man's assertions against the judgment of many of the ablest men of the century? Can there be any wonder that this Society, which promised so much, has accomplished literally nothing, when it has been handicapped by the influence of a man who freezes up all phenomena, ignores all conditions, and casts aside as of no moment the experiences of hundreds of thoughtful and wise people? To meet records such as Spiritualism presents with contemptuous insinuations of credulity and dishonesty is scarcely what could have been expected from anyone claiming kinship with philosophy or science.

I have only now to bring before your notice one other name, which has been sounded far and wide as that of a strong man, viz., Dr. Richard Hodgson. I do not for a moment place him in the same school as Podmore. There was a depth of power and application in him which, if for long it produced nothing satisfactory to himself, eventually landed him on the shores of certainty. For a season he seemed quite unfit to probe the claims which were made, that the dead could come into contact with the living. Some peculiar personal experiences attracted him to the occult, but he could not trust, could not rely on his own judgment. All professional mediums were alike fraudulent, and he had a special pride in his superior acumen to be able to get at the secret of all their tricks. He had a reputation amongst his *confrères* as the great detective, and they no doubt thought that he had annihilated Madame Blavatsky for ever when, in 1885, he issued his report on his return from India. He went out with an eye focussed to catch fraud, and had little difficulty in convincing himself that only chicanery was the stock-in-trade of that remarkable woman; and so, in after years, with Eusapia Paladino. Whatever Lodge, Myers, and the other experimenters might say, Hodgson *knew* she was but an arrant knave, and yet the much traduced Eusapia marches on her way, convincing and converting

Continental scientists daily. By going to America in 1887, as secretary for the American branch of the Society, Hodgson was placed in a new field of inquiry. He did discover that there was *one* professional medium who had genuine gifts; that a modicum of righteousness did exist after all. For nearly twenty years Mrs. Piper was the oracle on which the truth of a future life hung. According to Professor Hyslop, it cost the Society £1500 for these Piper investigations. It was a long, dreary search, made all the more difficult by the methods which were adopted. Hodgson might read about the experiences of other people, but they were of no value to him. It is doubtful if he ever accepted physical phenomena as having any reality. Crookes' statements, he admitted, were the best attested, but he could not accept them as true until many additional cases had been given. I have often wondered that the spirit people in association with Mrs. Piper did not give up his conversion as hopeless, but no doubt they saw the day of triumph ahead. Research dogmas had to be adjusted towards the plainest facts before they could be accepted. What a web of prejudice had to be destroyed before the spirit voices could sound clearly! Ultimately the inner and the outer man saw that what Spiritualists had fought for so long was true.

The ripening time had come at last, and Hodgson's detective faculty and scepticism were found to be but obstacles in the path of the spirits. No doubt the work of Stainton Moses and the *Spirit Teachings* were known to him in the period when his mind was holden; but Mrs. Piper's control, "George Pelham," changed the current of his life, so that when Stainton Moses had been translated and his group of helpers were free to work within Hodgson's sphere, he gave them the welcome of a true Spiritualist. He had pretty well done with the old state of suspicion, and was filled with the rapture which spiritual communion brings. He could hardly wait to die, and talked about that "other side" as if it were at his doors. "Imperator," the patient teacher, was recognised as an in structor from the beyond seeking to proclaim the highest conception of religion, and was no longer regarded as a part of the medium's sub-consciousness. In the face of a real being of intellect and righteousness the subliminal exposition had to melt away, and he caught the spirit of those whom he had previously sneered at for being satisfied with facts instead of theories.

Hodgson's conversion came as a surprise, it was so decided. Mrs. Sidgwick, his one time colleague, might hope that he would modify his convictions, but that could never be. The spirit people had given him real knowledge. He stood on a rock from which nothing could dislodge him. Four years before his translation he was able to say, as the outcome of a powerful conviction, "I think, for the rest of my life from now, should I never see another trance or have another word from 'Imperator' or his group, it would make no difference to my *knowledge* that all is well: that 'Imperator' and others are all they claim to be, and are, indeed, messengers that we may call divine." Nothing could be clearer than that he had found the pearl of great price, and was courageous enough to express his convictions in language which could be understood. I need scarcely refer to the messages which he has sent to the earthly friends since his translation. One day, it is to be hoped, these will be printed, free from the accumulation of useless wordiness in which the Research mode envelops everything. But it is not to be expected that Hodgson's acceptance of Spiritualism will affect those who still wait outside the gates of knowledge.

Of late a new group of investigators has been heard of, not allied specially with the Psychical Research Society, but successors to their spirit and modes. Dr. Maxwell writes pointedly about the reality of the phenomena; he is never in doubt, like

Sidgwick, about the raps and many other phases, and he has had sense enough to see that the medium's confidence and sympathy have to be won by the sitters throwing out sympathy, deference, and loyalty. Maxwell sets down the most conclusive evidence for intelligent spirits being the cause of the phenomena, but keeps harping about "personifications," what they say and do. He will not have the spirits—just yet; like Brewster, "spirit is the last thing he will give in to." Those who read will form their own conclusions, and many will recognise that we get nothing useful out of "collective consciousness," which is but a struggle on the part of a theorist to get out of a corner. Spiritualists know that the spirits are going to conquer, that Maxwell, Richet, Morselli, Flammarion, and others have all to travel in their own fog for a season only. It is satisfactory, at all events, that the members of this new school of Researchers do find that the phenomena are real. They have rehabilitated Eusapia and proved that the Cambridge experimenters were a body of weaklings. If we want to get at minds which can embrace the simple, disentangle the perplexed, and enlighten the obscure, we need to go back to some of the earlier observers of spiritual phenomena. The following words by Professor De Morgan are of rare value when we contemplate the work of the Society for Psychical Research. He says:

"I doubt whether inquiry by men of science would lead to any result. There is much reason to believe that the state of mind of the inquirer has something—be it internal or external—to do with the power of the phenomena to manifest themselves. It may be a consequence of action of incredulous feel ing on the nervous system of the recipient, or it may be that the volition—say the spirit, if you like—finds difficulty in communicating with a repellant organisation, or maybe is offended. *Be it which it may, there is the fact.*"

Words such as these are the outcome of an exalted and contemplative mind. This man had an inner conviction which was not related to fancy or imagination. The story of the spirits' coming back to earth, which captivated the minds of the many I have named, cannot be ruthlessly passed over; certainly it is not the *Proceedings and Journals* of the Psychical Research Society that will accomplish this. Twenty-five years spent in dreary talk has been a waste of time and scarcely justifies the continued existence of this Society. Its name has been a mask. I know that there are some Spiritualists who are simple enough to think that the men who form this Society are capable of sifting the grain from the chaff, but the unfortunate thing is that they have not been blessed with vision to recognise what is grain and what is chaff, and this pious opinion has to be rooted out from the minds of Spiritualists as having no relation to the actual facts. We, who have got volumes of indisputable evidence, have no need of patronage, no need to get closer to those who will not open their eyes, but persistently oppose the greatest revelation of the centuries. It was the facts of Spiritualism which at last brought Myers and Hodgson to see the light as we have done. We will not falter in our propaganda, but shall stand firm for the truth that the world of spirit is in touch with the world of matter. We know that this seemingly obscure thing, whose real glory has been unguessed, will one day mount the throne of the world and be recognised as the choicest, fullest, best gift of God to man.

I cannot do better than conclude with some words from Stainton Moses' *Spirit Teachings*:

> *The glorious tidings shall spread till the day*
> *comes when we shall be called upon to*
> *proclaim them from the mountain tops, and*
> *lo! God's hidden ones will start up from the*
> *lowly places of the earth to bear witness to*

*that which they have seen and known, and the
little rills that man has heeded not shall
coalesce, and the river of God's truth,
omnipotent in its energy, shall flood the earth
and sweep away in its resistless course the
ignorance and unbelief and folly and sin
which now dismay and perplex us.*

FOX

San Francisco

www.foxediting.com

www.ingramcontent.com/pod-product-compliance
Lightning Source LLC
Chambersburg PA
CBHW060326100426
42812CB00003B/897